Corporate Social Responsibility Series

Series Editor
Professor David Crowther, London Metropolitan University, UK

This series aims to provide high quality research books on all aspects of corporate social responsibility including: business ethics, corporate governance and accountability, globalization, civil protests, regulation, responsible marketing and social reporting.

The series is interdisciplinary in scope and global in application and is an essential forum for everyone with an interest in this area.

Forthcoming title:

Corporate Social Performance: A Stakeholder Approach
Stuart M. Cooper
ISBN 0 7546 4174 0

Perspectives on Corporate Social Responsibility

Edited by

DAVID CROWTHER and LEZ RAYMAN-BACCHUS
London Metropolitan University

ASHGATE

Published by
Ashgate Publishing Limited
Gower House
Croft Road
Aldershot
Hants GU11 3HR
England

Ashgate Publishing Company
Suite 420
101 Cherry Street
Burlington, VT 05401-4405
USA

Ashgate website: http://www.ashgate.com

British Library Cataloguing in Publication Data
Perspectives on corporate social responsibility.–
    (Corporate social responsibility series)
    1. Social responsibility of business
    I. Crowther, David II. Rayman-Bacchus, Lez
    658.4'08

Library of Congress Control Number: 2003111351

ISBN 0 7546 3886 3

Printed and bound in Great Britain by MPG Books Ltd, Bodmin, Cornwall

Contents

PART 3: THE ETHICS OF CORPORATE SOCIAL RESPONSIBILITY

List of Figures

List of Tables

List of Contributors

Rute Abreu is Professor of Project Valuation, Polytechnic Institute of Guarda, Portugal.

Thomas Clarke is Professor and Director of the Centre for Corporate Governance, UTS Sydney, Australia.

David Crowther is Professor of Corporate Social Responsibility, London Metropolitan University, UK; External Professor, Ansted University, British Virgin Islands; Founding Member, Association for Integrity in Accounting.

Fatima David is Professor of Social Accounting, Polytechnic Institute of Guarda, Portugal.

Roger Haw is President and Founding Director of Ansted Asia Regional Service Center, Malaysia; Founding member of Ansted University, British Virgin Islands; Council member and Life Fellowship of The Institute of Arts and Letters, London, UK; President of Ansted University Foundation and Board of Trustees, British Virgin Islands, UK; Diplomat to World Human Rights Service Council to United Nations, USA; International Advisory Board of World University, USA; Consulting Editor and Advisory Council, American Biographical Institute Inc., USA.

John Mahon is John M. Murphy Chair of International Business Policy and Strategy and Professor of Management, Maine Business School, University of Maine, USA.

Richard McGowan is Professor of Wallace E. Carroll School of Management, Boston College and Harvard Medical School Unit on Addictions, USA.

Branka Mraović is Associate Professor in Sociology of Organisations at the Faculty of Geodesy, University of Zagreb, Croatia.

John Peters is a Director of Emerald/MCB University Press, UK.

Marie de la Rama is a Research Assistant, Centre for Corporate Governance, UTS Sydney, Australia.

Lez Rayman-Bacchus is Senior Lecturer in Strategy and e-Business, London Metropolitan University, UK.

R. Seminur Topal is Professor of Yildiz Technical University, Istanbul, Turkey.

Chapter 1

Introduction: Perspectives on Corporate Social Responsibility

David Crowther and Lez Rayman-Bacchus

> If the confidence of the public in the integrity of accountants' reports is shaken, their value is gone. To preserve the integrity of his reports, the accountant must insist upon absolute independence of judgment and action. The necessity of preserving this position of independence indicates certain standards of conduct. (Arthur Andersen, 1932 – cited in Toffler, 2003)

For many people, particularly in the Western world the year 2002 will be the one in which corporate misbehaviour was exposed by the collapse of some large corporations. In particular the spectacular collapse of Enron and the subsequent fallout among the financial world – including the firm which Arthur Andersen himself founded in 1913 – will have left an indelible impression among people that all is not well with the corporate world and that there are problems which need to be addressed. This will be particularly the case amongst those adversely affected by this collapse, not least of whom are the former employees of the company who have lost their jobs, their life savings and their future pensions. Equally remembered however in other parts of the world is that 2002 was the tenth anniversary of the Union Carbide incident in Bhopal, India – the worst pollution incident in the history of the world. This incident killed thousands, left thousands permanently injured and an even greater number living a life of misery in the area surrounding the former plant. To date not one penny has been paid in compensation to those whose lives have been blighted by an incident caused by the lack of safety precautions which would be required in the Western world and which any socially responsible organisation would implement as a matter of course.

Issues of socially responsible behaviour are not of course new and examples can be found from throughout the world and at least from the earliest days of the Industrial revolution and the concomitant founding of large business entities and the divorce between ownership and management – or the divorcing of risk from rewards, as Crowther argues. But corporate social responsibility is back on the agenda of corporations, governments and individual citizens throughout the world. In this book for example Abreu and David consider practice in the European Community, while Mahon and McGowan consider practice in the USA. Clarke and de la Rama take a wider perspective in considering practice and performance in various Anglo-Saxon countries.

The term corporate social responsibility is in vogue at the moment but as a concept it is vague and means different things to different people. For example Topal and Crowther are concerned with bioengineering and its effects upon biodiversity and therefore upon the future of the planet. On the other hand Mraovich is concerned with the consequences of the networked society (Castells, 1996) while Rayman-Bacchus is more concerned with trust in, and legitimacy of, corporate behaviour and the constant tension between economic wealth and social wellbeing. On the other hand Haw makes the point that socially responsible behaviour is based upon individual behaviour and we cannot expect responsible behaviour from corporations unless we behave responsibly as individuals. All of these interpretations are found within this book. Indeed one of the purposes of the book is to explore different definitions and to arrive at a broad understanding of the range of concerns subsumed within the term corporate social responsibility.

Given the plurality of interpretations of corporate social responsibility contained in this book, this introductory chapter does not seek to knit them into some overarching big idea or single theme. We have chosen to let the individual chapters speak for themselves, and for the reader to draw their own conclusions from the arguments offered. Instead the discussions in this chapter ranges across a variety of themes, some of which resonate with particular ideas within individual chapters, while other themes are raised here without seeking to connect with the particular contributions. The first theme discussed here is the extent to which we can assess the accountability of organisations to a broader constituency by reference to an implicit or hypothetical *social contract*. In the process we show how social contract theory also helps bind the relationship between corporate social responsibility and ethical behaviour. Following this we raise questions about the scope and depth of commitment among corporate leaders to *social responsibility*. Assessing this commitment is made difficult given what appears to be a runaway free market ideology; a belief system that seems to be elevating the corporation above the nation state, and is being transmitted through corporate global expansion and USA led government sponsorship. We further develop this globalising process by considering the extent to which corporate and social exploitation of Internet technology is helping both corporate bodies and consumer and citizens transform our world into *a global village*. We then broaden this assessment of the role of Internet technology to consider the broader relationship between *technological innovation and social change*. In examining this relationship we show that technological development is underpinned by a utilitarian perspective, and at the same time technological change is unavoidably bound up with making moral choices. Lastly, we suggest that the wider debate about corporate social responsibility could be understood by *framing the arguments* in terms of a Hobbesian-Lockeian dichotomy, drawing in a consideration of the extent to which there is, or should be, an underlying utilitarian assumption, and how our rights might be affected.

The broadest definition of corporate social responsibility is concerned with what is – or should be – the relationship between the global corporation, governments of countries and individual citizens. More locally the definition is concerned with the relationship between a corporation and the local society in which it resides or operates. Another definition is concerned with the relationship between a corporation and its stakeholders. For us all of these definitions are pertinent and represent a dimension of the issue. A parallel debate is taking place in the arena of ethics – should corporations be controlled through increased regulation or has the ethical base of citizenship been lost and needs replacing before socially responsible behaviour will ensue? In the UK at the present the government seems to believe that citizenship needs teaching to our school children, presumably in the belief that this will manifest itself in the behaviour of corporations in the future. However this debate is represented it seems to us that it is concerned with some sort of social contract between corporations and society.

The Social Contract

A growing number of writers over the last quarter of a century have recognised that the activities of an organisation impact upon the external environment and have suggested that such an organisation should therefore be accountable to a wider audience than simply its shareholders. Such a suggestion probably first arose in the 1970s and a concern with a wider view of company performance is taken by some writers who evince concern with the social performance of a business, as a member of society at large. This concern was stated by Ackerman (1975) who argued that big business was recognising the need to adapt to a new social climate of community accountability, but that the orientation of business to financial results was inhibiting social responsiveness. McDonald and Puxty (1979) on the other hand maintain that companies are no longer the instruments of shareholders alone but exist within society and so therefore have responsibilities to that society, and that there is therefore a shift towards the greater accountability of companies to all participants.

Recognition of the rights of all stakeholders and the duty of a business to be accountable in this wider context therefore has been largely a relatively recent phenomenon.[1] The economic view of accountability only to owners has only recently however been subject to debate to any considerable extent. Some owners of businesses have however always recognised a responsibility to other stakeholders and this is evident from the early days of the Industrial Revolution. Thus, for example, in the nineteenth century Robert Owen (1816, 1991) demonstrated dissatisfaction with the assumption that only cost minimisation and the consequent profit maximisation was the only thing of concern to a business. Furthermore he put his beliefs into practice through the inclusion within his sphere of industrial operations the provision of model housing for his workers at New Lanark, Scotland. Further examples of socially responsible behaviour have continued to exist since these days. Thus there is evidence from throughout the history of modernity that the self-centred approach of accounting

---

1   Mathews (1997) traces its origins to the 1970s although arguments (see Crowther, 2002a) show that such concerns can be traced back to the Industrial Revolution.

for organisational activity only to shareholders was not universally acceptable and was unable to satisfactorily provide a basis for human activity.

Implicit in this concern with the effects of the actions of an organisation on its external environment is the recognition that it is not just the owners of the organisation who have a concern with the activities of that organisation. Additionally there are a wide variety of other stakeholders who justifiably have a concern with those activities, and are affected by those activities. Those other stakeholders have not just an interest in the activities of the firm but also a degree of influence over the shaping of those activities. This influence is so significant that it can be argued that the power and influence of these stakeholders is such that it amounts to quasi-ownership of the organisation. Indeed Gray, Owen and Maunders (1987) challenge the traditional role of accounting in reporting results and consider that, rather than an ownership approach to accountability, a stakeholder approach, recognising the wide stakeholder community, is needed.[2]

The desirability of considering the social performance of a business has not always however been accepted and has been the subject of extensive debate. Thus Hetherington (1973: 37) states:

> There is no reason to think that shareholders are willing to tolerate an amount of corporate non-profit activity which appreciably reduces either dividends or the market performance of the stock.

while Dahl (1972: 18) states:

> ... every large corporation should be thought of as a social enterprise; that is an entity whose existence and decisions can be justified insofar as they serve public or social purposes.

Nevertheless the performance of businesses in a wider arena than the stock market and its value to shareholders has become of increasing concern. In many respects this can be considered to be a return to the notion of the social contract.

Social contract theory is most often associated with the work of Hobbes (1651) and Rousseau (1762) where a contract, usually considered to be implied or hypothetical, is made between citizens for the organisation of the society and as a basis for legal and political power within that society. The idea is that for the legal and political system to be legitimate it must be one that the members of society would have rationally contracted into. Social contract theory has been applied to the question of business in society in a similar fashion by considering 'what conditions would have to be met for the members of such a society to agree to allow corporations to be formed' (Smith

---

2   The benefits of incorporating stakeholders into a model of performance measurement and accountability have however been extensively criticised. See for example Freedman and Reed (1983), Sternberg (1997, 1998) and Hutton (1997) for details of this ongoing discourse.

and Hasnas, 1999). The conclusions reached by the theorists include that the members of society would demand that the benefits outweigh the detriments implying a greater welfare for the society while remaining 'within the bounds of the general canons of justice' (Donaldson, 1982). This can be summarised into three basic requirements that relate to social welfare and justice. Hasnas (1998) suggests that:

> when fully specified, the social welfare term of the social contract requires that businesses act so as to 1) benefit consumers by increasing economic efficiency, stabilizing levels of output and channels of distribution, and increasing liability resources; 2) benefit employees by increasing their income potential, diffusing their personal liability, and facilitating their income allocation; while 3) minimizing pollution and depletion of natural resources, the destruction of personal accountability, the misuse of political power, as well as worker alienation, lack of control over working conditions, and dehumanization.

The justice term is less agreed upon but Hasnas suggests that one thing it should require as a minimum is that businesses do not 'systematically worsen the situation of a given group in society'. This obviously has a strong resonance with stakeholder ideas. Social contract theory has been criticised most usually because, as mentioned earlier, the contract is either argued to be implied or hypothetical. Therefore there is no actual contract (Kultgen, 1987), that members of society have not given any formal consent to such a contract, and that they would be surprised to learn of its existence. Donaldson (1989) freely admits that the contract is a 'fiction' but continues that this does not undermine its underlying moral theory.

Social contract theory is therefore grounded in moral theory, with a strong basis in ethics. In various chapters in this book contributors argue that there is a strong connection between corporate socially responsible behaviour and ethical behaviour.

Social Responsibility and the Free Market

It was as long ago as 1967 that Marshall McLuhan first stated that we now live in a global village and that technology was connecting everyone together. Much has changed since then in terms of technology and now with access to the Internet available to everyone we truly do live in a global village in which anyone can interact with anyone else wherever they are living and whatever time zone they are residing in. The Internet has changed the world as never before and this is having profound consequences for people everywhere.

Marshall McLuhan was prophetic in some of the other things which he had to say. When he was talking about this global village he also said that war would continue to be a feature of the world but that there would be an increasing emphasis upon economic war rather than physical war. Well physical war has not gone away but it might be argued that the reasons for wars in the present are to do with economic reasons at least as much as they are to do with imperialistic or ideological reasons – at least as far as governments and countries are concerned. But governments, as the epitome of the nation state are becoming less important. In Europe we have seen a number of new nations states becoming established and in one country, the UK we are possibly in process of breaking up the country into the smaller units of England, Scotland, Wales and a united Ireland. But this is beside the point, because what is becoming more important than governments and nation states is the multi-national company, operating in a global environment. Some of these multinationals are very large indeed – larger than many nation states and a good deal more powerful. Arguably it is here that the economic war for the global village is taking place.

Many governments throughout the world behave as if they recognise this and respond to the veiled threats from these corporations to relocate their operations by granting concessions of various kinds. Even the government of the United States – the most powerful nation on earth – behaves in this way. For them however the problem is that all their politicians are funded by these corporations and so they must behave as if they are on the payroll and must do as they are told. Needless to say these corporations are concerned with their own interests rather than with altruism and so American domestic and foreign policy is dictated by the needs of multinational corporations. And where America leads others must follow – or suffer the consequences – economic or physical.

One of the consequences of the acquisition of governmental influence by these corporations is the myth of the free market as being beneficial to all. It is widely accepted – almost unquestioningly – that free markets will lead to greater economic growth and that we will all benefit from this economic growth. Around the world people are arguing – and winning the argument – that restrictions upon world economic activity caused by the regulation of markets is bad for our well-being. And in one country after another, for one market after another, governments are capitulating and relaxing their regulations to allow complete freedom of economic activity. So the world might not yet be a global village but it is rapidly becoming a global market place for these global corporations.

We have all witnessed the effects of the actions of some of these global corporations. Recently we have seen the effects of the actions of some of these corporations within the United States itself – the champion of the free market. We have seen the collapse of the global accounting firm Anderson; we have seen the bankruptcy of major corporations such as Enron and World.com with thousands of people being thrown out of work and many people losing the savings for their old age which they have worked so long and hard to gain. And why has this happened? Basically the people running these corporations have been found out – they have been found to be deceitful liars and their lies have been uncovered. But the myth of the free market is grounded in classical liberal economic theory, as propounded by people such as John Stuart Mill (1848) in the nineteenth century, which, briefly summarised, states that anything is OK as long as the consequences are acceptable. And there is no alternative – at least if you listen to many. Indeed Francis Fukuyama (1992) argued that with the collapse of the Berlin Wall liberal democracy had triumphed and the end of history had arrived. Many people are familiar with this argument of Fukuyama – and have challenged the assertion – but most are less clear that he lamented this end of history.

But it is our argument that history has not ended and that there is an alternative to the myth of the free market and its presumed beneficial effects. The authors in this book believe that corporate social responsibility provides a way forward which negates the negative effects of an unregulated free global market. Some base their argument upon the importance of ethics and ethical behaviour – for each of us as individuals and for each corporation – for corporations are nothing more than a collective of individuals who have banded together for a particular purpose. All individuals have rights – rights to pursue their own ends and to seek to better their existence in whatever terms they define this idea of better. But with rights go responsibilities and obligations. For many corporations – and particularly for the managers of those corporations – this relationship between rights and responsibilities has been lost, with the rights maintained and the responsibilities discarded.

How did this go wrong? Crowther argues that this started to go wrong when the concept of limited liability was introduced for corporations – in the UK in the early part of the nineteenth century. The principle of limited liability was introduced to protect investors (i.e. shareholders) from the potential adverse consequences of the actions of the corporations in which they invested. One of the problems however must be associated with accounting and its use by organisation to record their actions.[3] The traditional view of accounting, as far as an organisation is concerned, is that the only activities with which the organisation should be concerned are those which take place within the organisation, or between the organisation and its suppliers or customers. Essentially the only purpose of traditional accounting is to record the effects of actions upon the organisation itself; an essentially inward looking position. Consequently it is considered that these are the only activities for which a role for accounting exists. Here therefore is located the essential dialectic of accounting – that some results of actions taken are significant and need to be recorded while others are irrelevant and need to be ignored. This view of accounting places the organisation at the centre of its world and the only interfaces with the external world take place at the beginning and end of its value chain.

It is apparent however that any action that an organisation undertakes will have an effect not just upon itself but also upon the external environment within which that organisation resides. In considering the effect of the organisation upon its external environment it must be recognised that this environment includes both the business environment in which the firm is operating, the local societal environment in which the organisation is located and the wider global environment. This effect of the organisation can take many forms, such as:

---

3   This recognition has recently led to the founding of the Association for Integrity in Accounting, the mission of which is to provide an independent forum to present and advance positions on a wide range of critical accounting and auditing issues, standards and regulations affecting the accountability and integrity of the profession and the public interest in maintaining trust and confidence in accounting. Information on the Association for Integrity in Accounting is available at http://www.citizenworks.org.

- the utilisation of natural resources as a part of its production processes;
- the effects of competition between itself and other organisations in the same market;
- the enrichment of a local community through the creation of employment opportunities;
- transformation of the landscape due to raw material extraction or waste product storage;
- the distribution of wealth created within the firm to the owners of that firm (via dividends) and the workers of that firm (through wages) and the effect of this upon the welfare of individuals.

It can be seen therefore from these examples that an organisation can have a very significant effect upon its external environment and can actually change that environment through its activities. It can also be seen that these different effects can in some circumstances be viewed as beneficial and in other circumstances be viewed as detrimental to the environment. Indeed the same actions can be viewed as beneficial by some people and detrimental by others.

A Global Village

It can be argued that things have not changed much in the 30 years since the arguments of McLuhan and the development of a social contract approach to business management were first made and the need for social responsibility is by no means universally accepted – or some of the things we have referred to would not have happened. But it is the view of the various authors of this that there are grounds for optimism. In the first place ethical and socially responsible behaviour is being engaged in successfully by a number of large corporations – and this number is increasing all the time. Secondly there is no evidence that corporations which engage in socially responsible behaviour perform, in terms of profitability and the creation of shareholder value, any worse than do any other corporations. Indeed there is a growing body of evidence that socially responsible behaviour leads to increased economic performance – at least in the longer term – and consequentially greater welfare and wealth for all involved, either actively or passively.

To return to the argument of Marshall McLuhan however, and the way in which technology is bringing about the global village then this provides one source of optimism. The increasing availability of access to the Internet has been widely discussed and its effects suggested, upon both corporations and upon individual members of society (Rushkoff, 1997). For corporations much has been promulgated concerning the opportunities presented through the ability to reach a global audience and to engage in electronic retailing; much less has been said about the effects of the change in accountability provided by this medium. Much of what has been said is based upon an expectation that the Internet and the World Wide Web will have a beneficial impact upon the way in which society operates (see for example Holmes and Grieco, 1999). Thus Sobchack (1996) argues that this technology will be more liberating, participatory and interactive than previous cultural forms while Axford (1995) argues that it will lead to increasing globalisation of politics, culture and social systems. Much of this discourse is concerned at a societal level with the effects of Internet technology upon society, and only by implication, upon individuals within society. It is however only at the level of the individual that these changes can take place. Indeed access to the Internet, and the ability to communicate via this technology to other individuals, without regard to time and place, can be considered to be a revolutionary redistribution of power (Russell, 1975) – a redistribution in favour of us all as individuals. Moreover the disciplinary practices of society (Foucault, 1977) breakdown when the Internet is used because of the lack of spatial contiguity between communicants (see Carter and Grieco, 2000 regarding the emerging electronic ontologies) and because of the effective anonymity of the communication which prevents the normalising surveillance mechanisms of society (Clegg, 1989) to intercede in that communication. Thus the Internet provides a space for resistance to foment (Robins, 1995).

Of particular interest however is the way in which access to Internet technology can redefine the corporate landscape (see Crowther, 2000, 2002) and change the power relationship between large corporations and individuals. In this respect the changes in these power relationships can be profound and even revolutionary, generating new and contested arenas of control and accountability. On the one hand the communicative freedom and immediacy offered by the technology provides a potential challenge to legitimacy and can give individuals the ability to confront large corporations and to have their voice heard with equal volume within the discourse facilitated by cyberspace. In this respect the power imbalance is being equalised and we are moving from a global marketplace to a truly global village.

On the other hand as the technological marriage of data communications (principally the Internet) and computing unfolds old ethical issues resurface in new clothes. One such is the collection of information about individuals. Corporations, governments and their agents have been collecting information on individuals since the dawn of social organisation. The harnessing of computers during the last quarter of the twentieth century has enabled a significant increase in the intensity of information gathering; a development that many saw as propelling democratic society toward an Orwellian nightmare. Others acknowledged the need of institutions to collect information, but worried about how to balance that need against the individual's desire for privacy (Johnson and Nissenbaum, 1995). As the twenty-first century dawns, an important feature of our modern global village is the quantum leap in scope of this information gathering. The application of information and communication technologies (ICT) is enabling faster information transmission (within and between global corporations), involving more parties (buyer, seller, information broker, government) and new kinds of informaton to be collected. The cost of collecting and storing this information is often a marginal cost to the collecting organisation. For example, consider the automatic deployment of *cookies* from host to website visitors, recording our interests, preferences and browsing behaviour. Given this scale of information gathering we need to evaluate the moral implications of a variety of new conditions. For example, we as online consumers want information tailored to our preferences but are unhappy to divulge personal data (Rayman-Bacchus and Molina, 2001). We find ourselves in a dilemma whereby we can experience a new level of personal service, but at the price of sacrificing private information. Furthermore, giving personal information could help the tailoring, but doing so also invites spam (junk e-mail) and other possible abuses.

Technological Innovation and Social Change

We live in a time when technological change is generally seen as progressive, and where the enterprising exploitation of technology is credited with helping to generate economic growth and social wellbeing. This time, the age of modernity, is characterised by a multitude of technological achievements that many of us take for granted: the automobile, aeroplane, satellite, gene therapy, embryo fertilisation, and so on. Modernity also dispensed with magic and tradition, replacing it with logic and reason, and a cultural and ethical hegemony of the developed West over the rest. In the context of a global village many of today's social responsibility controversies revolve around the validity of this cultural and ethical hegemony. For example, corporations, such as Motorola, thinking their global strategies to be progressive have found those strategies wanting in the face of regional or national identities.

Other social controversies centre on technological innovations, such as the Internet and genetic engineering. For example many of the issues raised in this book implicate technology, either directly or indirectly. However technological innovation is not a free floating agent of change, but a product of capitalist competition. Arguably the most significant organisational innovation in the recent history of modern democracies has been the corporation. As Green (1992) argues the development and exploitation of technological artifacts has taken place within the context of the firm, either working independently or as Constant (1987) shows within 'communities' or networks of firms and research centres. What kind of future competing firms may perceive, conceive and achieve are therefore central to technological advance and social change. Corporate action then reflects and shapes our assessment of the meaning and value of change.

Unger's (1994: 3) definition of technology as the 'intelligent organization and manipulation of materials for useful purposes' captures a commonly held utilitarian view of technology's value to society's economic and social wellbeing. This utilitarian perspective also underpins traditional management teaching, which presents technology as neutral artifact, asocial and value free, and as an instrument in the hands of competitive strategy (Rayman-Bacchus, 1996). While we quickly castigate corporations for failing to prevent disasters, we seem slow to take up arms against those responsible for less discernable but no less unacceptable consequences of technological developments. Pitt (1990) identifies for example the continued failure of many process industries to avoid polluting the environment, and the failure of power utilities to plan for the decommissioning of nuclear power stations. In the case of the latter, government must surely shoulder much of the responsibility. Consider too the consumption of designer wear in the West and the dubious employment conditions surrounding its production in developing economies. We seem to accept many of these failings as the price for progress, or as Pitt (1990: 385) says 'it is what the market wants'. These arguments reflect the economist's hedonistic commitment to satisfying 'preferences' or 'desires' (Griffin, 1986), whereby the interests of some override the interests of others. Modernity seems to host a sentiment that justifies inflicting suffering on some for the sake of the greater good.

Taking the broader *consequentialist* perspective – rather than the narrow hedonistic *utilitarian*[4] view – any moral evaluation of how we use technology depends on how our actions and attitudes contribute to an objective assessment of a better world (Griffin, 1986). From this view as long as policy makers and corporate leaders seek to maximise or at least achieve satisfactory economic and social outcomes, then their actions and motivations are morally right. However, there are three weaknesses to this consequentialist view. First, that any moral evaluations of actions and motivations rest on *objectively* conceived *good* outcomes that are independent of the evaluation. This proposition carries a strong requirement to look for universal principles to guide action. Postmodernists would criticise this universalism. While we like to think that there is a clear distinction between right and wrong, good and bad, knowledge is relative, secular and power dependent. Our observations and judgements made depend on our assumptions, presupposed social institutions of civil society, and world views. There is no single morality. Ethics is essentially a social and cultural phenomenon giving rise to different ethical positions. The second weakness is the maximising requirement; maximising on whose terms? Third, while the consequentialist position allows for personal bias , there remains a belief that this bias can be held separate from an impartially defined good outcome (Scheffler, 1988).

There can never be an outcome that is objectively good. As Rayman-Bacchus (1996), Schwarz and Thomson (1990) and others have shown social process is embedded in technology, giving it an interpretive flexibility. The development and exploitation of technology is inherently value laden, interest driven, and subject to claims and counter-claims about its moral integrity. Both policy makers and corporate leaders see positive outcomes in genetic engineering, but the outcomes they see are different: government sees technological advance, surplus food production and export potential, while corporations see the profit potential. Sceptics see the danger to our environment and health risks.

While rejecting any implied technological determinism, or social determinism, important social innovations do attend these and other technological innovations.

---

4   Detailed examinations of consequentialism and utilitarianism can be found in a number of texts. For consequentialism see Scheffler, S. (ed.) (1988), *Consequentialism and its Critics*, Oxford: Oxford University Press, and for utilitarianism see Kagan, S. (1989), *The Limits of Morality*, Oxford: Clarendon Press.

Consider the extent to which e-mail has become part of everyday life within the last decade, central to business communication and individual communication alike, and possibly central to social relations. For those with access to e-mail and real-time online chat the old temporal and spatial limitations on communication – and more broadly on cultivating social relations – evaporate.

Users of e-mail provides a trail of their thoughts and actions going back months and years. E-mail trails are easily monitored and stored, by employer and Internet Service Provider (ISP). Further, the UK government is currently pushing through legislation requiring ISPs to archive all e-mail traffic for up to twelve months, and make such information available in the interests of national security for the new war against terrorism. Paradoxically, while the Internet provides us with a freedom that subverts Foucault's Panopticon, our everyday dependence on e-mail combined with corporate surveillance of e-mail content, restores manipulative power to the corporation and government. While electronic media and e-mail in particular are enabling, they are at the same time disabling. With surveillance of e-mail traffic and content goes the power to classify what constitutes acceptable and unacceptable. Foucault would argue that through our dependence on e-mail we are still cooperating with our own subjugation.

The social innovations being facilitated by ICT, genetic engineering and other emerging technological developments hint at a possible future that postmodernist thinkers would recognise. For example as noted earlier, our contemporary world is characterised by anonymous communication. Our world is also subject to the colonisation of our perceptive senses by electronic media to a degree that is blurring any distinction between objects and their representation. The emergence of Internet lovers who never meet and often come to know each other through pseudonyms. As Lyon (1994: 16) puts it, 'the late twentieth century is witness to unprecedented destruction of meaning. The quest for some division between the moral and immoral, the real and the unreal, is futile'. For Lyon *Blade Runner* the movie is a metaphor for a world where one can no longer distinguish between 'replicants' (bioengineered people) and real (biological) people. His prognosis of an amoral world seems pessimistic but bear in mind that this view was offered on the eve of the World Wide Web, cloning and stem cell technology and. This view did not anticipate the subsequent explosion of digitised information and communication that we now witness, nor of the birth of *Dolly* the sheep, and therefore of the greater force of its argument today.

These examples highlight the inherent trade-off between rights and responsibilities, and the conflictual interests of employee and employer, citizen and government, consumer and corporation. Moreover, institutional pursuit of comprehensive information, and the relative ease of collecting and storing that information, may benefit society (national security, coordinated public services, efficient administration). Nonetheless we, as individuals, should never forget that such a project has a pervasive impact on our everyday lives and carries with it an ever present danger of blurring the distinctions between: what is relevant and irrelevant; and factual data and interpretation of that data.

Framing the Arguments

Much of the broader debate about corporate social responsibility can be interpreted as an argument between two positions: greater corporate autonomy and the free market economic model versus greater societal intervention and government control of corporate action. There is clear evidence that the free market proponents are winning the argument. They point to the global spread of capitalism, arguing that this reflects recognition that social wellbeing is dependent on economic growth. Opponents concede this hegemony but see the balance shifting in their favour, through for example greater accountability and reporting. Some opponents suspect the corporate team of cheating on their environments, both ecological and social, while others object fundamentally to the idea that a free market economy is beneficial to society. Which side is right? Resolving these arguments seem intractable if not impossible because they assume divergent philosophical positions. We do not propose to offer any definitive answers since any attempt to do so would itself involve make value judgements. We can though highlight the terrain upon which these arguments roam. Some reflection on the assumptions inherent in the arguments for and against greater corporate social responsibility therefore seem appropriate as a way of helping us make greater sense of the competing positions.

One frame of reference is to consider the arguments as being bound by two philosophical arguments, one Hobbesian the other Lockeian. These two positions also incur reference to ideas of *utilitarianism* and *rights*.[5] Thomas Hobbes is well known for offering the concept of the social contract. In this citizens would agree to vest absolute power in a sovereign power as the only way to avoid anarchy. In this citizens give up their individual rights, including control of liberty and property, and possible life. He argued that human self-interest is such that we would be willing to wage war on each other, the end result being a short and unpleasant life for all. This tradition accords with a utilitarian position: the pursuit of maximum welfare, and provides the test for whether corporate behaviour is morally right or wrong. Utilitarianism regards corporate activity as morally good if it maximises human welfare, and collective welfare may override individual welfare. This is a model of centrally planned economies and welfare economics and has been fashionable among socialist political parties and governments. Scandinavian economies have been admired for their success working in this tradition. From about the 1980s socialists around the world have been remodelling themselves into various forms of capitalism, more in keeping with the next model.

Locke's ideas represent a distinctly individualist position, of which American entrepreneurialism is the best example. In his political philosophy the individual's

---

5   A full discussion of rights cannot be accommodated here, but there are a number of useful sources, including: Dworkin, R. (1977), *Taking Rights Seriously*, Cambridge, MA: Harvard University Press; Gewirth, A. (1986), 'Why Rights are Indispensable', *Mind*, 95: 329–44.

rights to liberty and property are paramount to which end government intervention should be minimal. Moreover legitimate government holds power in trust from its citizens under a social contract, and may be removed by those citizens whenever they judge government to be failing. Within this tradition Milton Friedman (1970; Carson, 1993) argues that corporations have a legitimate right to pursue and maximise shareholder returns, the only constraint being to act within the law, in particular to avoid deceit, committing fraud and coercion. The legitimate pursuit of profit meets shareholder obligations, and benefits society; business managers are not competent to determine and pursue broader social goals and attempting to do so could be construed as taxing shareholders and undermining the role of government. The utilitarian view coincides with this tradition in seeing free market economics as the best guarantor of maximum wellbeing, but as already noted cannot at the same time provide for individual rights.

Critically, Locke (Laslett, 1967) writing in 1689, long before concerns of resource depletion, argued that a fisherman adds (economic) value by catching fish, but that he should not over-fish but recognise that fish is a common good and should therefore leave enough for others. Ironically today the free market economic model is being blamed for depleted fish stocks around Europe, and the European Union parliament has assumed responsibility for managing the competing interests of business and a natural resource. An important flaw with the free market economic model is that it does not recognise the existence of limits to exploitable resources or the cumulative effects industrial activity on the natural and social environment. Moreover, Friedman's constraints on business (no coercion, no deceit and no fraud) do not appear to recognise these limits. Arguably the addition of two other constraints is well overdue: to avoid resource depletion and environmental damage. Government might be better placed to coordinate the management of these two constraints, but recent history of Eastern European economies suggests otherwise. In any case global competition undermines national attempts to manage their own economies.

Conclusions

This book quite deliberately does not take any position on the debate surrounding corporate social responsibility. Indeed the perspectives of the contributors is too diverse to allow this to happen. This is of course deliberate and part of our wish to show the diversity of concerns which fall within the umbrella term. It is equally part of the objective of this book to show that a concern with corporate social responsibility is a worldwide issue which is being addressed by scholars in many countries. Thus the contributors to this book come from a number of different countries. Our aim is to present a spectrum of approaches from a variety of scholars from different countries and from different disciplines in order to show the diversity of the debate and the diversity of contributors. In doing so we hope to both broaden the debate and make it more inclusive by the facilitation of scholars from different countries, disciplines and ontologies in engaging with each other because it is our belief that this is a manner in which progress will be made.

The worldwide and wholesale transformation of political and economic values currently taking place shows our (human) fixation with liberty, property and the good life. Evidence suggests widespread belief that the economic and political institutions of the free market economy model holds out the better promise for the wellbeing of both individuals and communities. Nonetheless, governments, international agencies, business and consumers all need to bear in mind the force of historical contingency. Past social attitudes, business practices and institutional arrangements have delivered a legacy to us the full implications of which are still unfolding. Continued disclosure of corporate wrong-doing and negligence suggests that while corporate social responsible behaviour has improved, there remains much room for improvement. This book seeks to make a contribution to the debates within this important subject, by pressing for open and accountable corporate governance, societal consciousness of the issues and for government action to reflect a greater sensitivity to the place of business in society.

References

Ackerman, R.W. (1975), *The Social Challenge to Business*, Cambridge, MA: Harvard University Press.

Axford, B. (1995), *The Global System*, Cambridge: Polity Press.

Carson, T. (1993), 'Friedman's Theory of Corporate Social Responsibility', *Business and Professional Ethics Journal*, 2: 3–32.

Carter, C. and Grieco, M. (2000), 'New Deals, No Wheels: Social Exclusion. Tele-options and Electronic Ontology', *Urban Studies*, Vol. 37, No. 10: 1735–48.

Castells, M. (1996), *The Rise of the Network Society*, Oxford: Blackwell.

Clegg, S.R. (1989), *Frameworks of Power*, London: Sage.

Constant, E. (1987), 'The Social Locus of Technological Practice: Community, System, or Organisation', in W.E. Bijker, T.P. Hughes, and T. Pinch (eds), *The Social Construction of Technological Systems: New Directions in the Sociology and History of Technology*, Cambridge, MA: MIT Press.

Crowther, D. (2000), 'Corporate Reporting, Stakeholders and the Internet: Mapping The New Corporate Landscape', *Urban Studies*, Vol. 37, No. 10: 1837–48.

Crowther, D. (2002a), *A Social Critique of Corporate Reporting*, Aldershot: Ashgate.

Crowther, D. (2002b), 'The Psychoanalysis of On-line Reporting', in L. Holmes, M. Grieco and D. Hosking (eds), *Organising in the Information Age: Distributed Technology, Distributed Leadership, Distributed Identity, Distributed Discourse*, Aldershot: Ashgate: 130–48.

Dahl, R.A. (1972), 'A Prelude to Corporate Reform', *Business and Society Review*, Spring: 17–23.

Donaldson, T. (1982), *Corporations and Morality*, Englewood Cliffs, NJ: Prentice Hall.

Donaldson, T. (1989), *The Ethics of International Business*, New York: Oxford University Press.

Foucault, M. (1977), *Discipline and Punish*, trans. A. Sheridan, London: Penguin.

Freedman, R.E. and Reed, D.L. (1983), 'Stockholders and Stakeholders: A New Perspective on Corporate Governance', *California Management Review*, Vol. XXV, No. 3: 88–106.

Friedman, M. (1970), 'Social Responsibility of Business', *New York Times Magazine*, 13 September.

Fukuyama, F. (1992), *The End of History and the Last Man*, New York: The Free Press.

Gray, R., Owen, D. and Maunders, K. (1987), *Corporate Social Reporting: Accounting and Accountability*, London: Prentice-Hall.

Green, K. (1992), 'Creating Demand for Biotechnology: Shaping Technologies and Markets', in R. Coombs, P. Saviotti and V. Walsh (eds), *Technological Change and Company Strategies*, London: Academic Press.

Griffin, J. (1986), *Well-being*, Oxford: Clarendon Press.

Hasnas, J. (1998), 'The Normative Theories of Business Ethics: A Guide for the Perplexed', *Business Ethics Quarterly*, January: 19–42.

Hetherington, J.A.C. (1973), *Corporate Social Responsibility Audit: A Management Tool for Survival*, London: The Foundation for Business Responsibilities.

Hobbes, T. (1651), *Leviathan*, many editions.

Holmes, L. and Grieco, M. (1999), *The Power of Transparency: The Internet, E-mail and the Malaysian Political Crisis*, paper presented to Asian Management in Crisis Conference, Association of South East Asian Studies, University of North London, June 1999.

Hutton, W. (1997), *Stakeholding and its Critics*, London: IEA Health and Welfare Unit.

Johnson, D.G. and Nissenbaum, H.F. (eds) (1995), *Computers, Ethics, and Social Values*, Englewood Cliffs, NJ: Prentice-Hall.

Kultgen, J. (1987), 'Donaldson's Social Contract for Business', *Business and Professional Ethics Journal*, Vol. 5: 28–39.

Locke, J. (1689), *Two Treatises of Government* (2nd edn 1967), ed. P. Laslett, New York: Cambridge University Press.

Lyon, D. (1994), *Postmodernity*, Buckingham, Milton Keynes: Open University Press.

Mathews, M.R. (1997), 'Twenty-five Years of Social and Environmental Accounting Research: Is There a Silver Jubilee to Celebrate?', *Accounting, Auditing and Accountability Journal*, Vol. 10, No. 4: 481–531.

McDonald, D. and Puxty, A.G. (1979), 'An Inducement–Contribution Approach to Corporate Financial Reporting', *Accounting, Organizations and Society*, Vol. 4, Nos 1/2: 53–65.

McLuhan, M. and Fiore, Q. (1968), *War and Peace in the Global Village*, San Francisco: Hardwired.

Mill, J.S. (1848), *Principles of Political Economy*, London.

Owen, R. (1991), *A New View of Society and Other Writings*, London: Penguin.

Pitt, M. (1990), 'Managing the Future: Questions and Dilemmas', in R. Loveridge and M. Pitt (eds), *The Strategic Management of Technological Innovation*, Chichester, West Sussex: John Wiley.

Rayman-Bacchus, L. (1996), *The Practice of Strategy*, unpublished PhD Thesis, University of Edinburgh.

Rayman-Bacchus, L. and Molina, A. (2001), 'Internet-based Tourism Services: Business Issues and Trends', *Futures*, Vol. 33: 589–605.

Robins, K. (1995), Cyberspace and the World We Live In', in M. Featherstone and R. Burrows (eds), *Cyberspace/Cyberbodies/Cyberpunk*, London: Sage.

Rousseau, J. (1762), *Du Contrat Social*, translated as *The Social Contract*, many editions.

Rushkoff, D. (1997), *Children of Chaos*, London: HarperCollins.

Russell, B. (1975), *Power*, London: Routledge.

Scheffler, S. (ed.) (1988), *Consequentialism and Its Critics*, Oxford: Oxford University Press.

Schwarz, M. and Thomson, M. (1990), *Divided We Stand: Redefining Politics, Technology and Social Choice*, Hemel Hempstead: Harvester Wheatsheaf.

Smith, H.J. and Hasnas, J. (1999), 'Ethics and Information Systems: The Corporate Domain', *MIS Quarterly*, Vol. 23, No. 1: 109–27.

Sobchack, V. (1996), 'Democratic Franchise and the Electronic Frontier', in Z. Sardar and J.R. Ravetz (eds), *Cyberfutures*, London: Pluto Press.

Sternberg, E. (1997), 'The Defects of Stakeholder Theory', *Corporate Governance: An International Review*, Vol. 6, No. 3: 151–63.

Sternberg, E. (1998), *Corporate Governance: Accountability in the Marketplace*, London: IEA.

Toffler, B.L. (2003), *Final Accounting: Ambition, Greed and the Fall of Arthur Andersen*, New York: Broadway Books.

Unger, S.H. (1994), *Controlling Technology: Ethics and the Responsible Engineer*, New York: Wiley.

PART 1
THEORISING CORPORATE SOCIAL RESPONSIBILITY

Chapter 2

Assessing Trust in, and Legitimacy of, the Corporate

Lez Rayman-Bacchus

Introduction

Are we experiencing a crisis of confidence in the legitimacy of the corporation? The last 30 years of the twentieth century have been marked by a number of scandals and accusations of wrong-doing by corporations and business leaders within the UK and the USA. These accusations have been spurred by a variety of incidents, all seeming to turn on an abuse of privilege in relations with stakeholders. For example, the disclosure of information, attempts to massage corporate performance data (financial, environmental) and public opinion and influence on government policy.

Policy makers tend to see these scandals as a crisis, each time attributing them to one or more identifiable mechanisms including: lack of independent oversight of the board; the corrupting effect of stock-options; loopholes in the financial reporting process; monopolistic behaviour; and failings of the audit process. More recent revelations have damaged investor confidence, fickle at the best of times, to the extent that UK and US stockmarkets fell 30–40 per cent during 2002. Of course there have been many incidences of wrong-doing throughout the twentieth century, of which the more public have sparked government enquiries, recommendations seeking to further tighten up accountability, and regulation to prevent a repeat of past excesses.

In recent times we have seen a succession of enquiries and recommendations: the Cadbury Enquiry (1992) into Financial Aspects of Corporate Governance, followed by the Hampel (1998) and Turnbull (1998) Reports. While investor confidence always seems to return, public trust remains low, despite the many legislative remedies of the last few decades. A 1976 survey (The Harris Survey) of public trust in major US institutions showed a drop of public confidence in major companies from 55 per cent in 1966 to 16 per cent in 1976. A similar survey conducted in 2002 (The Golin/Harris Survey) showed that public confidence in US corporations was still significantly low down a ranking list, based on a survey where almost 70 per cent of people said they did not trust corporations today.

These instances of wrong-doing, legal moves and social attitudes suggest that the legitimacy of the body corporate is under threat. As Mason (1959) observed more than 40 years ago and Sutton (1993) has more recently restated:

> who selected these men, if not to rule over us, at least to exercise vast authority, and to whom are they responsible? The answer to the first question is quite clearly: they selected themselves. The answer to the second is, at best, nebulous. This, in a nutshell, constitutes the problem of legitimacy.

At a general level this paper is concerned with examining the principles that we draw on in pursuit of individual and collective interests, and in managing our relations with corporations. More specifically, this paper explores the basis for trust in corporations, and whether whatever confidence we do have in the body corporate is misplaced in the context of what we (whether as investor or citizen) know and can know about corporate moral intention and behaviour. This discussion also needs to be located in the wider context of major social movements, since corporate interaction with these contexts generate trust and legitimacy. The paper first locates the growth of corporate influence, drawing on the historical roots of the corporation, ideological criticism and contemporary political developments. Having established the centrality of the corporation to a capitalist way of life, the notions of trust and legitimacy are introduced before discussing the relevance of these concepts to the role of the corporation in shaping and reflecting social change. The focus of the analysis here is public trust in, and legitimisation of, the corporation, rather than relations between individuals or between organisations.

An Evolving Global Context

The suggestion of a crisis may seem dramatic, but the term is useful for capturing what appears to be 'a gradual and uneven splitting of the complex network of ideas' that form our social fabric of which the corporation is such a major part.[1] The slow unfolding of a number of socio-political movements going back more than a century, tied up with the perceived ever increasing power of the corporation, provides the backdrop for a rising awareness of the potential of the corporation for good and ill. This engagement between society and the corporation has during the last century increasingly fed our sense of doubt in the moral integrity of the body corporate. The activities of corporations have attracted respect and suspicion in equal measure for a very long time now. We may glean some insight into this apparent contradiction by briefly looking at corporate history, twentieth century political and social swings, and reflection on Marxist ideas on political economy.

---

1 Quotation borrowed from a different context: McHoul and Grace's *A Foucault Primer* (1993: 3).

Evolving Power of the Corporation

The corporations of seventeenth and eighteenth century Europe were created by governments for a range specific purposes, from instruments of colonial expansion to financing and managing public projects and works. At one end of the spectrum of influence, charters were granted to explore and exploit new territories (e.g., Casa de San Giorgio of Genoa, and the East India Company of Britain). As instruments of legitimate governments, and supported by private armies, colonial enterprises enjoyed demonstrable power within the territories under their administration. Other charters were granted for projects with a clear life expectancy, including building canals, bridges and water systems. These charters both fuelled and supported the industrialisation of nineteenth century Europe and USA. Popular demand oversaw the opportunity for incorporation to expand from being a privilege to being a right, and for purposes of serving private (shareholder) rather than public interests.

Over the last 300 years the corporation has evolved from being an instrument of government chartered for a specific purpose, to being granted a statutory life independent of government, with the right to carry out any legitimate (lawful) activity. During this time the close relationship between State and corporation has not dissolved but evolved. The corporation has, in its own right, become central to both our economic and social development. In the words of Sutton (1993: 4), the corporation remains 'as the primary agents for the advancement of capitalism, industrialism, and technical progress'. Indeed current debates about globalisation reflect fears that some corporations wield more political and economic influence than many nation states. Heilbroner (1988) for example, reflecting on the development of capitalism, observed that the corporation has evolved into a semi-autonomous economy within and beyond the legislative state.

Differing assessments of the competitive nature of capitalism highlight its unstable nature. In addition to the oft cited notion of competition, Marx's class conflict, Schumpeter's technological change, Keynes' view of changing demand/supply conditions, all testify to the lack of consensus on how corporate behaviour shapes capitalist industrial society. Indeed Marx and Weber, the two iconic sociologists of the nineteenth century, saw the emerging industrial society as (respectively) conflictual and cooperative. From a Marxian perspective the corporation is exploitative and antithetical to socially responsible behaviour. For some the state could and should play a part in harnessing capitalism to meet societal needs. Keynes, the twentieth century economist, saw an interventionist role for the state in managing the demand/supply cycle and thereby reducing if not removing social conflict. During the twentieth century whole sectors regarded by governments as having a strategic (national) significance, including employment and industrial competitiveness, have operated under various degrees of state control or regulation. Examples include the utilities, health, education, financing home ownership, steel and fossil fuel production.

The last two decades of the twentieth century have been marked by a sharp reversal of such policies by governments around the world, both right and left. Governments have been relinquishing control of state enterprises to the body corporate. More profoundly, government has been encouraging or creating new managerialist administrative frameworks within which to provide public services, including health, education, cultural and charitable services (Zan, 2001). There is a sense in which the body corporate has become a Hobbesian Leviathan. Commenting almost 100 years ago, Davis (1905) noted the growth of the corporation as a 'conspicuous feature' of the social development of Europe and America. Writing in the seventeenth century, Hobbes argued that the best way for subjects to ensure long term peaceful coexistence was to contract among themselves to gift the sovereign with their unconditional obedience (Hampton, 1986); giving a sovereign anything less than absolute power would be a recipe for civil unrest (Kavka, 1986; Gauthier, 1969). Paralleling Hobbes' prescription for the relationship between subject and sovereign in the seventeenth century, this paper suggests that we, the twentieth century citizenry of capitalist economies, have surrendered to the body corporate the determination of our long-term preservation. This proposition goes beyond the common view of corporate history that the rights of the individual corporation – and by extension all corporations – are granted under contract with us the citizenry, and by implication are revocable. We have become subjects of the body corporate, whom we rely on for all our needs, both economic and welfare. The new managerialist paradigm rests on the belief that the body corporate is the best guarantor of the individual's prosperity and wellbeing. Social policy is increasingly shaped by the body corporate and its managerialist rationality.

Demise of Socialism and Growth of Capitalism

Although some combination of respect and distrust have been in the making for a century, major socio-political change during the last forty years seem to have added impetus to the process of capitalist growth. These events have enriched the power of the corporation. Perhaps the most spectacular socio-political change has been the end of the Cold War. The political and economic sweeping away of the democratic-socialist divide has helped the spread of corporate globalisation, enabled greater mobility of labour and knowledge workers, and encouraged greater mobility of capital. The economic and political influence of the corporation has been further enlarged through the easing of legislative and financial controls, resulting for example in a flourishing of financial innovations in capital raising mechanisms, and technological innovations, most notably the development of the Internet and other Information and Communication Technologies (ICT).

The collapse of socialism and the end of the Cold War in the early 1990s were immediate and dramatic, resulting in a transformation of the political and economic relations between East and West. At the same time, and in part because of the apparent failure of socialism, the more economically secure economies have experienced a strengthening of democratic ideals and ideological commitment to capitalism. For example in the form of legislative attempts to further open up democracy – or create it out of the ashes of socialism, the promotion of the rights and freedoms of the individual and the pursuit of self-interest through the market mechanism. Capitalism did not simply step into the vacuum left by socialism; this strengthening of commitment to capitalism was already under way. Indeed capitalist economies were themselves experiencing a range of transformations, exhibiting characteristics that varied spatially and temporally. Reganomics (remembered for deregulation of USA industries) and Thatcherism (remembered for privatisation of UK state-controlled enterprises) of the 1980s, underpinned by an ideological commitment to classical liberalism, had overturned the 1960s and 1970s welfare liberalism of the UK and USA which seemed to be fostering economic decay and social unrest. Tinker (1991) offers a measured analysis of this movement through his periodisation study of capitalism. By examining the pattern of corporate social responsibility accounting between the 1960s and 1980s, he traced the movement of capitalism through various ideological manifestations: a preoccupation with mergers and acquisitions during the 1960s (Brilovian critique); followed by a concern that corporations be more socially accountable (caring society); followed by a swing away from supporting welfare programmes towards a market forces ideology during the 1980s (market re-regulation).

A new world order has emerged at the turn of the twenty-first century, confirming the USA as the most powerful state, economically and militarily. As (American) capitalism colonises the old socialist enemy the East-versus-West argument has evaporated.[2] During the last half of the twentieth century political arguments have shifted from debating the relative merits of a centrally planned economy against those of a market economy (Parkin, 1971; Lane, 1985), to arguments about *which* form of market economy.

Even before this very tangible political and economic collapse of the socialist economies, and their conversion to capitalism, other key ideological foundations were being called into question if not discredit. McHoul and Grace's (1993: 5) exposition of Foucault's rethinking of the concepts of discourse, power, and the history of ideas offers some insight into these changes. Foucault saw that since the 1960s, Marxist political economy had looked increasingly irrelevant.

> [T]he classical Marxist model seemed unable to cope with the new kinds of struggle emerging in so-called post industrial societies … centred as much on race, gender and ecology as on purely economic considerations such as class.

The class struggle of the nineteenth and early twentieth century, central to the Marxist thesis on capitalism, had by the late twentieth century evolved into a more complex division of labour and a fragmenting of old class distinctions, involving

---

2   Indeed American capitalism seems unconsciously to have succeeded in colonisation where American foreign policy failed in its attempts to stop the perceived spread of communism, the wars in Korea and Vietnam being two spectacular examples.

a diversity of struggles. In addition to these more complex and diversified forms of struggle, the industrial base of capitalism was also undergoing transformation. Knowledge-based forms of production had supplanted traditional heavy production industries as the industrial base in our way of life or 'form of social existence' (Poster, 1984; McHoul and Grace, 1993: 5). Moreover, important ideas underpinning Marxist political economy seemed increasingly out of place: the notion of an economic base supporting an ideological superstructure. Classical Marxism held that the real economic conditions of a society (the ownership and means of production) represented the base from which grew that society's culture, beliefs and laws. This model of society where material conditions (the economic base) determine ideas (the ideological superstructure) was now looking overly simplistic. For example, the technologies underlying the nuclear arms race were founded on scientific ideas. Furthermore those features distinguishing the industrial base from the superstructure in the post-industrial way of life of the late twentieth century, were now looking more arbitrary than a century earlier. The predicted overthrow of capitalism by the proletariat has not happened (at least not yet). Indeed capitalism has become stronger, while socialism seems retired. The corporation has evolved a more subtle and complex role in the capitalist economy than envisaged in Marxist thinking of the nineteenth and early twentieth centuries.

Tensions

The evolution of the body corporate, set in the context of contemporary political movements and ideological insights, give a sense of the power and influence enjoyed by the body corporate, and the increasing centrality of a managerialist discourse and practice in our way of life. However this corporate success is accompanied by much unrest and concern that the leviathan is out of control. While few would argue that capitalism has brought benefits, many would argue that these have come at a price, which highlights the tensions and conflicts inherent in capitalism. For some time now observers have expressed concerns about the scale of corporate influence. These concerns are reflected in recent headline grabbing protests, often violent, that have attended successive World Trade Organisation (WTO) ministerial meetings (held in Seattle, 1999 and in Genoa, 2001). These instances of civil unrest testify to a popular perception that globalisation is to blame for the widening gap between rich and poor nations. The WTO and member industrialised countries are suspected to be self-serving, supporting the interests of their corporations. Sections of society increasingly see the (global) corporation as being deeply implicated in this conspiracy; of being both sponsor and beneficiary of a programme that is not in the interests of either the southern hemisphere or the environment. Many see the rescue of Kuwait in 1991, and the invasion of Iraq by the USA and UK in 2003 as examples of political events being driven by corporate and economic interests.

With incomes larger than that of some countries, and operations that span more than 50 countries, one might plausibly argue that the global corporation has eclipsed many nation-states in its ability to influence local and regional politics. We have become acutely aware, in large part through the efforts of pressure groups and investigative journalism, of the potentially damaging influence of corporations. Companies are being held responsible for a range of social and economic ills, including: the pollution and destruction of our natural environment; the development of morally contentious technologies (GM foods, cloning); a suspicion of subverting the democratic process (funding political parties, favours to politicians); a widening gap between the rich and poor in our society; and impeding the economic growth of less developed countries. These undesirable effects constitute a crisis. As Sutton (1993: 7) has observed, the corporation is contributing to, and experiencing the effects of

> a systemic crisis that gained momentum with the end of the Cold War. These crises – restrictions on resources, religious and political tyranny, ecological degradation and so on ... cannot be resolved or even explained within the usual parameters of either political or business management.

If the corporation is so fundamental to our economic wellbeing, yet there remains a sense of suspicion that the body corporate is morally bankrupt, then issues of trust and legitimacy come to the fore. The question of trust in, and legitimacy of, the corporation arises because of on-going concern about the power that corporations exercise, and for some time now there has been a generalised weakening of trust in the corporation. Under ideal democratic conditions trust in corporate performance and behaviour is a precondition for the legitimate exercise of corporate power: if these corporations are to remain viable, they need our continued collective support. This erosion of trust seems to be based on a number of concerns: a sense that unknown corporations are exaggerating or purposefully making misleading claims about their performance, both economic and social; and that some corporations are pursuing aims and strategies, and exploiting technologies, that do not have public support (from armaments to hamburgers). These concerns are set against a background of shifting social values about the purpose of the corporation.

Trust and Legitimacy

The notion of trust has been shown to carry a variety of meanings and can be used in many ways. There is broad agreement that trust assumes interdependence between trustor and trustee. Trust is the trustor's attitude of dependence on another (the trustee) as the former takes the leap of faith required to get from the known to the unknown with the attendant risk and uncertainty. Furthermore, the trustor expects that the trustee will not exploit the vulnerability of the trustor's exposure to risk. Beyond these ideas writers assume divergent models of human behaviour. In their analysis of trust between organisations, Lane and Bachmann (1998) offer a useful summary of the varieties of trust that have been applied to organisations: rational or calculative trust (favoured by economists, agency theory and game theorists); shared values or norm-based trust; common expectations or cognitions based trust. These models of trust, either singly or in combination, have been applied at different levels of analysis: at a micro-level between individuals or organisations; institutions as sources of trust (Zucker, 1986), as distinct from trust or confidence in abstract systems (Luhmann, 1979); and societal trust (Fox, 1974; Fukuyama, 1995).

We gain some insight into corporate behaviour by considering four aspects of trust relations: the nature of deception; whether trust enhances corporate economic performance; whether personal trust is a valuable metaphor for institutional trust; and the extent to which trust relations are differentiated. These treatments are necessarily brief, but they serve to challenge assumptions. First, deception is commonly regarded as a conscious choice, but in an organisational setting, collective culpability can force individuals to involuntarily become party to the deception. Second, we might expect a positive relationship between trust and economic performance; greater trust leading to better performance. Corporate strategy certainly seeks to build customer confidence and lock in customers as part of its growth strategy. However the evidence shows the link between trust and performance to be complex and not necessarily positively correlated. Third, much theorising about trust treats the organisation as the individual writ large. In some sense individual personality is a useful metaphor for organisational culture, but there are significant problems with this approach in assessing trust relations. Fourth, close examination of trust relations shows that different stakeholder groups are likely to invest differing forms of trust in the same corporation; trust relations involve more than simply more or less trust.

Deception

As surveys repeatedly show, there is an established and significant level of public distrust of those in authority. Through individual experience and public disclosure of the particular, the investing community and a broad spectrum of citizens have become sceptical about all claims made by corporations. Corporations are expected to lie about any and everything; an expectation that is confirmed by the regular disclosure of corporate lying (in recent times Enron, Tyco, Arthur Andersen).

General trust has long been regarded as the glue that binds social cooperation (Simmel, 1950; Bok, 1978; Lewis and Weigert, 1985), and that without trust society is left with 'chaos and paralysing fear' (Luhmann, 1979: 4). Every lie helps undermine that general trust. Isolated instances of lying by executives are based on the assumption that most others are at the same time honest. These individuals may lie in pursuit of self-interest (promotion, bonuses, share option incentives), with 'little regard for good faith' (Bok, 1978: 23). Although Bok's evaluation of the practice of lying did not focus on the body corporate, her observations are nonetheless appropriate here since her analysis is aimed at those holding positions of trust. Moreover, as Bok (1978: 83) has observed, 'it is more often the case that persons or groups ... participate involuntarily in practices involving intentional deception. They are then forced to plan their strategy knowing that deception is possible or even likely.' The degree to which deception is widespread is a measure of corruption of the body corporate, and the uncertainty in the public mind of the level of deception weakens public trust further.

Corporate Economic Performance

The evidence is divided about whether trust enhances organisational economic performance. Williamson (1993) sees no useful relationship, while Kern (1998) sees no positive correlation between trust and organisational performance but see the possibility of too much trust, acting as a brake on organisational innovation and thus performance; the comfort and trust of familiar relations discourages experimentation.

Those suggesting that trust increases organisational performance argue that personal obligations and shared-value commitments dispense with the need for monitoring and control mechanisms against the risk of opportunistic behaviour by the trustee, thereby saving in transaction costs (Arrow, 1974; Granovetter, 1985; Barney and Hansen, 1994). The increasingly global reach of many corporations is not a product of increasing stakeholder trust, but of strategic alliances and networks between corporations. Such inter-organisational relations are seen to prosper where organisations enter into flexible and long-term relationships, the development of common frameworks for sharing knowledge, which if productive leads to high levels of trust (Ring and van de Ven, 1992). From a more sociological perspective, Fukuyama (1995) sees trust as a cultural phenomenon that is central to economic development at the societal level. In his view, capitalist East Asia has grown faster than the economies of Western democracies due to the former's greater reliance on trust, community and social commitments in contrast to the latter's culture of individualism. In addition, the institutional arrangements of individual countries produce varying degrees of trust, which accounts for differences in organisational compliance and economic performance between countries (Lane, 1997).

Corporate economic performance and trust do not appear to be strongly correlated. These analyses show that the concept of trust does not have uniform meaning and value but varies both with analytical lens and with the particular social arrangements being studied. This might be because performance is contingent on a wide variety of factors, and trust while desirable is not critical, since there are substitute mechanisms which we shall consider later.

Institutional Behaviour

Insofar as we may regard the corporation as one of a number of corporate institutions, most would agree that once an institution is put in place and becomes an established landmark, it is then seen as durable, taken for granted, and can be relied on to behave in predictable ways. Its predictability is born of the exercise of impersonal and formal procedures and rules. This impersonal character prevents the development of personal trust relations. More importantly, the predictability of behaviour makes the need for trust redundant. From this perspective we do not need to trust corporations to behave ethically because the regulatory framework, pressure groups and competitive forces ensure that they behave in ways that earn public confidence.

This however is a naive view of institutions, and particularly the corporation. There are useful parallels in the relationship between citizen and state and between citizen and corporation. Offe's (1999: 66) assessment of government institutions seems equally appropriate for corporate institutions. He regards institutions as,

> patterns of precarious and potentially contested cooperation'. [Institutional] rules can never provide for all contingencies and emergencies. ... [T]hey leave uncovered ... ever-present opportunities, as well as motives, for the opportunistic violation or subversion of institutions ...

Corporations are populated with persons, not robots, working in cooperation. First, administrators have to interpret the rules and make choices in light of particular circumstances. Rules can be interpreted broadly or narrowly, and at times have to be amended in light of unforeseen conditions. Second, individuals carry particular and often competing career and political agendas. From this, trust in institutions is no substitute for trust in individuals. However, while corporations loom large in our every-day lives, we as stakeholders cannot meaningfully assess our own confidence in these corporations as we might do with individuals, because we do not, and cannot, know what we need to know about any given corporation before deciding to invest our trust. Our modern democracies are very complex and while social trust is a necessary lubricant for the way we live, as Luhmann (1979: 46) observes 'it is all too obvious that the social order does not stand and fall by the few people one knows and trusts'. These arguments suggest that we cannot trust in either the corporation as an institution (due to the interpretive flexibility of rules and individual political behaviour) or the individuals (since we can know so few, and often have no personal relations with them).

Differentiated Trust

Stakeholders may have more or less interest in a corporation's activities, and more or less influence on the form and substance of that activity. Consequently individuals and organised groups (lenders, creditors, institutional shareholders, lobby groups, activists and pressure groups) are likely to take a range of positions of confidence in relation to the corporation.

The particular orientation of each stakeholder toward the corporation will dictate the nature of trust relations with that corporation. This intersection of stakeholder interest with the influence they have over corporate activity generates four possible positions of trust (Figure 2.1). In the first group will be those investing *active trust* (corporate executive group, senior managers, lenders, major creditors). They play, or seek, an active role in shaping the outcomes or processes of the corporation. Their vested interest and support for the corporation's strategy coincide. The second group of stakeholders (for example institutional shareholders and government) adopt a *neutral* position, possessing strong influence, but minimal direct interest. A change of circumstances could raise their interest, leading to a more active role in the corporate governance structure. A third group of stakeholders, such as community groups, may *actively distrust* the corporation.

These and other sectional interest groups may normally carry weak influence but have a keen interest in the corporation's activities. These groups may emerge from individuals banding together to fight a specific issue, perhaps affecting their local environment (for example mobile telephone antennae masts). They assume some level of social irresponsibility or unethical predisposition by the corporation. These groups tend to see their interests as being antithetical to those of the corporation. There is a fourth group that may be described as fatalistic. They share minimal or no interest in corporate activity, and have no sense of influence over such activity. This might be the state for most citizenry.

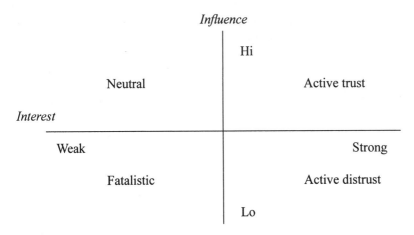

Figure 2.1   Trust relations matrix

Source: Adapted from Mendelow (1991).

While the matrix helps to highlight the differentiated nature of trust relations, it may overstate the homogeneity of stakeholder interests. For example, trade unions may occupy any of the quadrants, depending on their size and role in the corporate governance structure. Particular unions may have differing degrees of interest and influence over corporate activity. Furthermore trust relations are dynamic. Stakeholders' attitudes and behaviour change in response to changing circumstances, sometimes initiating change. Trust is a differentiated resource, the value and meaning of which is contingent on the nature of the relationship between corporation and stakeholder, and such relations may change over time. How corporations behave is influenced weakly by generalised trust, and influenced strongly by those holding political and economic sanction.

Alternatives to General Trust

Before leaving the discussion of trust, we should recognise the alternatives to general trust. In evaluating trust relations between stakeholders and the body corporate, there is need to distinguish between general trust as the basis for dependency, with alternative forms of relationship: grounded interest, predictability and delegation. These other forms of relationships may bolster confidence in the viability of a relationship, but there is a danger of confusing trust with these alternatives.

Grounded Interest

A central argument of agency theory or the shareholder model of corporate governance is that the trustee's motivations are grounded in the stakeholder's interests. The stakeholder's trust in the trustee (individual executive or the board) is based on the knowledge or belief that organisational and regulatory devices (governance systems) exist to compel the trustee to act in the stakeholder's interests. Management development and performance control mechanisms provide for the trustee to be competent to act in the stakeholder's interests. At the same time, the stakeholder need not be directly competent to judge the trustee. The stakeholder has the option of delegating much of their judgement to third parties, such as legal bodies and professional advisors.

Predictability

Corporations can be large and complex bureaucracies, and individual stakeholders, except institutional shareholders, cannot develop trust based on close (thick) and long-lasting relations with individual board members. First, these senior executives are typically once, twice, or thrice removed from consumer and investor. Second, many board members, especially Independent or non-executive members, are not there to foster such relations. Indeed they are there to provide arms length oversight. If the existence of trust requires grounding in relations with the organisation, but where the scope to develop such relations is accidental, then on what basis can we trust a corporation? There are two possibilities. One is to trust individual executives to be competent in their responsibility to fulfil our trust. The other is to trust in the role, incentives and corporate structure to deliver against our expectations. Neither is practical. The first requires us to invest an immeasurable amount of time and effort to know a large number of individuals. The second assumes that we can make sense of corporate structures and the many roles and incentives within them to be confident that the role holder will fulfil our trust. The reality is that while we might distrust corporations, we expect them to behave in the future much as they have behaved in the past. We base our expectations on this predictability.

Delegation

By giving someone control of some issue we delegate that concern. We, the consumer, stakeholder, citizen, collectively delegate to corporations the generation of wealth. Moreover, by delegating power to corporations we unavoidably enable them to influence other affairs, social, political, economical. We want corporations to accurately perceive our wants and develop products and services to meet our every whim, but we balk at the prospect of corporations gathering and using personal data for commercial gain. We delegate, but do not necessarily trust.

Assessing Legitimacy

As with trust, the notion of legitimacy is also multi faceted, and is reflected in differing views on its meaning. The concept has been given a self-justificatory emphasis (Maurer, 1971), and an emphasis on conformity to social norms (Dowling and Pfeffer, 1975). These interpretations share an evaluative emphasis, being concerned with whether an organisation's behaviour is acceptable to constituencies or not. This perspective may be distinguished from Meyer and Scott's (1983) emphasis on seeing legitimacy as concerned with constituencies being able to understand an organisation's behaviour. A prerequisite of *acceptance* in these terms must be *understanding*. Clearly these interpretations refer to differing parts of the elephant: corporations seek acceptance for their actions, just as much as constituencies want corporations to conform to certain norms of behaviour. For the purposes of this discussion two forms of legitimacy may be distinguished: competitive legitimacy and social legitimacy.

Competitive Legitimacy

Competing firms and their networks of supporting and complementary firms and organisations share certain experiences, assumptions and beliefs about the best way to compete. These similarities are reflected in common discernable practices and discourse, and lend support to such concepts as *strategic groups, industry recipes* and *organisational fields*. Such practice and discourse becomes institutionalised, generating acceptable and unacceptable competitive behaviour. Legitimate strategies therefore are those seen to develop within an institutional framework. Clearly corporate failure may be initiated when the actions of key stakeholders of a corporation influence other stakeholders to distrust, regardless of their interest (capital market, product market or organisational). For example when the CEO of Ratners the jewellers ridiculed its own products, its share value tumbled and sales plummeted. Ratners questioned its own legitimacy, and led to a loss of trust and economic viability.

Corporations seeking legitimacy for their aims and strategies, and in particular from potential investors and lenders, will be sensitive to this legitimating framework. When set against the importance of building competitive advantage through differentiation, Deephouse (1999) suggests that successful corporations strike a balance between conformance and deviation, but remain within legitimate boundaries. Developing this argument further, we may regard boundaries as social constructs where cognitive and emotional judgements determine whether corporate action is comprehensible and acceptable by stakeholders or wider constituencies. Moreover, it seems likely that social and technological innovation encourages both corporations and constituencies to continually push and stretch the envelope of legitimacy.

Social Legitimacy

Boundaries of legitimacy are blurred and corporations may find themselves negotiating that boundary, or actively attempting to redefine the boundary, in terms of changing constituency understanding and acceptance of their actions.

Stillman's (1974) observation that 'a government is legitimate ... only if ... government output are consistent with the value pattern of the society' might seem applicable to the corporation. We, as citizens, like to think that the legitimacy of the corporation rests on that corporation continuing to meet societal expectations, not just in terms of products and services, but also in terms of demonstrable ethical and socially responsible behaviour. Moreover while government power is legitimated through election, for a constitutionally determined period, in contrast, the corporation derives much of its power and legitimacy from a variety of organised stakeholder groups, without time limit. Clearly an assessment of governmental legitimacy includes a test of sustainability that is more stringent than that applied to the corporation.

Corporations invest much effort in creating, maintaining and repairing understanding and support from constituencies, and adopt a variety of strategies as deemed appropriate (Dowling and Pfeffer, 1975; Ashforth and Gibbs, 1990; Suchman, 1995). For example, Dowling and Pfeffer (1975) suggest three strategies that corporations may use. First, the corporation may change its behaviour to conform to constituency expectations, for example to cease employment of child labour. A second strategy is to attempt to change or manage public perception of its actions; an area that keeps the public relations industry busy. In the third strategy the corporation attempts to associate itself with symbols of legitimacy, such as publishing an environmental report alongside the annual report and accounts (Buhr, 2002). In this there is no attempt to change behaviour or to change public expectations.

Is trust a precondition for legitimacy of the corporation? At a general level if, in order for the corporation to be legitimate, we must trust in it, then the evidence is that corporations are not to be trusted, and are thereby not legitimate. Corporations continue to prosper as long as they are economically viable, without necessarily being legal or legitimate. Stakeholders, paying close attention to corporate strategy, are able to form a view about the competences and intentions of a few executives, and by extension the whole corporation. These stakeholders may genuinely trust, and therefore fund and support, the corporation. Others follow guided by a herd mentality, based in part on assumed superior knowledge of the first group, and in part on assumed expectations of others. More generally corporations survive and thrive as long as core stakeholders trust, and not too many other stakeholders actively distrust, the corporation. Generalised trust appears to have a less than critical role in legitimating the individual corporation. What then is the basis for the legitimate exercise of corporate power?

Max Weber (1968) in his well-known analysis of the basis of the cohesion of a community, offered three sources of legitimacy: traditions and customs, legal-rational procedures (e.g., voting), and charismatic leadership. From this perspective the voluntary support and cooperation of stakeholders toward corporations is a product of these elements in combination. First, if capitalism can be called a tradition – based on the continued development of our economic system through practice and belief in it, going back at least to the Middle Ages – then this custom and practice legitimates our continued support for the corporation. Second, legal-rational procedures provide an overt framework of legitimacy. Boards must follow predefined procedures in resolving major decisions, some of which requires shareholder approval (the appointment of the most senior corporate officers, including non-executive directors, remuneration). More widely, corporations carry statutory obligations to uphold prescribed standards across a range of activities, including product safety, supporting employee rights, accounting for their impact on the environmental (ecological and social). Third, confidence in the corporation is commonly bound up with the personality of the CEO, whose remarks can send share prices up as well as down.

Contested Legitimacy

An important weakness of Weber's sources of legitimacy is that they ignore the responsibilities of the corporation towards stakeholders. Corporations cannot legitimise themselves. They are accountable to stakeholders and institutions that set performance criteria beyond corporate control. Furthermore, while Weber's sources are important, and compliance with modern governance systems is mandatory, these considerations are still not sufficient to motivate support and cooperation from stakeholders. Trust is needed, especially where some widely shared sense of the public good is at stake; a public good which may be in conflict with corporate interests, for example the commercial disposal of nuclear waste.

We need to trust in the exceptional competency of the leadership, in the fairness of decision makers, in the impartiality of institutional procedures, that executives, working individually or in cooperation, do not act opportunistically to our disadvantage, and we need to trust in the values that the corporation espouses. Stakeholders have differentiated knowledge of these issues, and in any case not all stakeholders will support particular corporate aims and strategies equally. The corporation therefore experiences trust and legitimacy unevenly from its public, who will regard the corporation's aims and strategies as acceptable or unacceptable, and will have varying degrees of influence over the corporation. Institutional investors, pressure groups and incumbent managers all exercise influence, but such influence is clearly mediated by narrow sectional interests. For example the interests of institutional shareholders overlap only partially with those of the incumbent managers. Pressure group agendas vary widely but their concerns often bring them in conflict with incumbent managers, whether prosecuting ecological concerns, monitoring equal opportunity practises or monitoring respect for consumer rights.

Discussion: Change

The embeddedness of capitalist ideas within the liberalist ideology of western democracies provides for both the longevity of the corporation and paradoxically fuels the tensions and conflicts that drive shifting social expectations and corporate behaviour. Capitalist ideas are so embedded that while the corporation is subject to social change, it is at the same time an important source of social change. From this perspective the movement of commitment from one capitalist ideology to another is not, as some have suggested, driven by 'structural inequalities and disadvantages' that are internal to capitalism alone (Tinker, 1991: 36). Such movement is also a product of the embedded relations between capitalism and democratic ideals. Indeed Tinker's 'periodisation' study unintentionally highlights that corporate behaviour and societal expectation are bound together by the tensions between the interests of society and those of the body corporate.

While society exercises a *collective will* to rein in and regulate corporate freedom (through legislation, the activities of pressure groups and decades of tightening accountability), corporate influence is at the same time shaping social expectations. First, successive governments have led the adoption of the managerialist model to all parts of our social organisation. Second corporations routinely enrol accounting and marketing principles and practices in order to raise capital and manage investor perceptions. Mouck (1994) for example in his examination of three areas of corporate activity (technological innovation, advertising and influence over mass media) shows the potential of corporations for generating social change. Moreover, corporations employ a variety of strategies to create and maintain legitimacy, sometimes targeting underlying social expectations (Lindblom reported in Buhr, 2002).

Sources of Change

Such attempts to change social expectations are often contested. Further, legal statutes alone provide insufficient support for corporate action. For example the legitimacy of genetically modified (GM) foods is hotly contested. One argument to emerge has been that consumers do not understand the value of GM foods and overstate the dangers. Both Monsanto (corporation with R&D invested) and the UK government have been trying to educate consumers over safety concerns. Consumer groups in turn view claims in favour of GM foods with suspicion. There remains much distrust in this emerging sector as reflected in the slow and uneven acceptance of GM foods. Where economic viability relies on demand then trust and legitimacy are needed.

Trust relations are differentiated and corporate legitimacy is a contested terrain. The corporation need not be palpably engaged in illegal, unethical or socially irresponsible activity. Such activity simply needs to fall outside acceptable norms and values of the constituencies. These conditions generate scope for both corporate innovation and social change. What counts as legitimate corporate behaviour varies across a wide variety of social arrangements, some of those arrangements remaining stable, while others are in a greater state of flux. Legitimate corporate activity can also be contested where differing sections of society hold conflicting beliefs about the value or morality of such activity. These conflicts deepen when existing legal statutes, as the arbiter of last resort, are found to be inadequate in the face of changing social values and a widening envelope of the technologically possible. Sometimes the activity is regarded by sections of society as morally right even if illegal, as in the on-going debate about euthanasia. Even the reverse is possible, whereby some activity may be legal, such as the right to abortion, but the moral basis of which is contested by sections of society.

A Model for Change

We appear increasingly to expect the corporation to acknowledge and respect notions of community welfare and justice, alongside the creation of wealth. A common attitude of gratitude for corporate philanthropy during the early twentieth century has, by the late twentieth century, evolved to an expectation of corporate social responsibility. While developed and developing economies argue over the division of the global pie, it is the management of public services that is taking centre stage as governments seem increasingly unable to finance major public projects and welfare services. Both developed and developing nations want business to play a significant role in providing services that previously fell within the preserve of the state, from clean water and medical care to education and public transport.

Despite concerns about the legitimacy of business practices, and that the motives of corporations are anathema to the purposes of a public service, governments around the world have come to believe that the *modus operandi* of business is a model of efficient administration, customer centred, and will be more effective at delivering public services. In the UK this collaboration between state and the corporation is taking place under the banner of the Private Finance Initiative (PFI). Indeed the corporate model of business administration has become so entrenched that public services have been re-engineered to model themselves on the managerialist model. For example in the UK the organisation and management of local government, the National Health Service and the management of many schools, and in Italy the management of cultural services (Zan, 2002). The legitimacy of these re-engineered public services remain in question, in part because there appears to be a conflict of interest between maximising returns to shareholders and maintaining a high quality, low cost public service. In assessing corporate performance in these new settings policy makers seem to conflate the interests of shareholders and the requirements of good public service. This new corporatism is driven by the doctrine that market forces and business methods are the right bases on which to organise society.

Conclusions

The social organisation of developed democratic economies, such as the UK and other European states and the USA, is in crisis. Trust in, and the legitimacy of the corporation, a key element of this social organisation, is in question. Indeed there has been a sense of unease for some time now. I have tried to make sense of this crisis from three perspectives: the historical roots of the relationship between state and corporation; the consequences of the end of the Cold War and socialism for democratic states and capitalism; and through reflection on the role of the corporation through a re-examination of Marx's ideological assessment of the tensions between capital and labour.

Trust and legitimacy are important because the corporation is able to exercise significant power and influence, rivalling that of the state. Moreover, periodic and repeated determinations of corporate wrong-doing undermines general trust and invites speculation about the level of wrong-doing not uncovered. Such incidences confirm to all observers that there are good reasons for stakeholders to distrust corporate motives and practices. However, trust relations are complex. Corporations experience a range of different trust relations, all operating at the same time – active and passive trust and distrust – which vary according to the relationship between corporation and stakeholder. A lack of trust need not paralyse trust relations or the functioning of the corporation. Delegation, grounded interest and predictability mean that corporate life goes on without necessarily involving trust. Despite the lack of generalised trust in corporations they survive and prosper, as long as the corporation has the support of key stakeholders and there is minimal active distrust from other quarters.

Taken over the last 200 years the purpose and influence of the corporation has evolved, as has its relationship with the state. The corporation has grown from being an instrument of state political and economic policy, to becoming an independent institutional force for social, economic and technological change, rivalling many nation states by the end of the twentieth century. Some of these changes have been on a global scale filling the economic vacuum left by failed socialism. At the same time social values have developed in new directions, for example in work and leisure patterns, and attitudes to ecological damage.

These social movements are imbued with corporate influence, through for example technological change. Equally, corporate evolution reflects the development of social preferences, for example in employee rights and corporate social responsibilities, often enforced through legislation. The continual movement of social values means that expectations remain in some state of flux. Evolving social expectations also carries a paradox. On the one hand, a lack of general trust means that the legitimacy of the corporation remains under scrutiny and is always open to challenge.

On the other hand, the fruits of corporate activity provide a compelling argument for adopting the corporate model of administration to other activities in society, in particular the delivery of public services. According to this argument corporate enterprise and efficiency has generated an Aladdin's cave of consumer goods and services, accounting for the economic success of developed nations. Since governments – of both developed and developing nations – find themselves unable to either fund or manage public services, then perhaps the corporation is better able to carry that mantle.

Given the evolving nature of both corporate purpose and influence and social expectations, we might reasonably expect the emergence of some new form of social organisation, in both developed and developing economies. Based on observable developments in state policy and innovations in state-corporation relations, this paper suggests that a new form of capitalism seems to be emerging. As this new form of social organisation develops, business will play an increasingly central role in financing and managing public services. Perhaps more profoundly, business administration already established as a model of efficiency, will become the exemplar for how local and state government should be organised and managed.

References

Arrow, K. (1974), *The Limits of Organization*, New York: Norton.

Ashforth, B.E. and Gibbs, B.W. (1990), 'The Double Edge of Organizational Legitimation', *Organization Science*, Vol. 1, No. 2: 177–94.

Barney, J.B. and Hansen, M.H. (1994), 'Trustworthiness as a Source of competitive advantage', *Strategic Management Journal*, 15: 175–90.

Beetham, D. (1991), *The Legitimation of Power*, Basingstoke: Macmillan.

Bok, S. (1978), *Lying*, Hassocks: Harvester.

Buhr, N. (2002), 'A Structural View on the Initiation of Environmental Reports', *Critical Perspectives on Accounting*, Vol. 13: 17–38.

Davis, J.P. (1905), *Corporations: A Study of the Origin and Development of Great Business Combinations and of their Relation to the Authority of the State*, New York: Putnam and Sons (reprinted by Hein, New York).

Deephouse, D. (1999), 'To be Different or to be the Same?: It's a Question (and Theory) of Strategic Balance', *Strategic Management Journal*, Vol. 20, No. 2: 147–66.

Dowling, J. and Pfeffer, J. (1975), 'Organizational Legitimacy: Social Values and Organizational Behavior', *Pacific Sociological Review*, Vol. 18, No. 1: 122–36.

Fox, A. (1974), *Beyond Contract: Work, Power and Trust Relations*, London: Faber and Faber.

Fukuyama, F. (1995), *Trust: The Social Virtues and the Creation of Prosperity*, London: Hamish Hamilton.

Gauthier, D.P. (1969), *The Logic of Leviathan*, Oxford: Oxford University.

Giddens, A. (1978), *Durkheim*, London: Fontana.

Golin/Harris Survey (2002), *American Business Faces a Crisis of Trust*, Chicago: Golin/Harris International.

Granovetter, M. (1985), 'Economic Action and Social Structure: A Theory of Embeddedness', *American Journal of Sociology*, Vol. 91: 481–510.

Hampton, J. (1986), *Hobbes and the Social Contract Tradition*, Cambridge: Cambridge University Press.

Heilbroner, R. (1988), *Behind the Veil of Economics*, New York: Norton.

Kavka, G.S. (1986), *Hobbesian Moral and Political Theory*, New Jersey: Princeton University Press.

Kern, H. (1998), 'Lack of Trust, Surfeit of Trust: Some Causes of the Innovation Crisis In German Industry', in C. Lane and R. Bachmann (eds), *Trust within and between Organisations*, Guildford: Oxford University Press.

Lane, C. (1997), 'The Social Regulation of Inter-firm Relations in Britain and Germany: Market Rules, Legal Norms and Technical Standards', *Cambridge Journal of Economics*, Vol. 21, No. 2: 197–216.

Lane, C. and Bachmann, R. (ed.) (1998), *Trust within and between Organisations*, Guildford: Oxford University Press.

Lane, D. (1985), *Soviet Economy and Society,* Oxford: Blackwell.

Lewis, J.D. and Weigert, A. (1985), 'Trust as a Social Reality', *Social Forces*, Vol. 63, No. 3: 967–84.

Luhmann, N. (1979), *Trust and Power*, Chichester: John Wiley.

Lukes, S. (1972), *Emile Durkheim, his Life and Work: A Historical and Critical Study*, London: Allen and Unwin.

McHoul, A. and Grace, W. (1995), *A Foucault Primer: Discource, Power and Subject*, Malaysia: UCL.

Mason, E.S. (1959), *The Corporation in Modern Society*, Cambridge, MA: Harvard University.

Maurer, J.G. (1971), *Readings in Organizational Theory: Open Systems Approaches*, New York: Random House.

Meyer, J.W. and Scott, W.R. (1983), *Organizational Environments: Ritual and Rationality*, Beverley Hills, CA: Sage.

Mouck, T. (1994), 'Corporate Accountability and Rorty's Utopian Liberalism', *Accounting, Auditing and Accountability Journal*, Vol. 7, No. 1: 6–30.

Offe, C. (1999), 'How Can we Trust our Fellow Citizens?', in M.E. Warren (ed.), *Democracy and Trust*, Cambridge: Cambridge University Press.

Parkin, F. (1971), *Class, Inequality and Political Order*, London: MacGibbon and Kee.

Poster, M. (1984), *Foucault, Marxism and History: Mode of Production versus Mode of Information*, Cambridge: Polity.

Ring, P.S. and van de Ven, A.H. (1992), 'Structuring Cooperative Relations between Organisations', *Strategic Management Journal*, Vol. 13: 483–98.

Simmel, G. (1950), *The Sociology of George Simmel*, ed. K.H. Wolff, New York: Free Press.

Stillman, P.G. (1974), 'The Concept of Legitimacy', *Polity*, Vol. 10: 39–42.

Suchman, M. (1995), 'Managing Legitimacy: Strategic and Institutional Approaches', *Academy of Management Review*, Vol. 20, No. 3: 571–610.

Sutton, B. (ed.) (1993), *The Legitimate Corporation*, Bodmin: Basil Blackwell.

Tinker, T., Lehman, C. and Neimark, M. (1991), 'Falling Down the Hole in the Middle of the Road: Political Quietism in Corporate Social Reporting', *Accounting, Auditing and Accountability Journal*, Vol. 4, No. 2: 28–54.

Warren, M.E. (ed.) (1999), *Democracy and Trust*, Cambridge: Cambridge University Press.

Weber, M. (1968), *Economy and Society*, New York: Bedminster.

Williamson, O.E. (1993), 'Calculativeness, Trust and Economic Organisation', *Journal of Law and Economics*, Vol. 36 (April): 453–86.

Zan, L. (2002), 'Renewing Pompeii, Year Zero. Promises and Expectations from New Approaches to Museum Management and Accountability', *Critical Perspectives on Accounting*, Vol. 13: 89–137.

Zucker, L.G. (1986), 'Production of Trust: Institutional Sources of Economic Structure, 1840–1920', *Research in Organizational Behavior*, Vol. 8: 53–111.

Chapter 3

Limited Liability or Limited Responsibility?

David Crowther

Introduction

After the South Sea Bubble of 1720 and the losses involved, there was general public suspicion about the use of joint stock companies as a means of enterprise. Indeed Adam Smith (1776) questioned the ability and motivation of the directors of such a company to conduct the oversight of the assets of the company in an honest manner, stating:

> ... being the managers rather of other people's money than of their own, it cannot well be expected that they should look over it with the same anxious vigilance with which the partners of a private copartnery frequently watch over their own.

Of course this problem was one of the reasons for the development of financial accounting and reporting. This need was brought about by the need for a separation of the public and private actions of an individual and the need to record, and account for, the public actions because of the involvement of others in these public actions. Thus the medieval methods of bookkeeping, with the indistinguishability of public from private actions, was inappropriate to this modern world in which capitalist enterprise was beginning to arise. Capitalism required the ability to precisely measure activities and this was the founding basis of management accounting. Indeed it has been argued (Sombart, 1915) that capitalism would not have been possible without the techniques of double entry bookkeeping and its subsequent metamorphosis into management accounting. This accounting provided the mechanism to make visible the activities of all involved in the capitalist enterprise and to both record the effects of past actions and the expected results of future actions.

The modern world therefore saw the genesis of the modern firm as a mechanism which enabled individuals to combine in enterprise, and to combine capital and expertise from different individuals. It also saw the concomitant genesis of modern accounting in providing a representation of the actions of the firm, as distinct from the individuals comprising that firm. Thus the origins of corporate reporting can be seen to stem from the development of the firm as an individual entity as a means of reporting the activities of the firm to the owners of that firm. Indeed the Joint Stock Companies Act 1844 imposed upon firms the requirement to maintain accounts and to produce a balance sheet for shareholders. It was expected that such accounts would be published but this requirement to publish accounts was however repealed by the Joint Stock Companies Act 1856, with such accounts being required only for the internal purposes of the owners of the company. Nevertheless the development of the limited company as a form of enterprise necessitated the development of corporate reporting as a means of communication between the managers of the company and its owners. This need became increasingly apparent with the increasing size of such enterprises and the concomitant divorcing of ownership from management of such enterprises. This in turn was one of the drivers which led to the development of accounting practice and the development of corporate reporting. Thus by 1890 such enterprises were being accounted for on the basis of their being 'going concerns' as one of the main accounting principles (Newman, 1979), with accounting practice being based upon a separation of capital from income and profits from trading, both on the basis of a recognition of the divorcing of shareholding from management of the enterprise.

Thus by the start of the twentieth century it had been accepted that firms had a corporate identity which was distinct from that of their owners and that such firms embodied a presumption of immortality (Hein, 1978). Alongside this was the acceptance that control of the actions of the firm implied some liability for the effects of those actions and that the divorce of management from ownership necessitated some protection for the owners. This was achieved through the function of the audit of the activities of the firm and the Companies Act 1900 made compulsory the remuneration of such auditors. Although auditors are legally employed by the company it has never been made clear whether they are effectively employed by the shareholders, whose interests they are expected to protect, or by the directors, who have the managing role in the company. It is perhaps for this reason that the question of the impartiality of auditors has remained a constant source of debate into the present.

At the turn of the century it was generally accepted that accounting served the purpose of facilitating the relationship between managers and owners of a business, through its reporting function, but that the general public had no right to such information (Murphy, 1979). Thus the Companies Act 1906 stated that there was no requirement for companies to produce financial statements, although the Companies (Consolidations) Act 1908 amended this to require the production of a profit and loss account and balance sheet. This was further amended by the Companies Act 1929 which required the production of these, together with a directors report and an auditors report for the AGM. Subsequent legislation has extended the reporting requirements of companies to the format seen today.

Such corporate reporting has however been extended in addition to the satisfying of legislative requirements. Thus the period up to the Second World War saw an increasing use of accounting information for analysis purposes but with an emphasis upon the income statement. This period also saw the extension of the directors' report to contain information about the company which was not to be found in the financial statements. This information was however primarily concerning the past actions of the company as the emphasis in this period remained firmly upon the reporting of past actions as part of the relationship between the ownership and management of the firm. It is only in the post-war period that this emphasis changed from backward looking to forward looking and from inward looking to outward looking. Gilmore and Willmott (1992) have argued that this was a reflection of the changing nature of such reporting to a focus upon investment decision-making and the need to attract investment into the company in this period of expansion. The emphasis remained firmly upon the needs of the company however and only the emphasis had changed from informing existing investors to attracting new investors. Thus Jordan (1970: 139) was able to claim that:

> The purpose of accounting is to communicate economic messages on the results of business decisions and events, insofar as they can be expressed in terms of quantifiable financial data, in such a way as to achieve maximum understanding by the user and correspondence of the message with economic reality.

The users of such corporate reports, although no longer only the shareholders of the company and its managers, were however still considered to be a restricted set of the population, having specialist knowledge of and interest in such reporting. The identification of such specialists had however been extended to include both the accounting profession and investment professionals. Thus Cyert and Ijiri (1974: 29) were able to claim that:

> Financial statements are not just statements reporting on the financial activities and status of a corporation. They are a product of mutual interactions of three parties: corporations, users of financial statements, and the accounting profession ...

while Leach (1975: 13) stated that:

> In recent years there have been enormous changes in public interest in and understanding of financial statements. The informed user of accounts today is no longer solely the individual shareholder but equally the trained professional acting for institutional investors and the financial news media.

Thus there was at this time a general acceptance that corporate reporting should be provided for the knowledgeable professional rather than the individual (Mauntz and Sharif, 1961) and in order to satisfy the needs of these professionals corporate reports became more extensive in content, with greater disclosure of financial and other information. This pressure for greater disclosure was not however new and Mitchell (1906) argued that the accounts produced did not give an adequate basis for shareholder judgement.[1] All that has changed is the perception of who the reporting should be aimed at with a widening of the perceived intended audience from managers and shareholders

---

1   It is accepted that until the Companies (Consolidations) Act 1908 there was no legal requirement to produce a profit and loss account and balance sheet and so information might have been inadequate. The point is to show that the desire for further information has been a continuing theme of the discourse.

to include other professionals. There was however, throughout this time, little questioning of the assumed knowledge that the financial information is the most important part of the corporate report. The importance of the financial information contained in the reports has changed however and Lee and Tweedie (1977) claimed that the most important financial information contained in the report was details concerning profits, earnings and dividends. They equally claimed that the economic prospects of the firm are the most important information contained in the report (Lee and Tweedie, 1975) but were dismissive of the private shareholder in recording (Lee and Tweedie, 1977) that the majority read the chairman's report but nothing else.[2]

Limiting Liability

The developments in accounting, financial reporting and auditing were all designed to provide protection to investors in a joint stock company, with this being achieved by imposing a duty of accountability upon the managers[3] of a company. This was not however considered to be sufficient protection for potential investors in a business enterprise and further protection was introduced through the concept of limited liability. Limited liability means that the possible risk to any shareholder is a maximum of the amount paid for the shares plus any unpaid share capital (James, 1972). This limitation of liability is specified in the Memorandum of association (Smith and Keenan, 1969). The principle of limited liability was first introduced in the UK by the Limited Liability Act, 1855. According to Glautier and Underdown (1995) there was considerable opposition to the passing of this act but Parliament recognised the need to safeguard investors in companies. At the same time it recognised the potential for abuse and the requirements for stewardship and the disclosure of information to shareholders were linked to this limitation of liability, thereby safeguarding the shareholders of the company – at least in the minds of the legislators.

In legal terms a company is a person with the power to contract like any other individual[4] although the reality is that this power is vested in the managers of the company. The effect of this is that managers can enter into transactions for which they have no liability for non-fulfilment. Effectively by the introduction of this concept

---

2   This claim is in direct contradiction to the claim of Epstein and Pava (1993) that the majority of investors study the income statement and the balance sheet in some detail. This difference may reflect a change over time, a different investigative method, or a cultural difference (Epstein and Pava conducted their study in the USA). Epstein and Pava also studied the non-financial parts of the corporate report and found that some use was made of these also by shareholders.

3   Technically this duty is imposed in law upon the directors of a company in normal circumstances. In this chapter the word manager is used synonymously with the words director to imply someone with decision making power within the company without any necessity for partial ownership.

4   Wenlock (Baroness) v River Dee Co, 1887.

of limited liability risk was transferred away from the legal owners of a business and onto those with whom that business transacted. Equally the ability of managers to engage in those transactions on behalf of the business, without any necessary evidence of ownership – merely delegated responsibility – meant that most risk was thereby transferred away from the business. The potential rewards from owning a business became divorced from any commensurate risk – effectively separating the risk – reward relationship upon which finance theory is based.

This of course paved the way for the attraction of many more investors, thereby enabling the growth in size of business enterprises, and this was needed for the growth of large scale businesses such as the railways during the early days of the Industrial Revolution. It can be argued that the Industrial Revolution would not have happened without this introduction of limited liability as this made those investors secure in the knowledge that they were protected from any loss greater than the sum they had invested in the enterprise. Thus for relatively small levels of risk they were able to expect potentially great rewards and thereby escape from some of the consequences of the actions of the enterprise. Further actions have been taken since to alleviate corporations (and hence shareholders) from the risk associated with their investments. Buckminster Fuller (1981) describes lucidly the actions of successive US governments during the twentieth century which had the effects of transferring all risk to society in general through taxation, reduced regulation and through acting to bail out failed enterprises. Examples can be found in the actions of most other governments. So without risk corporations were able increasingly to do whatever they wished – and without responsibility anything became possible, even the lies of the present as no-one was accountable for their actions as long as economic growth – and profitability – continued. Thus we arrive at the present excesses. The link between rights and responsibilities had been severed and forgotten.

Constraining Managers – Agency Theory

Given that managers have both the ability to commit the organisation to whatever contracts and transactions they feel appropriate and a responsibility towards the owners of the business there was a need to ensure that this responsibility took place. It is normally accepted that Agency theory provides a platform upon which this can be ensured. Agency theory suggests that the management of an organisation is undertaken on behalf of the owners of that organisation, in other words the shareholders. Consequently the management of value created by the organisation is only pertinent insofar as that value accrues to the shareholders of the firm. Implicit within this view of the management of the firm, as espoused by Rappaport (1986) and Stewart (1991) amongst many others, is that society at large, and consequently all other stakeholders to the organisation, will also benefit as a result of managing the performance of the organisation in this manner. From this perspective therefore the concerns are focused upon how to manage performance for the shareholders and how to report upon that performance (Myners, 1998).

This view of an organisation has however been extensively challenged by many writers,[5] who argue that the way to maximise performance for society at large is to both manage on behalf of all stakeholders and to ensure that the value thereby created is not appropriated by the shareholders but is distributed to all stakeholders. Others such as Kay (1998) argue that this debate is sterile and that organisations maximise value creation not by a concern with either shareholders or stakeholders but by focusing upon the operational objectives of the firm and assuming that value creation, and equitable distribution will thereby follow.

The shareholder theory of the firm is often also referred to as agency theory as the role of the management of a firm is to act as the agents of the shareholders (the principals). The separation of ownership and control that is apparent in large modern-day (joint stock) companies, presently the most common way for a business to be organised, is another significant change since the days of Smith and Mill. It is this separation that leads to what is known as the principal – agent relationship. It is also argued that within this role it is only appropriate for managers (the agents) to use the funds at their disposal for purposes authorised by shareholders (the principals) (Hasnas, 1998; Smith and Hasnas, 1999). Further as shareholders normally invest in shares in order to maximise their own returns then managers, as their agents, are obliged to target this end. In fact this is arguing that as an owner a shareholder has the right to expect his or her property to be used to his or her own benefit. Donaldson (1982, 1989) disagrees and suggests that it can be morally acceptable to use the shareholder's money in this way if it is to further public interest. The ethical and moral acceptability of this suggestion is questionable and Smith and Hasnas (1999) point out that such an act would contravene Kant's (1804) principle. This principle states that a person should be treated as an end in his or her own right rather than as a means to an end. By using shareholders' money for the benefit of others it is argued that the shareholders are being used as a means to further others ends. This defence of shareholder theory is as ironic as it is compelling given that the exact same principle is often cited to defend stakeholder theory.

Assumed within agency theory is a lack of goal congruence between the principal and agent and that it is costly or difficult to confirm the agent's actions (Eisenhardt, 1989). In saying this it is suggested that, left to their own devices, the agents will prefer different options to those that would be chosen by the principals. The agents would make decisions and follow courses that further their own self-interest as opposed to that of the principal. This assumption that agents behaviour will be driven by their own self interest and nothing else has been criticised as being an overly simplistic conception of human behaviour (Williamson, 1985). It is argued that in addition to self-interested motives, altruism, irrationality, generosity, genuine concern for others … also characterise multi-faceted human behaviour. Sen (1987) agrees and actually states that 'to argue that anything other than maximising self-interest must be irrational seems altogether extraordinary'.

---

5   E.g. Herremans (1992), Tinker (1985).

It has been argued that shareholders should have rights to determine how their property be used, as should an owner of any asset under private property rights. Etzioni (1998) suggests that this view of shareholders property rights, which are both moral and legal, is 'widely embedded in the American political culture' and therefore needs no further introduction. Taking a step back Etzioni observes that such property rights are a social construct, as opposed to natural or inalienable rights, and as such society has the opportunity and the ability to change them if it is considered necessary. A closer consideration of what is meant by private property, as it has been socially constructed in present day Western societies, has been undertaken. Donaldson and Preston (1995) argue that the philosophy of property 'runs strongly counter to the conception that private property exclusively enshrines the interests of owners'. They specifically note the work of Pejovich (1990) as recognising that ownership does not entail unrestricted rights as they cannot be separated from human rights. Further, Honore (1961) suggests that the rights are restricted where the use would be harmful to others. Donaldson and Preston (1995) suggest that as property rights are restricted then they need to be founded on distributive justice. Interestingly Sternberg (1998) a proponent of shareholder theory, because 'it alone respects the property rights that are so essential for protecting individual liberty', also suggests that ethical business must also be based on 'distributive justice' along with 'ordinary decency' (Sternberg, 1994, 1998). Donaldson and Preston (1995) follow Becker's (1992) suggestion that the 'three main contending theories of distributive justice include Utilitarianism, Libertarianism and social contract theory'. Utilitarianism and libertarianism have already been commented upon as part of the historical roots of shareholder theory above.

Within the legal systems of the UK, the US, and most Western countries the managers of a business have a fiduciary duty to the owners of that business. This duty to shareholders is 'more general and proactive' than the regulatory or contractual responsibilities to other groups (Marens and Wicks, 1999; Goodpaster, 1991). These more general duties have also been used as a justification of the appropriateness of shareholder theories of the firm. The purpose and meaning of fiduciary duty were considered by Marens and Wicks (1999) who suggest that in actual fact this duty does not limit managers to a very narrow shareholder approach. They argue that the purpose of the fiduciary duty was originally designed to prevent managers undertaking expenditures that benefited themselves (Berle and Means, 1933). Further Marens and Wicks (1999) suggest that fiduciary duties simply require that the fiduciary has an honest and open relationship with the shareholder and does not gain illegitimately from their office. Therefore the tension between fiduciary responsibility and the responsibility to other stakeholder groups, the so-called stakeholder paradox (Goodpaster, 1991), is not as apparent as is often assumed. Further support for this argument is provided from the US courts. When shareholders have challenged management's actions as being too generous to other stakeholder groups then the court has 'almost always' upheld the right of management to manage. Management's justification or defence has often been on rational business performance grounds, such as efficiency or productivity, and the accuracy of such claims is difficult to prove. As such Marens and Wicks (1999) suggest that 'virtually any act that does not financially threaten the survival of the business could be construed as in the long-term best interest of shareholders'.

Thus agency theory argues that managers merely act as custodians of the organisation and its operational activities[6] and places upon them the burden of managing in the best interest of the owners of that business.[7] According to agency theory all other stakeholders of the business are largely irrelevant and if they benefit from the business then this is coincidental to the activities of management in running the business to serve shareholders. This focus upon shareholders alone as the intended beneficiaries of a business has been questioned considerably from many perspectives, which argue that it is either not the way in which a business is actually run or that it is a view which does not meet the needs of society in general. Conversely stakeholder theory argues that there are a whole variety of stakeholders involved in the organisation and each deserves some return for their involvement. According to stakeholder theory therefore benefit is maximised if the business is operated by its management on behalf of all stakeholders and returns are divided appropriately amongst those stakeholders, in some way which is acceptable to all. Unfortunately a mechanism for dividing returns amongst all stakeholders which has universal acceptance does not exist, and stakeholder theory is significantly lacking in suggestions in this respect. Nevertheless this theory has some acceptance and is based upon the premise that operating a business in this manner achieves as one of its outcomes the maximisation of returns to shareholders, as part of the process of maximising returns to all other stakeholders. This maximisation of returns is achieved in the long run through the optimisation of performance for the business to achieve maximal returns to all stakeholders.[8] Consequently the role of management is to optimise the long term performance of the business in order to achieve this end and thereby reward all stakeholders, including themselves as one stakeholder community, appropriately.

These two theories can be regarded as competing explanations of the operations of a firm which lead to different operational foci and to different implications for the measurement and reporting of performance. It is significant however that both theories have one feature in common. This is that the management of the firm is believed to be acting on behalf of others, either shareholders or stakeholders more generally. They do so, not because they are the kind of people who behave altruistically, but because they are rewarded appropriately and much effort is therefore devoted to the creation of reward schemes which motivate these managers to achieve the desired ends. Similarly much literature is devoted to the consideration of the effects of reward schemes on managerial behaviour (see for example Briers and Hirst, 1990; Child, 1974, 1975; Coates, Davis, Longden, Stacey and Emmanuel, 1993; Fitzgerald, Johnston, Brignall, Silvestro and Voss, 1991) and suggestion for improvements.

---

6   See for example Emmanuel, Otley and Merchant (1985).
7   Such owners are of course the legal owners of the business, that is the shareholders.
8   See for example Rappaport (1986).

Critiquing Agency Theory

The simplest model of agency theory assumes one principle and one agent and a modernist view of the world merely assumes that the addition of more principles and more agents makes for a more complex model without negating any of the assumptions. In the corporate world this is problematic as the theory depends upon a relationship between the parties and a shared understanding of the context in which agreements are made. With one principle and one agent this is not a problem as the two parties know each other. In the corporate world however the principles are equated to the shareholders of the company. For any large corporation however those shareholders are an amorphous mass of people who are unknown to the managers of the business. Indeed there is no requirement, or even expectation, that anyone will remain a shareholder for an extended period of time. Thus there can be no relationship between shareholders – as principles – and managers – as agents – as the principles are merely those holding the shares – as property being invested in – at a particular point in time. So shareholders do not invest in a company and in the future of that company; rather they invest for capital growth and / or a future dividend stream and shares are just one way of doing this which can be moved into or out of at will. This problem is exacerbated, particularly in the UK, by the fact that a significant proportion of shares are actually bought and sold by fund managers of financial institutions acting on behalf of their investors. These fund managers are rewarded according to the growth (or otherwise) of the value of the fund. Thus shares are bought and sold as commodities rather than as part ownership of a business enterprise.

If the principal agent relationship has ceased to exist then this leave managers without any great degree of accountability and able to act on their own in seeking to meet their own needs. In this chapter therefore it is argued that the role of management in shaping the organisation, determining its performance, and reporting upon that performance is much more central to an understanding of organisational behaviour than is a study of managerial reward schemes in the context of agency theory. The sole vehicle for communication – and no longer for accountability therefore has become the annual report and concomitant annual general meeting. Thus managers at the centre of an organisation are the authors of the script which becomes the corporate report. Thus as authors they shape that script and decide its contents. Furthermore they determine the image of the organisation which they wish to be portrayed to the readers of the script. They are then able to operationalise the production of that image through the corporate reporting mechanisms which are instituted within the organisation and through determining the format of the report actually produced. The purported nature of that corporate report is to inform shareholders, and other interested parties (who are thereby considered to be readers of the script and consequently stakeholders to the corporate reporting process), of the actions which have been taken by management in the preceding period on behalf of the shareholders, and the outcomes of those actions in terms of performance.

This report is intended to be forward looking and to signal to the readers of the script that the future will be an improvement on the present. Indeed an examination of corporate annual reports shows that the past has continually been dismissed as almost an irrelevance and certainly no basis for judgement concerning the future. Instead the future will be an improvement upon that past and this improved future will be brought about by the skills of the management team, who best know how to manage the resources of the business, despite overwhelming evidence to the contrary from the results of the preceding three years. Thus, for example, the following statement is made in the United Biscuits 1995 report:

> The group has been organised into three regions with their chief executives based at group headquarters, sharing central services. Group management can now concentrate on formulating strategy and monitoring performance more rigorously. Layers of management have been removed and the result is better communication, integration and allocation of resources.

Interestingly enough this suggests that these senior executives have not been performing optimally in the past if they are able to focus on performance monitoring more rigorously in the future. This meaning is however disguised in the more important image that strategy formulation is the most significant and most difficult role of management. Indeed this role is so demanding that it requires the separation of these executives, both spatially and in terms of obligations, from their actual areas of operation.

Management also demonstrates the power to reconstitute itself without reference to the owners of the business. Thus in addition to the restructuring mentioned above the following statement is also made by the chairman:

> As announced in last year's annual report, my predecessor Sir Robert Clarke retired in June 1995. Two non-executive directors have left the board, having contributed valuably to the debate on reshaping the business: Sir Charles Fraser has retired, and Tom Wyman resigned in March following our withdrawal from the USA. Executive directors David Hearn and Brian Chadbourne have also left the company. We welcomed as an executive director Malcolm Little, who has a solid record of achievement both in United Biscuits[9] and elsewhere, and whose steadying hand is already felt across our UK businesses. Gordon Hourston, formerly chairman of Boots The Chemist, has joined us as a non-executive director.

This kind of statement is common throughout all the annual reports of the organisations and indicates the general ability of management to reconstitute itself and determine its own succession without reference to anyone else. This example has been quoted because of the relatively extreme position of United Biscuits, in terms of poor past performance. It reinforces the argument that reference to the past has no place in determining the future of the organisation. Instead the future is all that matters. If management truly believed that they acted as agents for others, either shareholders exclusively or a combination of stakeholders, then the admissions of

---

9   This mention is surprising given the results of the company in preceding years.

failure which were being made at United Biscuits, as incidentals in the script, would cause them to tender their resignations or at the very least seek reaffirmation of their role in managing the organisation. This behaviour therefore provides one clue in the consideration of the role of management in any organisation.

In this respect therefore the managers of the organisation act as determinants of the religion of the organisation, as constituted through the rituals embedded into organisational behaviour. They can therefore be likened to the priesthood because of the central role which they play in determining the religious functions to be performed. Thus, in the context of atemporal continuity, the priesthood of the organisation is able to determine its own succession and perform the appropriate initiation rites into its select body. Some new priests have however already been initiated into priesthood in other organisations and the transition is therefore relatively simple.

Part of the myth creation role of corporate reporting is designed to foster the myth that managing an organisation is a difficult task which requires a unique set of skills which few people possess. Fortunately for the future of any particular organisation, the management of that organisation are in possession of this unique set of skills, and the semiotic is intended to create this image. This message is evident in all the corporate reports considered but the poorer is the reported performance the more is the need to emphasise the possession of these skills. The case of United Biscuits has been considered at length but other examples exist. Thus for example in 1995 the chairman of Northern Foods makes the following statements:

> I have referred in recent reports to the intensity of competition and resultant structural changes in UK food retailing. Our performance this year reflects a marked acceleration of this change, which has led to significant sales and profit reductions in our businesses ...
>
> We have clear strategies in place in both our operating areas. In dairy, we lead the growing supermarket milk sector and are completing major investments which will give us significant competitive advantage ...
>
> The food retailing climate in the UK remains intensely competitive and the decline of the doorstep and small shop sectors continues. Nevertheless, our scale, low cost base, product profile, financial strength and management capability gives us confidence that we are in a strong position to meet these continuing challenges and to achieve long term growth in shareholder value.

Thus the message is reinforced that management of a business is complex but the particular management of the particular organisation have the requisite skills and ability to manage such a difficult operation; moreover they are foresighted enough to have strategies in place which will show just rewards in the future. Such statements can be found throughout the landscape of corporate reporting. This then provides a clue as to the reason for the reports giving the message that environmental performance and financial performance are incompatible and that one must trade off with the other, despite the argument above that the two conflate into a common concern. The reason for the image of incompatibility is in the myth creation role of corporate reporting and the need to continually create and recreate afresh the myth of the organisation and its religion, and to reaffirm the role of the priesthood in the organisation.

Thus the corporate myth is intended not just to portray the organisation as atemporal and omnipresent but it is also designed to affirm the priesthood in power. This is achieved through the creation of the rituals of organisational religion already referred to but also by means of creating an image of the difficulty of managing the organisation so that it becomes apparent that only the priesthood have the necessary skills to achieve this management. The more difficult this task appears to be the more apparent it becomes that the task needs to be delegated to those with the necessary skills – the current management team as portrayed through the semiotic. Thus managing the conflicting and oppositional demands of financial and environmental performance becomes one additional burden which the priesthood must bear on behalf of the owners of the business and this provides a motivation for the segregation of the script into its environmental and financial constituents. Naturally the shareholders will be expected to demonstrate their gratitude to the priesthood for assuming this additional burden and the rewards of management for their efforts will need to be commensurate with their burden.

It must be remembered however that managers are not only the authors of the script but are also part of the audience, not only as managers but also as other stakeholders. Thus one way in which the other stakeholders interact with the script and its authors is through the managers themselves acting as representatives of those other stakeholders. Thus managers are able to interpret the response of those other stakeholders to their own actions by considering their own responses. This gives the motivation and means to legitimate their actions, as managers, being undertaken on behalf of the other stakeholders to the organisation. Legitimation of activity in this way, by means of self-referential discourse, is of course dangerous and can lead to self delusion. The fact that such discourse is unquestioned among the rest of the audience however supports the validity of legitimation in such a manner.

It has been claimed elsewhere (Crowther, 2002) that this performance takes place upon the corporate reporting stage but in the chapter it is argued that this drama is played out on what is described as the Mythic Stage. On this stage the frame is atemporal but the action is linear. Thus on this stage the authors create the corporate reporting script which in turn creates the myth of organisational existence. This myth of organisational existence creates in the minds of its readers the notional of atemporality but also of a better future because of the priesthood. This in turn creates the myth of the godhead. This second myth, that of the godhead, is the real purpose of the creation of the dialectic of corporate reporting. Through the creation of this myth the authors of the script are enabled to achieve individuation through their self-belief in their own essentiality to the myth of organisational existence. This is achieved through the creation of the semiotic which presents the managers of the organisation as essential to the future of the organisation. This therefore enables the managers themselves to believe this desire on behalf of the stakeholders to the organisation to secure the desirable improved future, which is of course dependant upon the managers of the organisation remaining as managers. The Mythic Stage can be depicted thus:

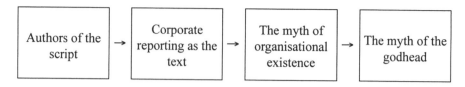

Figure 3.1   The Mythic Stage

Upon this stage the audience is not involved in any interaction but nevertheless have an important part to play. Their part is that of affirmation of the myths and, through this affirmation, worship of the godhead. Thus the myths continue to be created in atemporal continuity (Berger, 1974, Horne, 1986). For this affirmation to take place it is of course necessary that the audience accept the myths as reality and so the text of the corporate report is designed to create the necessary images of the organisation to ensure this acceptance, and this takes place in the manner previously considered. It is also necessary that the motivations of the audience as individuals are recognised and thus the semiotics of the reporting suggests through appropriate images of interaction and that the audience has an actual part to play in the unfolding of the script. This semiotic of interaction, and the concomitant creation of the binarisms in the script is necessary to the maintenance of the myth of organisational existence which is in turn necessary to the myth of the godhead. Thus the audience is included in the community of the organisation as a part of the organisation and the horizon is ringed by the unifying myth of organisational existence (Nietsche, 1956).

In return for their acceptance of the myths and their worship of the godhead the audience is presented with rewards which are great in the present but are promised to be even greater in the future. These rewards are partly financial, in the form of increased value of their investment and dividends, partly in terms of welfare through the knowledge that the organisation is responsible in terms of its interaction with the environment, and partly in terms of self-esteem through the knowledge of inclusion in the wonderful, well managed community of the organisation. Thus the full Mythic Stage can be represented as shown in Figure 3.2.

On this stage the shareholders of the organisation have been relegated from the central role of ownership of the business, with the consequent power to delegate or withhold the power of management of the business to others, to a peripheral role of investing in the business and affirming the role of the managers in leading the business into the future. Thus the managers are able to declare to these shareholders that changes have been made, even to the constitution of that management itself, in the manner already described, without the need to refer such matters to them as the owners of the business. Their role as mere investors is to affirm the action already taken through their engagement in one of the principle rituals of organisational religion, the Annual General Meeting. Even in this ritual the role of these investors is merely to affirm the actions and wishes of the priesthood. Thus in some of the annual reports (e.g.

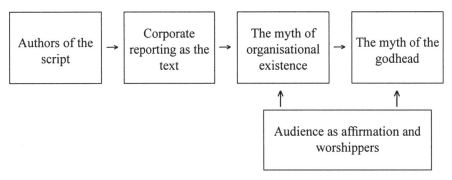

Figure 3.2   The full Mythic Stage

Hazlewood Foods) the order of service for this ritual is presented as predetermined and consists firstly of the need for affirmation of the actions of the priesthood.

Thus the first items on the order of service (i.e. the agenda) always include:

- to receive the accounts and reports of directors;
- to declare a dividend;
- to re-elect or confirm the appointment of directors.

Although the form of the AGM is legally prescribed, the essential feature of this view of the meeting as a religious rite is that it is assumed that the appropriate responses, as prescribed in the religious rites, will automatically follow in the form of affirmation by the audience as worshippers of the organisational religion. The receipt of this affirmation is so taken for granted that the necessary actions have already been implemented.

The acceptance of the existence of this Mythic Stage upon which the play is performed provides an explanation of corporate reporting and the way in which such reporting is structured. Such acceptance need not however be judgmental as it does not mean that its existence is either good or bad, as there is no need for any such polarisation. It merely provides a semiotic of corporate reporting. This semiotic does however have implications when the internal performance reporting system is re-examined.

According to Campbell (1972: 245):

> The function of ritual is to give form to human life, not in the way of a mere surface arrangement, but in depth. In ancient times every social occasion was ritually structured and the sense of depth was rendered through the maintenance of a religious tone. Today, on the other hand, the religious tone is reserved for exceptional, very special 'sacred' occasions.

In this chapter however it is argued that that religious tone has been maintained, but in a context which most would identify as a secular context. Of more interest however is the way in which epic stories have changed their origins and functions in modern society. Instead of uniting society they have now been usurped for the dividing of society and privileging some at the expense of others. This of course has always been the function of religion and the new religion, of managerial supremacy, has appropriated the concepts of the myth and the epic story to promote their hegemony.

Previously epics stories have recounted the adventures of the hero who acquires knowledge and skills which will be used for the benefit of society. Now managers have cast themselves in the role of the hero – who already has the necessary skills for his epic adventure. Such skills as are not possessed can of course be readily acquired from the consulting organisations which are ever ready to sells their nostrums (Carter and Crowther 2000) to whoever wishes to purchase them. In the past the people recounted tales of the hero but now the hero recounts tales about himself. In the past the hero was deemed by the people to be so but now the hero is self-styled. Indeed the heroic role is no longer sufficient and these people have also assumed the role of the godhead, no longer is material reward sufficient for the hero now he also demands also worship and obeisance. And we have let it happen. The modern hero has committed the perfect crime (Baudrillard, 1996) in which he is rewarded while others are punished – those who have allowed this to happen.

As Baudrillard (1996: 1–2) states of the perfect crime:

> This is the story of a crime – the murder of reality. And the extermination of an illusion – the vital illusion of the world. The real does not disappear into illusion; it is illusion which disappears into integral reality … Though the crime is never perfect, perfection, true to its name is always criminal … But perfection is always punished: the punishment for perfection is reproduction.

References

Baudrillard, J. (1996), *The Perfect Crime*, trans. C. Turner, London: Verso.

Becker, L.C. (1992), 'Placed for Pluralism', *Ethics*, Vol. 102: 707–19.

Berger, P. (1974), *Pyramids of Sacrifice*, Harmondsworth: Penguin.

Berle, A. and Means, G. (1933), *The Modern Corporation and Private Property*, New York: Commerce Clearing House.

Briers, M. and Hirst, M. (1990), 'The Role of Budgetary Information in Performance Evaluation', *Accounting, Organizations and Society*, Vol. 15, No. 4: 373–98.

Buckminster Fuller, R. (1981), *Critical Path*, New York: St Martin's Press.

Campbell, J. (1972), *Myths to Live By*, London: Souvenir Press.

Carter, C.J.G and Crowther, D. (2000), 'Unravelling a Profession: The Case of Engineers in a Regional Electricity Company', *Critical Perspectives on Accounting*, Vol. 11, No 1: 23–49.

Child, J. (1974), 'Managerial and Organisational Factors Associated with Company Performance – Part 1', *Journal of Management Studies*, Vol. 11: 73–189.

Child, J. (1975), 'Managerial and Organisational Factors Associated with Company Performance – Part 2', *Journal of Management Studies*, 12: 12–27.

Coates, J.B., Davis, E.W., Longden, S.G., Stacey, R.J. and Emmanuel, C. (1993), *Corporate Performance Evaluation in Multinationals*, London: CIMA.

Crowther, D. (2002), *A Social Critique of Corporate Reporting*, Aldershot: Ashgate.

Cyert, R.M. and Ijiri, Y. (1974), 'Problems of Implementing the Trueblood Report', *Journal of Accounting Research* supplement.

Donaldson, T. (1982), *Corporations and Morality*, Englewood Cliffs, NJ: Prentice Hall.

Donaldson, T. (1989), *The Ethics of International Business*, New York: Oxford University Press.

Donaldson, T. and Preston, L.E. (1995), 'The Stakeholder Theory of the Corporations: Concepts, Evidence and Implications', *The Academy of Management Review*, Vol. 20, Issue 1.

Eisenhardt, K.M. (1989), 'Agency Theory: An Assessment and Review', *Academy of Management Review*, Vol. 14: 57–74.

Emmanuel, C.R., Otley, D.T. and Merchant, K. (1985), *Accounting for Management Control*, London: Chapman and Hall.

Epstein, M.J. and Pava, M.L. (1993), *The Shareholder's Use of Corporate Annual Reports*, London: JAI Press.

Etzioni, A. (1998), 'A Communitarian Note on Stakeholder Theory', *Business Ethics Quarterly*, October, Vol. 8, No. 4: 679–91.

Fitzgerald, L., Johnston, R., Brignall, S., Silvestro, R. and Voss, C. (1991), *Performance Measurement in Service Businesses*, London: CIMA.

Gilmore, C.G. and Willmott, H. (1992), 'Company Law and Financial Reporting: A Sociological History of the UK Experience', in M. Bromwich and A. Hopwood (eds), *Accounting and the Law*, Hemel Hempstead: Prentice Hall: 159–91.

Glauter, M.W.E. and Underdown, B. (1994), *Accounting Theory and Practice*, London: Pitman.

Goodpaster, K.E. (1991), 'Business Ethics and Stakeholder Analysis', *Business Ethics Quarterly*, Vol. 1, No. 1: 53–73.

Hasnas, J. (1998), 'The Normative Theories of Business Ethics: A Guide for the Perplexed', *Business Ethics Quarterly*, January: 19–42.

Hein, L.W. (1978), *The British Companies Acts and the Practice of Accountancy 1844–1962*, New York: Arno Press.

Herremans, I.M., Akathaparn, P. and McInnes, M. (1992), 'An Investigation of Corporate Social Responsibility, Reputation and Economic Performance', *Accounting, Organizations and Society*, Vol. 18, Nos 7/8: 587–604.

Honore, A.M. (1961), 'Ownership', in A.G. Guest (ed.), *Oxford Essays in Jurisprudence*, Oxford: Clarendon Press: 107–47.

Horne, D. (1986), *The Public Culture: An Argument with the Future*, London: Pluto Press.

James, P.S. (1972), *Introduction to English Law*, London: Butterworth.

Jordan, J.R. (1970), 'Financial Accounting and Communication', in G.G. Mueller and C.H. Smith (eds), *Accounting: a Book of Readings*, New York: Holt, Rinehart and Winston.

Kant, I. (1804/1981), *Grounding for the Metaphysics of Morals*, trans. J.W. Ellington, Indianapolis, IN: Hackett Publishing.

Kay, J. (1998), 'Good Business', *Prospect*, 28 (March): 25–9.

Leach, R.G. (1975), presentation at the launch of *The Corporate Report*, July.

Lee, T.A. and Tweedie, D.P. (1975), 'Accounting Information: An Investigation of Private Shareholder Understanding', *Accounting and Business Research*, Autumn: 280–91.

Lee, T.A. and Tweedie, D.P. (1977), *The Private Shareholder and the Corporate Report*, London: ICAEW.

Marens, R. and Wicks, A. (1999), 'Getting Real: Stakeholder Theory, Managerial Practice, and the General Irrelevance of Fiduciary Duties owed to Shareholders', *Business Ethics Quarterly*, April, Vol. 9, No. 2: 273–93.

Mauntz, R.H. and Sharif, H.A. (1961), *The Philosophy of Auditing*, American Accounting Association.

Mitchell, T.W. (1906), 'Review of Corporate Reports: The Report of the American Locomotive Company', *Journal of Accountancy*: 106–25.

Murphy, G.J. (1979), 'The Evolution of Corporate Reporting Practices in Canada', in E.N. Goffman (ed.), *Academy of Accounting Historians Working Paper Series Vol. 1*: 329–68.

Myners, P. (1998), 'Improving Performance Reporting to the Market', in A. Carey and J. Sancto (eds), *Performance Measurement in the Digital Age*, London: ICAEW: 27–33.

Newman, M.S. (1979), 'Historical Development of Early Accounting Concepts and their Relation to Certain Economic Concepts', in E.N. Goffman (ed.), *Academy of Accounting Historians Working Paper Series Vol. 1*: 157–86.

Nietsche, F. (1956), *The Birth of Tragedy*, New York: Doubleday.

Pejovich, S. (1990), *The Economics of Property Rights: Towards a Theory of Comparative Systems*, Dordrecht: Kluwer Academic Publishers.

Rappaport, A. (1986), *Creating Shareholder Value*, New York: The Free Press.

Sen, A. (1987), *On Ethics and Economics*, Oxford: Blackwell.

Smith, A. (1776), *The Wealth of Nations*, many editions.

Smith, H.J. and Hasnas, J. (1999), 'Ethics and Information Systems: The Corporate Domain', *MIS Quarterly*, March, Vol. 23, No. 1: 109–27.

Smith, K. and Keenan, D.J. (1969), *Essential of Mercantile Law*, London: Pitman.

Sombart, W. (1915), *The Quintessence of Modern Capitalism*, New York: E.P. Dutton and Co.

Sternberg, E. (1994), *Just Business: Business Ethics in Action*, London: Little, Brown and Company.

Sternberg, E. (1998), *Corporate Governance: Accountability in the Marketplace*, London: The Institute of Economic Affairs.

Stewart, G.B. III (1991), *The Quest for Value*, New York: HarperCollins.

Tinker, T. (1985), *Paper Prophets: A Social Critique of Accounting*, London: Holt, Rinehart and Winston.

Williamson, O.E. (1985), *The Economic Institutions of Capitalism*, New York: Free Press.

Chapter 4

The Power of Networks: Organising versus Organisation

Branka Mraović

Do not let them seduce you. (Berthold Brecht)

Introduction

The key feature of the global age is represented, on one hand, in the form of material constitution of the new planetary order, and, on the other hand, in the form of creating a new social life. The paradigm shift that is taking place in the world economic and political order announces the decline of the modern theories of power, i.e. what was in Modernity considered as transcendent to productive and social relations is now being formed inside and immanent to these processes. The binary structure of power cannot exist in the reality of multiple and interconnected networks that push the political synthesis of the social space in the field of virtual communication. The global project of network power is entirely virtual, boundless and flexible, and its identities are hybrid and fluid. The basic position in this chapter is that the project of globalisation did not derive from modernity, but that it is a project created within capitalism beginning immediately after World War II, with two fundamental assumptions that needed to be dealt with: firstly, the development of Information Technology constituting the technical basis of virtual communication; secondly, the fall of the Berlin Wall as the metaphor of the fall of socialism announced the processes of formation of national states, which turned this part of the world into one of the greatest investment opportunities in the last decade of the twentieth century.

The information society is based on global networks and computer communications, creating a wide range of virtual communities imposing a new type of logic – the network logic. The world is getting ever smaller each day, while the space of manoeuvre of business organisations is getting bigger. At the same time, in the new network landscape, information technologies, including the Internet, provide a technical support for a greater justice and equality on the virtual highways, thus affirming the voice of individual. However, a real trap of today's world is borne out of the fact that we all – individuals, groups, communities – come to adopt mutual views by means of the control imposed by those who create and own the networks. The possibilities to control, misguide and manipulate are infinite. But owing to the very same technologies, the word 'control' gets a completely new meaning. The Internet insiders agree that no one can fully control the Internet, which in itself opens up a huge potential for human agency to productively use the technologies, just as it opens up the question of a new interpretation of the concept of agency itself.

If the key word changing the nature of business in the corporate world of the 1980s was 'quality', and of the 1990s 're-engineering', then surely, as Bill Gates (1999: xxv) claims, the year 2000 and beyond will be marked by the word 'speed':

> Going digital will put you on the leading edge of a shock wave of change that will shatter the old way of doing business. A digital nervous system will let you do business at the speed of thought – the key to success in the twenty-first century.

The new level of electronic based intelligence functions as the human nervous system, and has evolved from the ever improving Internet technologies enabling a world wide connectivity. In the digital age, connectivity has a much wider meaning than the process of simply putting individuals into contact. What is at stake here is that the Internet creates a new universal space for information sharing, collaboration and commerce.

> A digital nervous system is the corporate, digital equivalent of the human nervous system, providing a well-integrated flow of information to the right part of the organization at the right time. A digital nervous system consists of the digital processes that enable a company to perceive and react to its environment, to sense competitor challenges and customer needs, and to organize timely responses. (Gates, 1999: xx)

Gates uses the phrases 'Web workstyle' and 'Web lifestyle' to emphasise the impact of employees and consumers taking advantage of these digital connections. These emerging hardware, software and communication standards will change the forms in which business is operated as well as the consumers' behaviour.

There is no doubt that the digital technologies will entirely change the structures of organisations, and as a result, the relations of power within the organisations. Furthermore, in the global age we are faced with a justified call for rethinking organisational concepts and behaviour. A postmodernist view of the organisation is radically different from the existing paradigms and interpretations in that its major emphasis is on the dominance of community as the agent of local need (Crowther, 2002). Also, what is brought about by the developments in the technological and informational architecture of society is a compression of space and time, resulting in the fact that organisations as temporal or geographical entities have ceased to have any meaning whatsoever. Hence there is a need to redefine the concept of locality in the sense that it divorces from geographical proximity. This equally applies to organisations as micro-societies, as well as to the society at large.

> When considering the question of organisations and the identity of the constituents of such an organisation therefore, and their relationship with the macroculture and with societal

structure, this suggests that the local structure has dominant importance to the individual and his/her sense of community is defined circumstantially. (Crowther, 2002: 240)

The new understanding of the community creates a need for a different type of organisational structure 'in order to cater for needs of the individual constituents of that organisation who aggregate for one common purpose while atomising (or aggregating with different individuals) for others' (Crowther, 2002: 241). Within such a perspective, organisational structure excludes the territorial basis of its existence, that is, through mediation of information and communication technologies, the organisation becomes a virtual organisation existing within a virtual context, as the need for such a context arises. By removing territorial boundaries from an organisation, there arises a question of the redefinition of the concept of organisation in terms of organising local societal structures.

In the following pages we would like to tell a story of how the modern organisation has given way to the paradigm of organising, whereby we point out that it is the change of the paradigm of power which is the milestone that enabled the transfer.

The Networking Logic of the Informational Society

The novelty that the processes of globalisation, as essentially economic processes, with the inherent political and social consequences, brings about is that they transfer the power battle field into the environment of information technologies. It is characteristic of the global age in which we live, work and realise our various interests that the dominant social functions have been organised around networks. The networks constitute a new social morphology in all societies, and the proliferation of network logic significantly modifies both activities and their results in the processes of production, knowledge, power and culture. Castells (2000: 500) describes the phenomenon as follows:

> I would argue that this networking logic induces a social determination of higher level than of the specific social interests expressed through the networks: the power of flows takes precedence over the flows of power. Presence or absence in the network and the dynamics of each network vis-à-vis others are critical sources of domination and change in our society: a society that, therefore, we may properly call the network society, characterized by the pre-eminence of social morphology over social action.

The paradigm of information technologies has provided a material basis for a pervasive expansion of networks along the entire social structure. It pervades the core of life and mind, while the networks constitute a new social morphology in a way in which the network logic represents a distinctive feature of the global era. Hence Castells (2000) has a reason to use the term 'network society' as he wants to emphasise the 'pre-eminence of social morphology over social action'. According to him, the new IT paradigm consists of the following elements:

- information is its raw material – these are technologies to act on information, not just information to act on technology;
- pervasiveness of its effects – information is an integral part of the totality of human activity;
- the networking logic;
- flexibility; and
- convergence of specific technologies into a highly integrated system.

> … the development of Internet is reversing the relationship between circuit switching and packet switching in communication technologies, so that data transmission becomes the predominant, universal form of communication. (Castells, 2000: 72)

The information technology paradigm evolves towards its openness as a multi-edged network. Therefore, comprehensiveness, complexity and networking are its decisive qualities.

The topology defined by networks determines that the distance (or intensity and frequency of interaction) between two points (or social positions) is shorter (or more frequent, or more intense) if both points are nodes in a network than if they do not belong to the same network. On the other hand, within a given network, flows have no distance, or the same distance, between nodes. Thus, distance (physical, social, economic, political, cultural) for a given point or position varies between zero (for any node in the same network) and infinite (for any point external to network). The inclusion/exclusion in networks, and the architecture of relationships between networks, enacted by high-speed-operating information technologies, configure dominant processes and functions in our societies. (Castells, 2000: 501)

A network operated social structure:

- is a highly dynamic open system;
- is capable of expanding with no limitations;
- is of variable geometry,
- unifies and commands;
- includes and excludes; and
- acts in timeless space.

The integrated, global capital networks are sources of huge and dramatic reorganisations in power relationships because the switches that connect the networks, and using signal codes in the process, have an ability to shape, guide and misguide societies. The networks are appropriate instruments of capital economy, and their interrelations and crossings reflect the relations between corporations and small firms, sectors and geographical entities. The new social organisation is defined by the evolution aiming towards the network forms of management and production, and its main ingredient is information.

A convergence of social evolution and information technologies has created a new economy organised along the global networks of capital, management and information. The environment in which the selfness realises itself in the informational society is the global networks and computer communications, creating a wide range of virtual communities imposing a new type of logic – the network logic. The concept 'informational society' is much wider than the concept of 'network society'. Castells (2000) makes an analytical distinction between the concept of 'information society' and 'informational society'. The former represents a type of society in which information has a function to communicate knowledge, and as such, it constitutes the cultural history of mankind, and the latter represents a distinctive form of social organisation in which data production, processing and transmission are major sources of wealth and power.

Information technology differs in definition to computing in that it includes not only computing technology but also data communications. Consequently, communication technologies are inherently important in allowing information systems to be linked together nationally and internationally within the global environment (Elliot and Starkings, 1998). Computer networks are not mere technical facts, but social catalysts in the first place, which significantly affect human relationships, especially when it comes to economic relations and power relations that we find in the organisational culture of the global age. Although investments into IT are huge, and although these technologies are primarily introduced with the aim to increase productivity, the research studying their economic justification show that IT gives much better results in the battles for control rather than in being a measure of corporate profitability. The term 'computer paradox' comes from the Nobel prize economist Robert Solow who said: 'We see computers everywhere but not in the productivity statistics' (in: Strassman, 1997: 24). Hence power struggles do not arise from economic development only, but also from opportunities to access communication channels. The new system of wealth production comprises of the global networks made of markets, banks, government agencies, industrial centres and research institutes, which, due to information technologies, are able to have prompt communications with one another, exchanging data, information and knowledge.

From Organisation to Organising

If the corporations are the factor vital for the future of society in the Global Age, then it is obvious that the changed reality calls for new scientific responses. The main weakness of the new age democracy, states Albrow (1997), comes from the fact that solutions to organisational dilemmas are approached in such a way so that they are seen, wrongly, as technical issues, which comes from the assumption that they are simply side effects of business efficiency and free markets. In the mid-1990s, it became clear that neither big corporations nor the Welfare State were the dominant forms of social organisation. Hence social transformation becomes a key issue in the ever changing world, which means that what is needed is a reflexive account, and an organisational reconstruction capable of offering theoretical and methodological 'tools' with which to cope with the fundamental question of the global age: *Does the organisation simply serve the interests of the powerful?*

The twentieth century structural principles, lying in the background of all types of organisation and determining the path of rationalisation of society as a whole, are going through a speedy transformation nowadays. This in turn sets an agenda for the issue of change of organisational form, but it also brings forth a need for a new evaluation of some of the issues belonging to the debates on modern and post-modern organisation.

The Constitutive Principles of Modern Organisations

An account of modern organisations, Giddens (1987) argues, is intricately related to the 'problem of order'. However, what is not at stake here is the issue of the ways in which social cohesion is possible in the context of diverse and conflict-based individual interests, as the functionalists would think; what is at stake is that the 'problem of order' is an issue of time-space distanciation. The organisation 'within' time-space and the organisation of time-space is something that is characteristic of all societal systems.

> What, then, is an organization? It is a social system which is able to 'bracket time-space', and which does so via the reflexive monitoring of system reproduction and the articulation of discursive 'history'. (Giddens, 1987: 153)

Organisations started to proliferate only with modernity, and so they represent specific features of modern culture. Modern organisations have the following features:

* intensification of surveillance as information collation and retrieval;
* links with specifically designed locales; and
* the relation between locales and the timing and spacing of activities through various sectors of organisations (Giddens, 1987).

That was the time when organisations were said to depend on rational principles, when the range and size of the organisation reflected the power of rationality and when it was expected that a unique organisational form should dominate worldwide. They operated in the context of monopoly capital, world modernisation and bureaucratisation (Albrow, 1997). Weber was the greatest representative of the grand narrative of the Western civilisation as a process of rationalisation (Weber, 1964).

Although hierarchy is a constitutive element of modern organisations, it in itself implies an opposite tendency related to the recapture of power by those on the lower levels. According to the 'dialectic of control' developed by Giddens (1984), the tendency is a characteristics of all power relationships. Regardless of how strong is the power of one individual or group over another, the resources are always available, which enables the subordinate to reciprocally influence those in power.

All organisations are characterised by the mobilisation of two types of resources, the administrative and the allocative. Although literature on modern organisations tends to give preference to the former, Giddens is much more focused on the latter, because the authoritative resources in turn presume surveillance. It is possible to identify two aspects of surveillance in all organisations. One is surveillance as the accumulation, coding and retrieval of information; the other is surveillance as the direct supervision of the activities of some individuals as groups by others. What links the two forms of surveillance is the relation between the accumulation of 'organisational history' and that of personal histories or personal data.

Just like an inventory recording history, so does a file enables recording the knowledge of the world, and as such it is used for two primary purposes:

*   files are means by which the organisation includes itself into history and ensures control over future. Within organisations, files are the key for intensification of surveillance;
*   as they show an entire overview of an individual's activities, files become a medium of structuring in order to regulate conduct in time and space.

As Foucault notices in *Discipline and Punish*, which gives an account of the development of hospitals in the eighteenth century, the keeping of registers formed an integral part of the process which forced the hospitals to adjust to a regime of disciplining. 'Discipline' includes the procedures of writing which enable that an individual could be located in the general register. In this way, the individual is kept 'under the gaze of a permanent corpus of knowledge'.

Foucault's analysis sheds light upon previously neglected or disregarded dimensions of the governance and management of power relations, enabling us to appreciate how order and organisations are sustained and realised (O'Doherty and Willmott, 2001). As Ackroyd and Thompson (1999) point out, his work provides an insight into the cultural mechanisms for smothering dissent and colonising the employees.

Hardt and Negri (2001a) argue that Foucault's work has made it easier for us to see the epochal transition of forms from the disciplinary society into the society of control, the process happening towards the end of modernity thus giving way to post-modernity. Although we do not agree with the authors' opinion that it is possible nowadays to give a Weberian account of the contemporary world, we would like to point out that their controversial *Empire* gives a sophisticated account of bio-power. Foucault's concept of bio-power is crucial for understanding the transformation from binary structures to network power, and it is this change that has happened in the power paradigm that has opened up an alternative path to the modern organisational paradigm.

Disciplinary power governs in a way that it structures parameters and limitations to thinking and practice, regulating and sanctioning normal and/or deviant behaviour. Unlike the disciplinary society in which social command is construed by the mediation of institutions, the society of control sees mechanisms of command becoming immanent to the social field and distributed by means of communication systems and information networks directly to the minds and bodies of the citizens. Bio-power is a form of power governing social life from the inside so that it absorbs, interprets and revalues the life, using in the process the flexible and fluctuating networks. Therefore, power is expressed as control stretching along the depths of consciousness and bodies of the citizens, and along the entire social relations at the same time. Social control over the individual is exercised not only through consciousness and ideology, but also within the body and with the body, with life becoming an object of power. However, the process is not about taking over the economic or cultural spheres of society, it is about penetrating into the very social *bios*, crashing down the linear and totalitarian form of capitalist development. The activities of corporations are defined no more by the help of abstract commands and organisations of unequal exchanges. It could be said that the activities directly structure territories and populations. Transnational corporations indirectly distribute labour among different markets, allocate resources functionally and organise hierarchically diverse sectors of the world production. A complex apparatus, selecting investments and directing financial and monetary manoeuvres, dictates a new political structuring of the world. Therefore, big industrial and financial powers produce not only goods but also subjectivities: they produce needs, social relations, bodies and mind, that is, as Hardt and Negri emphasise, they produce producers. Communication is the factor at the same time maintaining and organising the process of globalisation. It organises the process by means of structuring and multiplying internal connections along the networks. Political synthesis of the social space is fixated in the field of communication. This is the reason why the industries of communication have taken such a central position.

Considering the fact that bio-power is based on the issue of production and reproduction of the social being, there is a need for a new theory of subjectivity which acts through knowledge, communication and language. 'If we regard language as situated in social practices, and if we reject the distinction between consciousness and the unconscious followed by the structuralist and post-structuralist authors, we reach a different conception of the human subject – as agent' (Giddens, 1987).

Postmodern Organisation and its Political Implications

In the changing realities of the 1980s and 1990s, dynamic networks gain their impetus, enabling companies to downsize and outsource, and allowing for the development of matrix 'adhocracies'. In this way, small business firms become part of greater networks, while 'organisation' ceases to be a dominant organisational entity. Therefore, postmodern organisation relativises all organisational structures. The postmodern condition of organisation, however, is not a specific type of organisation. The reason for this, as Albrow (1997) points out, lies in that the configuration of the principles, practice and structure characteristic of the modernity and the modern organisation completely went to pieces. In the process it is the principles that suffered most. No decision came to be based upon principles, and the actors could use a whole display of options – mergers, delayering, downsizing, outsourcing. The location of principles is now moved outside the organisation and into the direction of social movements. Hence the principles come to belong to the sphere of value choices and commitments to collective goals outside the sphere of employment. Therefore, Albrow argues, postmodernity is a condition, and not a realisation of a project, as is the case with modernity. The greatest achievement of postmodernity comes from the fact that it ended the Modern Age in a way profound enough.

Unlike Albrow, who does not recognise the postmodern organisation as a distinctive entity, a position we hold in this paper, some authors take another direction. What is characteristic of such debates is that the dichotomy modern/postmodern organisation is taken as something given *a priori*, that is, the legitimacy for a new specific form of organisation is found in the level of its differing nature in relation to the modern organisation. In other words, postmodernist organisation is a term the authors use to define a contrast in relation to Weber's modern representation. The approach is also taken by Clegg (1992), who meticulously analyses organisational characteristics of the system of economic embeddedness characteristic of Japanese companies, and who concludes that postmodern organisation forms are implicit in these developments.

The Japanese success of the 1980s triggered a huge interest of the Western researchers into Japanese organisations, which soon became the beacons of the postmodern age. Certainly, there are evident differences and they may well sketch one political conjecture for postmodern organisation premised on stable private capital formation, production-centred strategies of economic calculation and high degrees of labour market segmentation' (Clegg, 1992). On the other hand, Aglietta (1979) came to believe that 'Fordism', as the foundation of modern organisation, would be increasingly limited to less developed industries and would tend to be located in the less developed zones of world economy as capitalism becomes ever more institutionalised.

It is hard to distinguish postmodern organisation from its political implications. What is at stake here is that the concept of postmodern arrangements is often, and we believe unjustifiably, related only to a 'free' market variant of organisational forms. The 1980s revival of neo-conservative liberal analysis sought to find recipes for success in deregulation, in de-unionisation or enterprise unionism and in state intervention oriented to curbing the excess of democracy, administrative overload, ungovernability and so on (Clegg, 1992).

In this way, an inevitable use of black and white accounts of the new processes becomes a norm, whereby the freedom of a few is positioned in a relationship of conflict to the restrictions imposed on the majority, which narrows down the possibilities for discussions on alternative concepts. Consequently, Clegg justifiably points out that the debates on the Pacific examples, such as Japan and the East Asian NICs should be balanced with the discussions on the economically less liberal and more social democratic options, such as Sweden and OECD countries. The fact that Sweden has a relatively well organised labour movement opens up the possibility of bargained corporatism in which employees via their organisations and institutions try to impose their political preferences on employers and the government.

If we take a comparative analysis of the postmodern and modern organisation, then it is important to note a wide range of dimensions such as skill formation, capital formation, as well as the ways in which they represent a framework for a variety of organisational operations through (contrasting modes of rationality). 'Within the core enterprises and countries control will become less authoritarian in the workplace as new forms of market discipline substitute for the external surveillance of supervision, changes fostered by extensive de-regulation' (Clegg, 1992: 159). There is no doubt though that capital stability is a key variable when the organisation chooses which form of rationality to construe. The distinctiveness of the Swedish strategy, however, shows that there is more than one way of achieving any particular outcome. In other words, which option the organisation will take depends upon an understanding of civil society and representative democracy.

Constituting Elements of Configuration of Globality

Nowadays, it is difficult to give a coherent overview of both organisational change and organisational science, argues Albrow (1997), for two reasons: the new science postulates the same assumptions as the old one, substituting one superior rationality with another, or it defies to give final views of organisations, be it old or new ones. He does not accept the distinction modern/postmodern organisation as he does not want to be caught in the dilemmas coming out from the break of 'the old modern' viewpoint on the congruence between organisation and science, and consequently puts both the modern and postmodern paradigm into a historical narrative. Today we are faced with the break up of the 'old modern forms of organisations', which means that we need to focus on the new global age as we try to find out answers to the question why it differs from the Modern Age. In which ways are the global levels of social organisation inherent in the everyday lives of individuals, and in the organisations for which they work – now this is the mega-question of the present time. In other words, we need to see the epochal character of the time we live in.

In doing so, we have an intellectual choice to view existing organisational theory as a break up of objectivity, or alternatively, as an expression of pluralism and diversity of organisational theory. Albrow made an important contribution to the understanding of the latter. The contemporary age does not impose a logic on organisational forms, as it does not function from the level of principles. What is clear is that in the age of globality, efficiency cannot be linked to only one type of organisational structure or to one type of socio-political system. In the new historical period we live in, capitalism has lost its coherence, increasingly becoming 'an unorganised capitalism' (Offe, 1985; Urry and Lash, 1987). The same decentring takes place in organisations, and their normal condition seems to be a continuous process of restructuring. The process of privatisation of state industries is concerned more with a hybridisation of organisational types rather than with a simple transfer of ownership.

It is the fluidity and variety of organisational forms that has been the major reason for departing from researching into organisational structures and turning to studying the praxis of organising. Today it could be hard to find an alternative to the widely accepted notion of the organisation as an existing outcome of organised practices (Albrow, 1997). It is the contingent and unstable nature of organisations in the age of globality that diverts the researcher's attention from 'the organisation' to 'organising' as an ordering practice.

Therefore, in the age of globality there is no unified model of organisation, or of network, which could put aside other models, much in the same way as there is no paradigm for movements. According to Albrow, the features which make globality the constitutive figuration of our time are the following:

- risks for global environment;
- nuclear armament;
- global systems of communication;
- globalised world economy;
- social movements accepting the social values of globality.

Taken together, they reach epochal transformations creating organisational limits. Global values make resistance legitimate, thus promoting collective responses to structures and forces which could potentially be a threat for the future of our civilisation. Hence it is quite understandable that the focus on organisation as such is being transferred towards organising. An immediate result is a diversity of organisational structures, which means that globalisation can hardly be viewed as a uniform process. In this way, Albrow concludes, globality has created such conditions in organisations which free them to a great extent from the 'iron cage of modernity'.

Definition of Organisation: Primacy and Centrality of Power

It is well known among researchers that there is no agreement on the definition of organisation, as well as on the attitude towards possibility of dialogue between various orientations. We believe that, in today's conditions of globality, the latter becomes a significant issue. Unlike Burrell and Morgan (1979), who should take credit for clearly formulating the alternatives to the dominant functionalist tradition which in the late 1970s hardly managed to cope with the spirit of the time, Deetz (2000) holds that it is more productive to focus on the differences and similarities among research perspectives, and not to deal with classifications. Hence, it is much more important to ask the question of *how* organisational science is practised, and the answer to it Deetz seeks in an analysis of constitutive moves of discourse in organisations. He finds it detrimental to reduce the concepts to categories or to reduce the delicate concepts to definitions. A similar view is taken by Silverman (1994), who points out the harmful effects of closing sociologies into schools. Communication along the paradigms is possible and desirable, assuming that various groups, in mutual interaction, try to build up a world together, whereby the criteria for the evaluation of various research programmes should be the moves they make towards the completeness or incompleteness of the projects that are the subject of interactions. As we gradually learn socially the positive effects of diversity – beyond 'separate but equal' and integration – 'organisation science can also benefit from better discussions' (Deetz, 2000).

Structuralism and Critical Theory gave important contributions to an understanding of the causes of exploitation, manipulation and domination during the long history of the metamorphosis of capitalism. In this way, the authors prepared the ground for the key question (which they themselves did not tackle), and closely related with the issues: *Why do people endure the living conditions which degrade them? What makes us to accept the unacceptable?* A response to this is possible only with the help of new analytical 'tools', and it is here that poststructuralist understanding of structure may open up new horizons. Structure is the explanation itself, that which *makes* sense, not that which *gives* sense. It follows from this that structure cannot be seen as determining action because it is not real and transcendent, but a product of human mind (Jackson and Carter, 2000). Consequently, no form of organisation or order seems to be inevitable, which opens up a space for organising a social order with a more 'human touch'. Therefore, the target of a future analysis should be the human mind and the way in which it is subjected to ideological constructions embodied in various forms of organisations.

Poststructuralist theories, with their focus on the primacy and centrality of power in the analyses of organisations and organisational behaviour, have made an important step forward by argumentatively questioning the views that organisational activity should be taken as functional, rational and hence neutral. To the contrary, organisations are in the first instance political sites realised in conditions of struggle and domination, so there is a need then to take them as part of the general system which Foucault calls 'governance'. Foucault points out that all interactions are characterised by an exercise of power, which lies in the individual subjects as they try to gain control so that they would be able to give preference to *their* point of view – in essence, so that they could gain the power to signify. It is not the structure that which is experienced, but the force of other people's desires. Hence it makes sense to speak about the production of truth.

> Truth is centred on the form of scientific discourse and the institutions which produce it; it is subject to constant economic and political incitement (the demand for truth, as much as for economic production as for political power): it is object, under diverse forms, of immense diffusion and consumption (circulating through apparatuses of education and information whose extent is relatively broad in the social body, not withstanding certain strict limitation); it is produced and transmitted under the control, dominant if not exclusive, of a few great political and economic apparatuses (university, army, writing, media); lastly, it is the issue of a whole political debate and social confrontation ('ideological struggles'). (Foucault, 1980: 131–2)

However, Foucault takes great care to show that power 'comes from below', that is, that global and hierarchical structures of domination within a society depend on and operate through more local, low-level, 'capillary' circuits of power relationship. In his 1974 lectures 'Truth and Juridical Forms' and also in 'Lives of Infamous Man', he suggests that innovations in forms of social control arose partly through initiatives or demands of minority groups and the humbler strata of society' (Gordon, 2001).

Poststructuralist approach recognises a functional use of power in the process of achieving desired ends. What the approach questions is the desirability of the ends themselves, the purposes for which organisational forms are made and how they are sustained. Jackson and Carter (2000) emphasise that organisations cannot be adequately defined without understanding the key role of power, that is, when it comes to organisational behaviour, then the behaviour is about using disciplinary power or being subject to it. 'From a poststructuralist perspective, power is the power to ordain significations, to prescribe how signifiers should be understood, or to prioritise one set of meanings and, by implications, repress all others' (Jackson and Carter, 2000).

New research is focused on organisations as processes and not entities, which means that its main target are activities and purposes of organising itself as a common principle in all organisations. Hence poststructuralist authors are more interested in *similarities* among all types of organisations, similarities related to their role in sustaining the system of governance and capitalist regime of truth. The research is focused on both aspects, i.e., on the organisation's external relations towards society as a whole, and especially on the social effects of corporate colonisation, rationalisation of society, and the domination of the public sphere, as well as on the internal relations in the concepts of domination by instrumental reasoning, discursive closures, and consent processes (Deetz, 2000).

The new research is concerned with the concept of disciplinary networks – matrices of power, as opposed to the concept of hierarchical power, as the former enables us to focus on the *quality* of operation of power in organisations, that is, on the *how* organisations exercise their superordinate function in the system of governance. Translated into the language of praxis, exercising of power means imposing a worldview advocated by the powerful who have usurped the 'right' to speak on behalf of the powerless, as the latter's right to their own opinion has been denied. In this way, the analyses of power within organisational context are transferred onto the discursive level. Yet even if we speak about the powerful and the powerless, a relatively neutral language is used. What should be noted, as Jackson and Carter (2000) point out, is that the exercise of power makes victims. Lyotard defines victims '... as those who are spoken of in a language which is not theirs, language in which the signifieds, and often even the signifiers, are not shared: victims are those who are the objects, those who are talked about but cannot themselves talk. This is precisely the case with conventional approaches to organisational behaviour' (Jackson and Carter, 2000).

Discourse is related to the experiences people have at work, yet it does not include an interpretation of the nature of that experience, because managers and management academics are the ones with the power to signify, and they also use a technical jargon. The discourse defines experience for itself, not what it means. This is an act of supreme power.

As Derrida (1998) points out, this abiding 'alienation' appears to be constitutive. Yet, an essential question here is whether it is possible to alienate language, and whether perhaps what all this is about is 'the structure of alienation without alienation'? From the fact that the language we speak is at the same time the language of the Other (I have only one language and it is not mine), there come structural limitations of language 'possession', of the peculiarity and property of language, as well as our responsibility for its use (Derrida, 1998).

Factors Influencing Construction of Meanings at Work

The authors, whose theoretical postulates are rooted in Critical Theory and poststructuralism, have given a significant contribution to an unveiling of the dominant thesis that the function of organisation is production of goods and services, as they have shown that the organisation's principal purpose is to maintain and increase the existing power relationships in capitalist systems of production. 'Human resource management' and accounting have proved to be an excellent evidence for detailed arguments in this field.

Human Resource Management

With his analysis of the *In Search of Excellence* phenomenon, Guest (1992) comes to a conclusion that this type of managerial literature is successful due to its ability to present a coherent, positive and optimistic philosophy about management. Focusing on values and emotions as central to behavioural science, Peters and Waterman (1982) choose a position in which 'people issues' in organisations are generally tackled in a subjective and intuitive way. Their insistence on 'soft' variables provides them with a double alibi: on one hand, objective evidence is not necessary or even needed, while on the other hand, since they do not see a conflict between personal growth and organisational growth, the issue of power in this kind of discussion is not an issue at all.

A similar philosophy of 'relying on own resources', that is, of an explicit use of managerial discourse, is advocated by Kanter (1990), who holds that the key to corporate renaissance lies in the initiatives developed by and within the organisation. Hence, if environments and structures are open to innovations, natural human innovation can do wonders. The idea is, Kanter (1995) says, how to manage global challenges so as to become the masters of changes, not their victims. What the author omits to say, however, is whom she considers 'we', and this is intelligently shrouded in the veil of qualitocracy made of three factors – concepts, competence and connections; that is, the global market cares for the 'quality' and not the 'brand' of the product's origin. In a similar vein, Kanter says that power battles will not be fought among nations but among global networks, yet the author does not enter into analysing *how* these new networks will operate.

Excellence literature represents, on one hand, an American response to the challenges posed by recession and an increasing threat from competitors, and on the other hand, it is an addition to continuous efforts to find new strategies that would reduce costs and increase profit. An immediate impetus for the concept, based on the 'American dream' ideology and an intensifying of values such as 'quality of working life', was the 1980s crisis of the US management caused by its failing to compete with Japan.

What is at stake here is continuous effort of management to redefine itself, as well the meaning of work and the ways employers treat their employees. On the other hand, if we consider the inherent need of capital to expand itself over its limits, then we see that the consequences of export/import of managerial techniques get the status of a first class political, moral and theoretical issues, which makes the cultural context an extremely important variable in analysing organisational behaviour. Mabey and Iles (1996) point out that 'human resource management' should be taken as a new form of managerial control, whose power does not derive from its impact on performance, but from its capability to involve current social values and political priorities into intra-organisational relations. So new techniques and a new language are used in the construction of meaning, which enables a total control of the ways organisations are discussed and understood, and of the ways in which organisational purposes and dynamics are conducted and formed. What is being neglected in these techniques, however, is the existence of diverse cognitive maps and personal agendas of the individuals involved. Also, there is little evidence that would support the thesis that human resource management has a positive impact on the work of organisations. This means that an interpretation of the meaning of human resource management requires an understanding of dominant values, economic priorities and cultural context of the country in which human resource management is being introduced.

Based on the results of an international team research on the nature of human resources management in seven European countries (UK, France, Spain, Germany, the Netherlands and Sweden), and on the managerial implications of the Single European Market, Clark and Mallory (1996) also came to a conclusion that human resource management should be taken as culturally relative. The data obtained in the research show that American managerial ideas, models and theories has lower applicability and relevance in those countries which do not share the same cultural values. When it comes to the phenomenon of power, the strongest distinctive feature is individualistic and collective cultural context.

A similar position is held by Adler (1997: 47), who defines the individualism vs collectivism dichotomy in the following way:

> *Individualism exists* when people define themselves primarily as separate individuals and make their primary commitments to themselves ... *Collectivism* is characterised by tight social networks in which people strongly distinguish between their own groups (in-groups, such as relatives, clans and organisations and other groups).

The Anglo-American human resource management insists on moving from the management–trade unions relationship to the management–employee relationship (the unitarian approach). In highly collectivist cultures, managerial practice accepts the fact that working tasks are designated in terms of team-work, so that team members share responsibility and rewards for their achievements. Instead of imposing 'universal' theories from one culture to another, Clark and Mallory suggest a model for understanding a 'European' human resource management, which they see as an interaction of three factors:

- international institutionalised context;
- national culture; and
- national institutionalised context.

This model diverts the focus from the ethnocentric approach to a more polycentric approach in comparative research on human resource management.

Accounting as a Technology of Control

A characteristic of this electronically operated global capitalism is that it is structured with the help of information networks in the timeless space of financial flows. Money has become almost totally independent of production, escaping into the networks of high-order electronic interactions. Capital network unifies and has command over specific centres of capital accumulation, structuring and conditioning the behaviour of capitalists in global networks. By acting directly through financial institutions, financial capital, 'mother of all accumulations that is the global financial network' (Castells, 2000: 504), determines the fate of industry and economy all over the world. It is no surprise that it incites emotions, passions and criticism. But, in any case, it does call for organised responses.

It is evident that what is thought to be the concept of good performance depends on the point of view taken by the distinctive stakeholders' groups. This, however, opens up the debate about the presentation of accountancy data, use of language and control of accounting discourse. For Morgan (1988), accountancy is an 'interpretative art', while Puxty and Tinker (1995) point out the need for policing accounting knowledge to recognise the material nature of language. Language is not a mere communication device, but it is a central constituent of the communication world. Hence the control of the signifier through the socialised gatekeeper is in essence a control of the material world. Control over the process of production of knowledge is not only a control over communication media, but also over the materiality of the accounting knowledge itself. The way in which language is used in accounting journals, whether it presents or misrepresents the material world, becomes an ideological means which supports capital, as well as a means of censoring 'dangerous minds'. This is the way in which academic community manipulates a certain 'thing', and not with the description of the thing. 'The key point here is that what appears at first to be merely an ideological state process becomes, in its operation, part of a repressive state process' (Puxty and Tinker, 1995: 258). Since discourse constitutes the central form of academic life, to control scientific discourse is the same as to control scientific life itself.

It is obvious that the accounting profession need reform, and this is where the main intention, initiative and action undertaken by the American SEC stems from in order to recognise once again the primary accountability of the profession towards the public interest. Hendrickson (2001) points out the harmful consequences which economic power of the AICPA and major accounting firms have regarding the accounting profession and accounting education. As a matter of fact, they use their economic power to establish domination over their surroundings by controlling the system of accounting education but also by the regulation of public accounting in order to protect and intensify their own private interests. Moreover, the greater their economic power, the smaller their concern for their own accountability as regards public interests. Hendrickson shows similarities with such authors who see the way out in a need to redesign the system of accounting education in such a way that would help this profession to regain its dignity. It is first and foremost related to the provision of relevant and reliable accounting reports, which is not only the essential prerequisite for functioning of the capitalist market, but also could contribute to the creation of the spirit of trust indispensable for functioning of the community.

Agency and Motivation in IT Environments

There is no doubt that the social relations between labour and capital have radically been transformed. At its core, capital is global. Networks converge towards a meta-network of capital, integrating capital interests at a global level. By contrast, although there is a unity of labour process within the complex global networks, labour is, in principle, local and disaggregated in its performance, individualised in its capacity, fragmented in its organisation, diversified in its existence, and divided in its collective action. In this way labour and capital increasingly tend to exist in different spaces and times, because the global capital is no longer dependent on specific labour, but is ever increasingly dependent on accumulated generic labour led by virtual global networks (Castells, 2000).

The important thing coming out of these processes is indeed global interdependence of the labour force in the informational economy. Castells, however, is not optimistic about the processes, and claims that the network society is characterised by a pre-eminence of social morphology over social action. A similar viewpoint is held by Albrow (1997) who argues that events cannot be controlled by human agency any more. The modern man has never been under such a dictate of the environment as he is in the age of globality. Unlike the two distinguished authors, we believe that the global processes open up a space not only for new forms of workers' resistance, but also for new methods of struggle. It was long ago that Touraine (1983: 10) emphasised that 'human societies possess an ability not only to reproduce themselves or adapt to the changing environments, by means of learning mechanisms and political decisions, yet what is more they have the ability to create and change their own directions, to *set their goals and create their own normativity*. The key concept of his analysis is the agency aimed at gaining control over a particular social field. Our society is not only the discourse of the state, but it is primarily a hierarchical system of agency. He recognises social movements as the actors of collective actions, which represent specific, and yet the most significant type of struggle in the 'postindustrial' and 'programmed' society. This in turn assumes a greater capability of the labour movement to adjust to a networking logic as a major source of social cohesion in the global capitalism.

Information technologies give new form and meaning to the concept of agency, which requires new efforts to clarify the explanatory validity of the concept. It is in this that we see a major benefit that praxis could gain from social theories in the present time.

The action frame of reference created by Silverman (1987) proves a time tested analytical tool. Relying on the Kuhn's concept of science and Schutz's critique of Weber, Silverman emphasises that the behaviour of members of an organisation cannot be sufficiently analysed with the help of the structural variables, and that subjective perceptions and meanings related to the expectations of individual actors should be considered. Hence he gives two major objections to contemporary accounts of organisations: first, organisational aims and rules are 'out there', that is, they exist separately from the ways in which the actors define situation; second, it is believed that agency can be explained through aims and rules, without taking into account the fact that micro-interactions are always the reflections of larger social processes.

According to the approach developed by Silverman, agency within organisation is a result of an interaction of three groups of factors:

- an institutionalised bank of knowledge outside of organisation which various actors bring into it;
- systems of roles within organisation; and
- various levels of actors' involvement, aims and definitions of situations.

Therefore, organisations are not rigid systems of power, but it is the actors who could be more or less continually involved in the efforts to sustain or change the existing power relationships. Organisational change can be understood either as the change of the rules of the game (through the system of roles within organisation) or as the change of actors' loyalty to the rules (through changing the extent of their engagement in the organisation). Social relationships in the organisation come from the interactions of their members, and can show various levels of consensuses and conflicts, cooperation and coercion, all in line with the nature of the actors' expectations and aims.

The basic task of the agency approach is to interpret the ways changes come out of the interactions. The attention is focused on the nature and sources of meanings that actors assign to their working roles. The main idea is to understand how interpretations of situations are changed by actors, and to interpret what is going on in organisations as a result of their motivated action, whereby their aims are formed by their previous expectations. In this way it is possible to divert the focus from the micro-issues of agency of certain actors towards the macro issues of the system of expectations, which establishes itself as actors follow their goals in the context of meanings and symbolic resources that they accept from a wider social structure. Social change, be it in the sense of the involvement of actors, or in the sense of expectations, occur as a result of social actions in which the members have different symbolic resources available, so their intention is to change the accumulated knowledge within a wider social context. An important contribution of the agency perspective is reflected in the fact that it provides an insight into the way in which the social world is construed and sustained.

Collins (1981) advocates a strategy of micro-translation which reveals empirical realities of social structures as patterns of repetitive micro-interactions. Considering the fact that micro-evidence indicates that the human cognitive ability is limited, it should be noted that in situations in which the individual actors are faced with new complex events, they rely to a great extent on tacit assumptions and routine, all of which are supported with the help of social coalitions within the organisation. Individuals continually negotiate with the coalitions in interaction ritual chains, in which conversations create symbols of group memberships. Each encounter is a 'marketplace' in which the individual tacitly matches conversational and emotional resources brought about by previous encounters. This highlights the fact that the entities seated in the individual, such as personality and attitude, are reflected as situational ways of action in conversational encounters, and that personality and attitude are stable in so far as the individuals go through the same type of repeated interactions. The main value of the micro-translation of the entire social structure in the interaction ritual chains lies in that the method offers 'tools' for interpreting both of the aspects, the inertia and the dynamics of the macro-structure, whereby Collins insists on the non-cognitive foundations of these interactions.

Simultaneously with the introduction of the new information technologies and 'generalised-culture producing specialists', we can, Collins argues, think about a historical introduction of 'new emotion-producing technologies'. From this point of view, changes in the technological infrastructure are decisive, because they change the number of people who can assemble for ritual purposes, and because they change the ability for 'impression management or dramatisation'. Various combinations of these emotional technologies, and the level of their concentration or dispersion among the population, are decisive factors in the struggle for power in any historical society. In the conditions of internet technologies, however, 'emotional impression management' becomes a global issue, and as such, we believe, opens up a huge space for constructive uses, as well as for manipulations and abuses in the processes of organising.

Any organisation involves authority manifested in the power of some people to impose orders that others should carry out. The foundation of authority is communication, which indicates the negotiative nature of the power as such. Organisational authority is based on the mutual orientations among the members of a group. From the micro-translation point of view, the social world is construed from aggregates of individual chains of interactional experiences meeting at crossroads in time and space. The major activity in the situations is conversation. What is important in any conversation, from the point of view of social membership, Collins emphasises, is not the content but the extent to which the participants can really sustain a common activity focused on the content. Consequently, the content is a means for establishing a membership. Conversation is a ritual in which all those who accept it share an organisational solidarity and the same cognitive symbols that keep the group together.

Participants of a successful conversational ritual have common conversational and cultural resources, and are able to sustain a mutual emotional tone, whereby the emotional participation is stratified in such a way so as the group can be divided into emotional leaders and followers. Conversational topics have two different implications for the reproduction of social structure. Some conversational topics are generalised and have the effect of a common participation in a horizontally organised cultural community sharing the same viewpoints. Others are particularised in the sense that they focus the attention of the population onto particular individuals, and as a result could change the organisational centre of power coalitions.

Emotional energies are an essential prerequisite for a successful interaction, whereby conversational rituals can be egalitarian or asymmetric. The egalitarian rituals are stratifying in the sense that the insiders are accepted while the outsiders are rejected; here the stratification exists in the form of a coalition against the excluded individuals, yet a domination of one coalition over another is possible. The asymmetric conversations are stratified from the inside, that is, here it is one individual who sets the emotional tone and invokes a cultural reality, while the rest represent the audiences.

The advantage of a model of interaction ritual chains can be seen in that the reciprocity of relationships between individuals turns into something that is variable, not constant; the individuals participate to an extent that the emotional dynamics of a particular coalition membership is appealing to the them. On the other hand, the 'new ritual technologies' change the quality of emotions across the society. Consequently, the changes can in turn change the nature of social movements and the dynamics of political and economic action.

Information technologies offer a wide range of opportunities and techniques for mobilising positive emotional energies along the entire social body. Unlike Castells, for whom capital is fluid, mobile and proactive, while workers purely reactive, Munck (2000) points out an important argument that labour should not be understood as a passive recipient of capital and government strategies. Furthermore, as Brown (2000) demonstrates, workers from different parts of the world also come into competition as a collective resource rather than as individuals, not only in situations where companies are deciding where to inwardly invest but also in circumstances where companies are deciding to relocate to another part of the world.

It seems that economic globalisation has created common ground for the struggles of workers in many countries, and that cultural globalisation minimised or relativised the former barriers of difference, or distance between labour movements. Hence trade unions were 'going global' in the methods they used in their strategies in the 1990s. Therefore, globalisation has created a whole new range of sites of resistance to capitalism and has helped generate a whole new repertoire of labour strategies and tactics. The raising of labour activities to the level of international communication is an important quality step forward, in the sense of learning to interpret language, because all social struggles are the struggles related to interpretation on the discourse level. 'International labour organisations will play a role in this discursive construction of the new reality, and the Internet will probably be a privileged medium' (Munck, 2000b: 391).

By affirming the voice of the individual the Internet provides mechanisms for the creation of a new global solidarity that enables redistribution of power within society (Crowther, 2002). Inspired by the thesis developed by Munro (1999) that one of the most effective ways of affecting a change is to stay outside and try to affect the stream of conduct at distance, Crowther believes that the Internet provides means that could affect the dominant relations of power in the corporate world. In this context, corporate reporting becomes a crucial issue, as it can be seen then whom organisations are accountable, and who has authority to evaluate their performance. What is revolutionary about this technology is that it provides a potential change of legitimacy in the sense of opening space for the individual to defy dominating coalitions of power and become an equal participant in the cyberspace discourse. On the practical plane, the Internet is an instrument by which the selfness could activate its operating principle: resistance against a big corporation. Stakeholders have increasingly greater access to information that makes them more capable to cooperate virtually in the form of pressure groups, thus contributing to changes in corporate reporting and conduct. These changes are brought about, as some authors (eg McDonald and Puxty, 1979; Robey and Sales, 1994; Crowther, 2002) think, because companies are not mere instruments of shareholders, but their accountability towards a wider social community comes from the fact that they are part of that community. In the new network landscape, information technologies, including the Internet, become an omnipenetrating social force providing mechanisms that enable the shift of power from those who abuse it to those who are their victims. In this way, owing to the Internet, the issue of the control of the controllers assumes some real foundations nowadays.

Conclusions

The novelty that the processes of globalisation, as essentially economic processes, with the inherent political and social consequences, brings about is that they transfer the power battle field into the environment of information technologies. Owing to a rocketing development of the Internet technologies, a new, global space for the expansion of dynamic networks has opened up. The networks enable companies to transform themselves and to become a part of a greater network, so that the 'organisation' ceases to be a dominant organisational entity. The rational principles lying in the background of the modern, Weberian organisation, which aimed at a single organisational form to dominate worldwide, have lost their *raison d'être*. In the age of globality, the principles are moved out of the organisations into the direction of social movements. Hence they belong to the sphere of the value choices, and to commitment to collective goals outside the field of employment. Globalist values make a resistance legitimate, thus promoting collective responses to structures and forces which could potentially be a threat for the future of our civilisation. In the reality of multiple and interconnected networks, the modern organisation has given way to organising; the author holds that the change in the paradigm of power, as a major milestone, has enabled the transfer. Poststructuralist theories, with their focus on the primacy and centrality of power in the analyses of organisations and organisational behaviour, have made an important step forward by argumentatively questioning the views that organisational activity should be taken as functional, rational and hence neutral. On the contrary, organisations are in the first instance political sites realised in conditions of struggle and domination, so there is a need to take them as a part of the general system which Foucault calls governance. Foucault points out that all interactions are characterised by an exercise of power, which lies in the individual subjects as they try to gain control so that they would be able to give preference to their point of view – en essence, so that they could gain power to signify. New research is focused on organisations as processes and not as entities, which means that its main target are activities and purposes of organising itself as a common principle in all organisations. Hence poststructuralist authors are more interested in similarities among all types of organisations, similarities related to their role in maintaining the system of governance and capitalist regime of truth. The concept of hierarchical power is opposed by the analyses of power in organisations, which is now transferred onto the discursive level. Relying on the poststructuralist understanding that structure cannot be seen as determining agency because it is not real and transcendent, but a product of human mind, the underlying message of this chapter is that no form of organisation or order seems to be inevitable. This position opens up a space for the kind of organising reaching towards the constitution of social order with a more 'human touch'. Information technologies are not mere technical facts, but primarily they are social catalysts; by penetrating into the core of life and the mind, computer networks expand the manoeuvre space available to human actors, providing us with a new form and meaning of the concept of human agency. Diversity of organisational structures comes as an immediate result of the mentioned processes, which means that globalisation can hardly be taken as a uniform process.

References

Ackroyd, S. and Thompson, P. (1999), *Organizational Misbehaviour*, London: Sage Publications.
Adler, N. (1997), *International Dimensions of Organizational Behavior*, Cincinnati: South-Western College Publishing.
Aglietta, M. (1979), *A Theory of Capitalist Regulation*, London: New Left Books.
Albrow, M. (1997), *Do organizations have Feelings?*, London and New York: Routledge.
Brown, P. (2000), The Globalisation of Positional Competition?, *Sociology*, Vol. 34, No. 4: 633–53.

Burrell, G. and Morgan, G. (1979), *Sociological Paradigms and Organisational Analysis*, London: Heinemann.

Castells, M. (2000), 'The Information Age: Economy, Society and Culture', Volume I: *The Rise of the Network Society*, Oxford: Blackwell Publishers Ltd.

Clark, T. and Mallory, G. (1996), 'The Cultural Relativity of Human Resource Management: Is There a Universal Model?', in T. Clark (ed.), *European Human Resource Management*, Oxford: Blackwell Publishers Ltd: 1–33.

Clegg, S.R. (1992), 'Modernist and Postmodernist Organization', in G. Salaman (ed.), *Human Resource Strategies*, London: The Open University and Sage Publications: 156–87.

Collins, R. (1981), 'On the Microfoundations of Macrosociology', *American Journal of Sociology*, Vol. 86, No. 5: 984–1014.

Crowther, D. (2002), *A social Critique on Corporate Reporting: A Semiotic Analysis of Corporate Financial and Environmental Reporting*, Aldershot: Ashgate Publishing Ltd.

Deetz, S. (2000), 'Describing Differences in Approaches to Organization science: Rethinking Burrell and Morgan and Their Legacy', in P.J. Frost, A.Y. Lewin and R.L. Daft (eds), *Talking About Organization Science: Debates and Dialogue from Crossroads*, London: Sage Publications: 123–52.

Derrida, J. (1998), *Monolingualism of the Other or The Prothesis of Orign*, trans. P. Menah, Stanford: Stanford University Press.

Elliott, G. and Starkings, S. (1998), *Business Information Technology: Systems, Theory and Practice*, London and New York: Longman.

Foucault, M. (1977), *Discipline and Punish*, trans. A. Sheridon, London: Penguin.

Foucault, M. (1980), *Power/Knowledge: Selected Interviews and Other Writings 1972–1977*, ed. C. Gordon, trans. C. Gordon, L. Marshall, J. Mepham and K. Soper, Harlow: Pearson Education.

Gates, B. and Hemingway, C. (1999), *Business @ The Speed of Thought: Succeeding in the Digital Economy*, London: Penguin Books.

Giddens, A. (1984), *The Constitution of Society*, Cambridge: Polity Press.

Giddens, A. (1987), *Social Theory and Modern Sociology*, Cambridge: Polity Press.

Gordon, C. (2001), 'Introduction', in J.D. Faubion (ed.), *Essential Works of Foucault 1954–1984*, trans. R. Hurley and others, London: Allen Lane, The Penguin Press: XI–XLI.

Guest, D. (1992), 'Right Enough to be Dangerously Wrong: An Analysis of the *In Search of Excellence* Phenomenon', in G. Salaman (ed.), *Human Resource Strategies*, London: The Open University and Sage Publications: 5–19.

Hardt, M. and Negri, A. (2001), *Empire*, Cambridge, MA: Harvard University Press.

Hendrickson, H. (2001), 'Some Comments on the Impact of the Economic Power Exercised by the AICPA and the Major Accounting Firms', *Critical Perspectives on Accounting*, Vol. 12, No. 2: 159–66.

Jackson, N. and Carter, P. (2000), *Rethinking Organizational Behaviour*, Harlow: Pearson Education Ltd.

Kanter, R.M. (1990), *The Change Masters: Corporate Entrepreneurs at Work*, London: Unwin Hyman Ltd.

Kanter, R.M. (1995), *World Class: Thriving Locally in the Global Economy*, New York: Simone and Schuster.

Kuhn, T. (1962), *The Structure of Scientific Revolutions*, Chicago: University of Chicago.

Lyotard, J.F. (1988), *The Differend – Phrases in Dispute*, trans. G. van den Abbeele, Manchester: Manchester University Press.

Mabey, C. and Illes, P. (1996), 'Human Resource Management in the UK: A Case of Fundamental Change, Facelift or Façade?', in T. Clark (ed.), *European Human Resource Management*, Oxford: Blackwell Publishers Ltd: 34–64.

McDonald, D. and Puxty, A.G. (1979), 'An Inducement–Contribution Approach to Corporate Financial Reporting', *Accounting, Organizations and Society*, Vol. 4, Nos 1–2: 53–65.

Munck, R. (2000), 'Labour and Globalisation: Results and Prospets', *Work, Employment and Society*, Vol. 14, No. 2: 385–93.

Munro, R. (1999), 'Power and Discretion: Membership Work in the Time of Technology', *Organization*, Vol. 6, No. 3: 429–50.

O'Doherty, D. and Willmott, H. (2001), 'Debating Labour Process Theory: The Issue of Subjectivity and the Relevance of Poststructuralism', *Sociology*, Vol. 35, No. 2: 457–76.

Offe, C. (1985), *Disorganized Capitalism*, Cambridge: Polity.

Peters, T. and Waterman, R. (1982), *In Search of Excellence*, New York: Harper and Row.

Puxty, T. and Tinker, T. (1995), 'The Sociology of Knowledge as Praxis', in T. Tinker and T. Puxty (eds), *Policing Accounting Knowledge: The Market Exuces Affair*, Princeton: Markus Wiener Publishers: 241–70.

Robey, D. and Sales, C.A. (1994), *Designing Organizations*, Boston: IRWIN.

Schutz, A. (1964), *Collected Papers, Vols I, II*, ed. M. Natanson, The Hague: Nijhoff.

Silverman, D. (1987), *The Theory of Organizations*, Aldershot: Gower.

Silverman, D. (1994), 'On Throwing Away Ladders: Rewriting the Theory of Organizations', in J. Hassard and M. Parker (eds), *Towards a New Theory of Organizations*, London: Routledge: 1–23.

Strassman, D.A. (1997), *The Squandered Computer: Evaluating the Business Alignment of Information Technologies*, New Canan, CT: The Information Economic Press.

Touraine, A. (1983), *Sociologija društvenih pokreta*, trans. M. Radović and D. Kuzmanović, Beograd: Radnička štampa, La Voix et le Regard (1978), Paris: Editions du Seuil.

Urry, J. and Lash, S. (1987), *The End of Organized Capitalism*, Cambridge: Polity.

Weber, M. (1964), *The Theory of Social and Economic Organization*, New York: The Free Press.

PART 2
PRACTISING CORPORATE SOCIAL RESPONSIBILITY

Chapter 5

Social Performance in Government: Choosing Fiscal Health over Physical Health?

John Mahon and Richard McGowan

Introduction

In 1994, the Food and Drug Administration (FDA) was considering classifying cigarettes as a nicotine-dispensing device thereby putting manufacturing and selling of cigarettes under FDA jurisdiction. The FDA is the governmental agency at the Federal (national) level responsible for safety of food and drugs. This proposal was extraordinary controversial as it would, with the change in classification, allow the FDA to exercise broad authority over all aspects of the cigarette business. In a *New York Times* article about this proposal, Anna Quindlen remarked, 'Whether talking about addiction, taxation (on cigarettes) or education (about smoking), there is always at the center of the conversation as essential conundrum: How come we're selling this deadly stuff anyway?' (*New York Times*, 15 October 1994: A15).

An excellent question that has many answers, but in many ways Quindlen provided several of those answers. The sale of cigarettes is tied directly to the tremendous revenue opportunities that it affords both the federal and state governments, and in the providing of employment. But besides the revenue possibilities, legislators also trot out economic theory that implies price increases due to excise tax increases will also dramatically decrease smoking. This raises a curious dichotomy for state (and federal) governments: tobacco contributes to state and federal revenues (via various forms of taxation) and these revenues can be used for the welfare of the people; yet cigarettes also pose a serious health risk to the population requiring state and federal expenditures to deal with these consequences of product use. Therefore do state leaders emphasise fiscal health (the taxing aspect of the product) or do they emphasise physical health (of the citizenry, both those that smoke and those that do not)? If 'emphasise' seems to be too strong a term, then how do governments make trade-offs in fiscal versus physical health?

Are cigarettes taxed merely for revenue or are cigarettes taxed in such a way that there is drastic reduction in smoking? As the general public has soured on smoking over the past 20 years, many state governments have implemented numerous anti-smoking laws and increased their excise tax rates in the hopes of decreasing cigarette consumption.

The question that Quindlen posed about the cigarette industry could also be levelled at the alcohol Industry, and these issues are not confined to just the United States. Alcohol and tobacco are products that are available worldwide. Indeed, the impact of tax revenues from these products may be even more important in lesser-developed nations than in the United States. The social costs of these products are also high worldwide, and governments are faces with tough choices as to what is the 'responsible' course of action. We do not always think of governments being involved with social responsibility – but they are, and we should consider them as we raise and discuss issues of social responsibility.

In fact, the sale of alcohol was abolished in the United States during the Prohibition Era. It was an experiment that most historians classify as a disastrous public policy measure. The sale of alcohol was eventually again permitted but with limitations and of course with the imposition of excise taxes. In regards to alcohol perhaps these most prominent public policy measures that have been enacted during the past ten years have been the passage of anti-drunk driving laws. But overall the motto that governments employ in regards to both cigarettes and alcohol is 'Doing well while doing good!'

This chapter addresses some of the issues of legislation, taxation and consumption that define the markets for cigarettes and alcohol. The first issue that will be analysed is just how effective have excise tax increases been in affecting tobacco and alcohol products—that is, are states who purport to represent the public welfare actually achieving reduced sales of these products? We will confine our analysis to the two most successful segments of these industries, namely cigarettes for tobacco and beer for alcohol. By analysing monthly state level sales data, we will be able to ascertain the effects that these measures have had on cigarette and beer sales. The second issue that needs to be addressed is why these industries have reacted quite differently to this government interference in their respective industries. In so doing we provide a sense of the tactics these industries use that other governments can expect in dealing with cigarettes and alcohol.

Cigarette Industry

During 2002, 12 states raised their cigarette excise tax (American Lung Association's 'State Legislated Actions'). The previous high was in 1993 when six states raised their excise tax rates. In fact, the median state excise tax rate increased from $.41/pack to $.48/pack. So it appears that the excise tax has become a potent and more frequently used weapon by anti-smoking forces in state legislatures. It should also be noted that in both years, state governments were experiencing declines in revenue. Hence, the dual purpose of the excise tax increase is once again confirmed.

Yet, these two goals of an excise tax increase could be in conflict. For if indeed the excise tax increase is successful in causing a significant decline in cigarette sales, then the state might actually take in less revenue – a trade-off they might not be willing to make. This scenario depends of course on the amount of the decline and the size of the excise tax increase. As a consequence, states are faced with the clear trade-off between fiscal health and physical health.

Another effect that excise tax increases could have is to force cigarette firms to hold down potential prices increases or not increase prices at all. The rationale behind this scenario is that cigarette firms would not wish consumers to be confronted with an increase in both the excise tax and retail price. Hence, cigarette excise tax increases could potentially hamper the profitability of the cigarette firms.

In order to evaluate a particular state's cigarette excise tax policy, we examine these two questions.

1. What are the effects of the excise tax increases on sales of cigarettes?
2. What are the effects of excise tax increases on the pricing policies of these industries?

Excise Tax Increases and Cigarette Sales

In order to answer the first question, a sample of five states was chosen. We believe that these five states represent a broad array of responses to cigarette taxing that can be mirrored in other national governmental decisions and approaches. ARIMA Intervention Analysis will be utilised to analyse the monthly sales data. The selection of these states involved several factors including location, tax level, American Lung Association (ALA) clean indoor air rating, border state's policies, and the timing of a state's most recent excise tax rate change were considered. For the excise tax position of each state and the American Lung Association rating of each state, there appears to be a correlation between the legislative actions and tax levels, so choosing states that represent consistent policy was practical for the analysis, as well as for the discussion of policy in the next section.

An attempt was also made to choose states from the traditional, regional designations of American geography. New Jersey represents the northeast; Delaware the mid-Atlantic and other regional low volume tobacco producing southern states; Kentucky is the sample for large volume tobacco producing southern states; California is the West Coast's representative. Florida was chosen to represent the scattered states that have many external factors affecting consumption. A complicating factor was that some states, though perhaps more representative of a region, had changed their excise tax rate too recently or too long ago to allow for a meaningful model to be built. The demands of ARIMA intervention analysis include modelling the data before the intervention, and a date too early in the data set would yield an insignificant base model; too late in the data and the post-intervention analysis would be meaningless. States such as New York, which made a decisive increase in the excise tax rates, were disqualified for this reason.

All told, much care was taken in the process of selecting the thoroughly analysed states. The models are to be considered unique to each state, but the implications of the models can be extended to states and to nations that have different characteristics. The ultimate goal of this section is to establish a framework from which to analyse a given state's (or nation's) decisions on the cigarette tax issue. All of the statistical results have been included for the interested reader in the Appendix at the end of this chapter.

California

California has long been considered one of the leaders in legislative and fiscal measures designed to limit or reduce smoking. Even in the United States, California is considered an outlier with regards to health and safety issues. This state tends to be a leader in these issues and often what happens in California ripples through the nation over time. California was one of only four states to receive the American Lung Association's highest rating for clean indoor air, their most 'comprehensive' designation. The designation is awarded based on the number and degree of regulations a state has passed. Of the 14 laws deemed most important by the ALA, California has passed 12, most to the highest degree possible. The only two regulations yet to be passed are for Jury/Courtrooms and Restrooms (bathrooms). California is the only state to receive the comprehensive designation, and simultaneously have an excise tax rate in the highest tier. On 1 January 1999 California changed their tax rate per pack to 87 cents, an increase of 50 cents over the previous level. Taxing and legislating at these levels appears to be part of a larger effort to curb the use of cigarettes, and seems to demonstrate an emphasis on physical health.

It is obvious by simply looking at a plot of shipments of cigarettes to California that there has been a decline in the shipped volume of cigarettes. It is also probably safe to assume that the legislative and tax climate that the state has imposed has played a significant role in the reduction of shipments. What is unclear from a simple visual inspection is the degree to which changes affect the actual consumption of tobacco in California. The January 1999 change offers a unique opportunity to study the effect of an excise tax rate change on the demand for cigarettes in a state that has an established track record in cigarette consumption deterrence.

To test the effect of the change, an ARIMA intervention was run on the shipment data. The various intervention types (step, pulse, hump) were tested, and consistent with our expectations, the pulse yielded the most significant results. The test results show that in the month when the excise tax rate increased there was a significant decrease in the number of cigarettes shipped to California. Based on the assumption that cigarette shipments are an accurate proxy for cigarette demand, this implies that demand for cigarettes in the first month also decreased. The second month after the change is marked by a dramatic decrease in the significance of the impact. This may be a reaction to the phenomenon of cigarette smokers hoarding cigarettes purchased at a lower price in the period immediately before the rate change. Giving additional weight to this possibility is the fact that in the third month (March 1999), the significance of the intervention increases substantially. From this period until the end of the data set in December 2000, the change in California's excise tax rate remains significant, but at steadily diminishing levels of significance.

This diminishing significance tells us several things. First, California's change in excise tax rates was initially successful in reducing the demand for cigarettes. Though as suggested earlier, and discussed more thoroughly later, this is not always the objective of legislators, it is nonetheless a benefit of the change. Secondly, we find that California has been successful in cultivating a climate that does not encourage cigarette smoking. Compared to other states with less developed anti-smoking legislation, the change in California's excise tax rate played a substantial role in reducing consumption, despite the fact that the change in the rate was not one of the biggest in the country over the period of the data set. In fact, because of the anti-smoking climate, California was probably more successful in reducing smoking with a smaller change in the tax rate than a state with a more pro-smoking environment would be. Third, the diminishing significance of the change in the excise tax rate is indicative of the acclimation of smokers to the new price point. As consumers of this addictive good become more familiar with the higher price point, and as their addiction places a greater demand on them, the consumers appear to relent and consume at levels closer to their original consumption decision. This is a crucial observation, as it suggests that tax increases can yield increased revenues for the state over time. While the motives may be questionable, and the results of diminishing significance, the data supports the widely held notion that California has proven to be one of the most effective states in the quest to eliminate cigarette smoking. They have done so with a combination of excise tax and smoking regulation strategies and tactics. This suggests that a two-pronged approach (taxing the product and limiting the use of the product) has a definitive impact on smoking, but has also resulted in increased fiscal health as well.

Delaware

When most people think of Delaware, they think of a small state on the Atlantic, not a state that is especially hard on tobacco. Boasting an excise tax rate of only 24 cents, up a mere 5 cents on 1 January 1991, Delaware does not appear to be a state that is attempting to tax tobacco out. They did, however, earn a 'moderate' rating from the ALA at the end of 2000. The passage of diminished versions of 13 of possible 14 clean indoors non-smoking laws resulted in a placement in the ALA's most commonly awarded category. How, or if, the decisions of the Delaware legislature affected the consumption of cigarettes with limited legislation and low excise tax rates is to be determined here.

Once again, an ARIMA Intervention Analysis was attempted to determine the effective-ness of the Delaware excise tax change as a method of deterring consumption. Based on a simple plot of the data, one did not expect there to be a significant and sustained decrease in consumption because of the tax change. The real test of the ARIMA intervention model is to see if the pattern of consumption, such as trend or seasonality, is altered by an event. As in all cases, the different types of interventions were analysed, and the pulse method emerged as the most significant of the models. The results for Delaware are actually quite compelling, in many ways because they validate some of our concerns for issues that might affect the data.

The excise tax change in Delaware was a significant event that affected the consumption of cigarettes with no lag, i.e. the effect was seen immediately. The change in shipments was substantial, and lasted for ten months, heading rapidly towards insignificance in the final months of effectiveness. Then consumption picked up again briefly, but still at a diminished rate from the pre-tax periods.

Next, over one year later, the model picks up on another significant development that affected consumption. Not surprisingly, this change was called the Marlboro Friday event that resulted in much lower list prices for the premium brand cigarettes; ultimately this event briefly simulated consumption. The final event of real interest is the third intervention the model identified. This intervention coincided with the Attorney Generals' settlement of cigarette manufacturer liability, commonly known as the Master Settlement Agreement. This event caused a very substantial increase in the price of cigarettes, and resulted in another decrease in consumption. The validation of earlier suspicions that these events could compromise or help the legislators who hoped to eliminate cigarette smoking through legislation was not surprising, but was unexpected in the sense that it does not appear in the data for all states. Fortunately, the relatively low taxing and limited regulating of Delaware created a set of data that allowed the SCA programme to identify these interventions.

The results of the Delaware analysis add credibility to the argument that the legislators in many states are not seeking to tax away cigarettes. It may be that fiscal health trumps physical health. All to often, cigarettes are seen as a stream of revenue that can line state coffers. Despite the temporary decreases in consumption, the expectations of higher revenues are sustained by the return to smoking after the consumer becomes 'conditioned' to the new price. Unfortunately for Delaware, events beyond their control further reduced the consumption of cigarettes and diminished the prospects of additional cigarette tax revenue.

Florida

Unlike the hard pressing legislators of California, Florida has positioned itself as a state in the middle of cigarette regulation. The legislative and taxation decisions that have been made are among the most average in the nation, which is to say, unremarkable.

Florida is a dramatically different state from almost any other state in the country. The large number of elderly and retired complicates the analysis in that they may be more likely to smoke because they will not bear the full consequences of their actions. Their consumption decisions, while not healthy, is also not myopic. Even if the elderly do not dramatically discount future periods, the limited number of future periods reduces the total expected long-term costs they will bear. In addition, there is very little use for large, non-bequeathed sums of money after death, so such consumers would also not be as price sensitive. How this affects the ability of legislators to reduce smoking statewide is a complicated question, so for purposes of this analysis, it is sufficient to recognise this unique demographic feature of the Florida population.

Once again, our first impression of a plot of the volume of cigarettes shipped to Florida is that the rate of decrease is slower than a more proactive state such as California. Even the simple trend line reveals that the rate of decrease in Florida is slower than the rate in other states. We also see the absence of a sudden drop in the volume shipped. This suggests that consumers did not perceive the magnitude of the change, only 9.9 cents, as a significant change in price. The implications of their perceptions are critical because the goal of this investigation is to determine if there is any significant change in consumption because of the price change. The most likely to react first would be the most price sensitive of consumers, generally agreed to be the young and poor populations.

As in previous cases, an ARIMA intervention model was run, and all forms of the intervention were tested. As expected, none of the ARIMA Intervention models proved to be significant. Even though it produced the most significant model according to the traditional measures of ARIMA modelling, the pulse model never indicated that there was a period where the change in the excise tax rate ever affected consumption by the smokers of Florida.

In light of the many considerations such as demographics, incidences of trade loading during the period of the excise tax change, the effects of tourists, and the possibly conflicted objectives of the legislature, the non-effect of the excise tax change in Florida is not surprising. The constituency in Florida will need to clamour for change before the legislators make any major decisions regarding the future of tobacco in the state. Perhaps surprisingly, the state has been known to hand out large settlements in jury cases to those adversely affected by cigarettes' negative qualities. It is possible that such a grassroots movement for a smoke-free Florida is beginning, but until the legislature takes decisive action, Florida will continue to be an enclave of consumption among non-tobacco growing states on the East Coast.

Kentucky

For every state that has attempted to discourage consumption of cigarettes through legislation and taxation, there is a state like Kentucky that has made virtually no attempts to reduce cigarette smoking. Only four states have passed fewer clean indoor air laws than Kentucky, which has passed only two of the fourteen analysed prohibitions on indoor smoking. The restrictions have been placed on smoking in schools and, ironically, in government buildings. The ALA has rewarded this minimalist approach with their 'minimal' clean indoor air rating.

Not surprisingly, Kentucky has also made very little effort to curtail smoking through excise tax manipulation. In fact, the excise tax on cigarettes in Kentucky is a mere 3 cents, up only 0.5 cents – in July 1970. Kentucky offers an opportunity to study the smoking of cigarettes in a state that does not attempt to dissuade the general population from consuming through the traditional methods that other states have chosen to employ.

By simply looking at the plot of Kentucky's monthly cigarette shipments for the last 20 years, it is clear that they are unlike any of the previously analysed states. Where California, Florida, and Delaware all had an apparent downward trend in consumption over the data range, Kentucky lacks such a pronounced decline. In fact, there has been a pronounced upward trend in shipments. On average, there have been an additional 13,033,000 cigarettes per month shipped to Kentucky with a pronounced spike in shipments from 1995 to 1999. Without a change in the excise tax rate during the data period, a simple ARIMA model was developed.

Clearly, the assumptions that a legislature can implicitly condemn or condone the smoking of cigarettes through their collective action appear to be true. That is, the exercise of political will can be oriented to social responsibility. The lack of any effort by the Kentucky government to reduce smoking, or even more pragmatically raise revenue through higher taxation, has produced a culture that accepts and apparently advances smoking. The consequences are not negligible. Kentucky has the second highest smoking related death rate in the United States at just over 444 per 100,000. Kentucky residents lose an average of 14.2 years of their life to smoking, also the second highest figure in the nation. The lung cancer death rate in Kentucky in 1997 was 53.2 per 100,000; no other state was higher than 48.1 (*Investment in Tobacco Control: State Highlights 2001*, 2002). Clearly there are physical health consequences to inaction. Of course, it is not surprising to learn that Kentucky is one of the top tobacco producing states in the country. Brown and Williamson, the third largest seller of cigarettes in the United States calls Lexington, Kentucky home. It would be naive to ignore the connection: tobacco is a cash crop (and a major employer) and that cash can easily be used to curry favour at many levels of the government.

New Jersey

In many ways, New Jersey is like almost any other state in the Northeast: relatively high excise tax rate and a solid position for clean indoor air. In addition, New Jersey sees both sides of interstate competition for excise tax revenue: they lose revenue from consumers who purchase their cigarettes in Pennsylvania and Delaware, but gain revenue from smokers who come from the higher taxing state of New York. New Jersey has settled on an 80 cent per pack tax on cigarettes, which is a doubling of the previous rate of 40 cents. The new tax level has been in place since January of 1998. New Jersey has also earned the ALA's 'moderate' rating by passing 10 of the 14 clean indoor air laws. As in all the other cases where the most recent excise tax change occurred within the data range, an ARIMA intervention model was developed to explain the consumption patterns of New Jersey residents. Once again, it was no surprise to discover that the ARIMA Intervention Model was insignificant. Despite the doubling of the excise tax, the intervention proved to be insignificant (meaning that the regular ARIMA model would be more appropriate). There may be a litany of possible reasons for this. But a plausible theory is that the rate of decrease in shipments for New Jersey, already one of the highest in the nation at an average rate of just over 40 million fewer cigarettes per month, was too steep to support an additional shock. One might maintain the change in price was not large enough to entice them to stop smoking their already depressed quantities; a substantially larger excise tax increase would be necessary to make the next step in reducing smoking. As mentioned previously, New Jersey is a good proxy for the northeastern region where the culture is firmly anti-smoking. Perhaps because of the absence of a long history with the tobacco crop, or possibly because the generally high population densities of northeastern states combine with the absence of smoke-welcoming establishments, there has been a general trend towards higher taxation and greater legislation. Of course, the proximity of the states has fostered a high level of competition between state treasuries. It is suspected that some states deliberately tax competitively. Simply put, this behaviour limits the ability of states to reduce their smoking populations. In the next section, we wish to examine how an excise tax increase affects the pricing policy (the tactics of their response) of the cigarette firms.

Excise Tax Increases and Cigarette Pricing Policy

Since excise taxes form such a high percentage of the retail price of cigarettes (30 per cent of the average nationwide retail price according to the Tax Foundation) economists hope to use the excise tax increases as an indicator of oligopolistic behaviour on the part of the cigarette industry. If the cigarette industry was behaving in oligopolistic manner in the face of an excise tax increase, then the industry would raise prices despite the increase in the excise tax rate.

Jeffrey Harris, a MIT economist who is also a physician, has been one of the most vocal critics of the cigarette industry. Harris has repeatedly charged that 'Cigarettes are sold in this country by a six-company oligopoly that has demonstrated the market power to raise prices at will' (Harris, *New York Times*, 30 January 1987: 57). Harris bases his contention that the industry uses excise tax increases as an excuse for 'pushing up the retail price of cigarettes far beyond the levels justified by the excise tax hike' (*Business Week*, 9 February 94: 21). Harris has pointed that price hikes far outpace increases in excise tax rates even during this period of excise tax in-creases. Harris' contention that cigarette firms are using excise tax increases as an excuse for 'unjustified' price hikes is one that needs to be examined. As we have noted earlier, the cigarette excise tax rate varies greatly from to state. As a result of these differences in excise tax rates, it would be interesting to investigate whether the cigarette firms have developed different pricing strategies in order to deal with these different levels of taxation.

In order to test whether or not cigarette firms did exhibit oligopolistic behaviour we test the following hypothesis using ARIMA Intervention Analysis for the two previous discussed excise tax increases. One large excise tax increase will be tested (California) while a small excise tax will also be analysed (Florida).

H_0: The percentage of the retail price for cigarettes, which excise taxes account for, will not significantly increase when an excise tax increase is imposed.

California

California has recently and drastically raised its cigarette excise tax to show its commitment to a credible anti-smoking strategy. California currently has the twelfth highest excise tax rate in the country. When California raised its excise tax to $.87/ pack in 1999, it was the highest in the nation. An increase in the cigarette excise tax rate (which more than doubled the rate) ought to have had a significant impact on the pricing policy of cigarette firms. This large cigarette excise tax increase had a major impact on any planned price increases by cigarette firms. The ARIMA Intervention Analysis confirms California's large excise increase of $.56/pack had a statistically significant impact in forcing the cigarette firms to slow the rate with which they raised the price for cigarettes. The Appendix at the end of the chapter contains the statistical results for the interested reader. Clearly cigarette firms respond strategically to tax increases.

Florida

Florida's anti-smoking policy has relied on a combination of anti-smoking laws (a moderate rating) and a moderate excise tax rate. In June 1990, Florida raised its excise tax rate from $.30/pack to $.399/pack, slightly above the US median rate at that time. It appears that this small excise tax increase had no significant effect on the pricing strategies of the cigarette firms in Florida. The ARIMA Intervention analysis confirms this observation. Although there was a very slight rise in the percentage of the retail price accounted for taxes, this rise was statistically insignificant. Hence, it appears that a small cigarette excise tax increase plays into the hands of the cigarette firms.

Conclusions with Regards to Fiscal Health Approaches by Governments

What these results have shown so far is that the large cigarette excise tax increases are a very potent weapon in reducing cigarette sales and restraining the oligopolistic behaviour of the cigarette firms. So the questions now become why haven't more states enacted larger excise taxes? What sort of political strategy have the cigarette firms employed in trying to mitigate the effects of cigarette excise tax increases?

There are a number of possible answers to the first question. First, there appears to be a correlation between the number of smoking prohibition laws and the excise tax level. As the number of smoking prohibitions increase, the anti-smoking climate of a state also increases over time. As the anti-smoking climate increases, huge increases in the cigarette excise tax become more politically acceptable especially in times of severe financial need. The other factor involves the actions of neighbouring states. Clearly, if a state unilaterally raises its cigarette excise tax, it risks the possibility that a neighbouring will claim some its market share for cigarette sales. In other words, legislators must take into account the problem of smuggling. Recall that Kentucky's cigarette sales are actually increasing and this increase is no small part due to smuggling activities. So once a neighbouring state significantly raises its excise tax legislators in an adjacent state are faced with the strategy of either claiming some of the smokers of that neighbouring state or enacting a similar excise rate increase. Keeping the excise tax low has some positive benefits for the adjacent state. That state is able to enhance revenues from tobacco sales (improved fiscal health) and not incur the health costs (no change in physical health in the state) in later periods of such sales as those burdens are dealt with in the other state. This is an unambiguous fiscal benefit without the associated health care costs. Obviously if the anti-smoking climate has been cultivated, then the excise tax increase becomes the favoured strategy.

As for the cigarette firms, their political strategic response has increasing become a regional one. The northeast part of the United States and the West Coast have been ceded to anti-smoking forces. In some ways, the general societal view of smoking has coalesced around smoking being unhealthy. As such, these societal mores are difficult to combat politically in any meaningful way. The cigarette industry's strongholds are the south and southwestern states, where societal mores are more supportive of smoking and more opposed to anti-smoking campaigns. The Midwest is the one section of the country where the cigarette industry and the anti-smoking forces are still in conflict.

Another industry that faces the threat of the excise tax as well as public measures to reduce consumption is the alcohol industry. In the next section we will examine how one segment – the beer industry has fared in dealing with similar public policy measures.

Beer Industry

Over the past 30 years, the brewing industry in the United States has changed drastically. In the 1970s, after nearly 200 years as an industry in the United States, national brands began dominating the production, distribution, and marketing of beer. It was during this period that Anheuser-Busch and Miller Brewing dominated the industry through marketing and regulatory activities. These two firms alone accounted for well over 60 per cent of all beer sold in the US.

Then the 'beer revolution' of the 1980s and 1990s took place. Even though industry analysts predicted otherwise, micro and regional brewers redeveloped in the 1980s and began making beer for specialised tastes. This specialised segment of the beer industry accounted for no more than 5 per cent of beer sales but at least 10 per cent of the profit.

Government policy towards the beer industry during the 1980s and 1990s was greatly influenced by the rise of these microbreweries. Once again, the excise tax is the principal public policy measure that states utilised in regulating the beer industry. Once again, the tax has a duel purpose: raise revenue and control consumption.

Two things are striking about this. First, there is a wide disparity of excise tax levels on beer, much like those on cigarettes. But this is where the similarity ends. In the case of cigarettes, taxes accounted on average (median) for slightly over 35 per cent of the retail price. However, for beer, taxes account on average (median) for slightly over 20 per cent of the retail price. Clearly, cigarettes are taxed at a much higher rate than beer.

But what is even more remarkable is the fact that there exist proposals to roll back the beer excise tax at both the federal and state level. At the federal level, over 100 Congressional Representatives have co-sponsored a bill to roll back the federal excise tax on beer from $18/barrel (about $.05/can) to $9/barrel. An example of state action in this area is New York that will roll back its excise tax on beer starting in September 2003. The federal government and the state governments have viewed the cigarette excise tax as a source of revenue that can be tapped periodically. Meanwhile, any increase in the beer excise tax is viewed at best as a last resort revenue measure and for the most part Congress and state legislatures are trying to find ways to lower the tax.

Excise Taxes and Beer Sales

In this section, monthly sales data will be analysed to ascertain the effect that increases in beer excise taxes had on beer sales for the states of Hawaii, Illinois, and New York. Two criteria were used to select these states. The first criterion is the size of the beer excise tax. Hawaii has one of the highest excise taxes on beer ($.92/gal.), Illinois has a moderate size beer excise tax (.185/gal.) while New York has a low excise tax ($.12/gal. and it is to be lowered even further). The other criterion is the number of microbreweries and micro-pubs that are operated in the state.

This 'micro' business criterion was chosen because the presence of such operations brings jobs and other positive aspects to their respective locations. The expectation is that changes in state tax codes have less effect on beer drinkers in New York, a state that is more influenced by microbreweries than states with less craft-beer influence such as Hawaii. That is, sales in states with many micro and regional brewers should not be drastically reduced by increases by the size of beer excise taxes because those beer drinkers care more about the taste and brand of beer they drink than drinkers in states that might not have regional breweries.

Hawaii

Hawaii has some of the highest state excise taxes in the country, and it is not home to any large brewing operations. Since the recent demise of the local brands Primo, Pali, Diamond Head and Maui Lager, the vacuum in Hawaii's beer supply has been filled by the big national brands, none of which are committed to brewing in the Islands. This is partly because of the cost of bottling, distance from raw materials sources, the high cost of doing business there and the even higher tax on alcohol production.

Hawaii is one of the last states in the country to have sanctioned brewpubs, and that allowance comes with strict quotas. According to Jeff Scott of www.beerexpedition.com only 14 breweries exist in all of the Hawaiian Islands, nine of which are brewpubs. Nonetheless, Hawaii provides beer drinkers with a perpetual 'beer season' of barbecues, luaus and festivals. The weather and culture contribute so much to year-round beer consumption that in order to meet demand, Oregon-based Gordon Biersch, operator of a Honolulu brewpub, must ship extra beer from Oregon due to the strict quotas placed on Hawaiian production.

Beginning in July 1994, Hawaii's excise tax rate has been calculated and based off the previous year's revenue so that a 1 per cent increase in revenue is generated each year. This procedure lasted until 1998, at which point the tax was $0.98 per gallon of beer and $0.09 higher than the tax of 1989. As seems to be evident in Figure 10, Hawaiian beer sale peaks decline over the mid-1990s and begin to flatten or even climb slightly after July 1998. Such a pattern would be expected as tax rates rose each year between 1993 and 1998 and then stabilised after this period.

The ARIMA intervention analysis that best fits this data, however, does not support this idea. Specifically, the time series was identified as an ARIMA $(0,1,1)(0,1,1)_{12}$. Regular and seasonal differencing achieved stationarity in the series. The MA parameter was estimated without a constant and statistically tested with the following results: $\theta = 0.64558$ ($t = 5.385$) with 80 degrees of freedom. Because the t-value for the excise tax variable is insignificant at $t = 0.1428$ and $p = 0.8868$, this data suggests that the model $y_t = \omega \, B \, S_t^{(T)}$ does not apply.

This model, were it applicable, would have explained a sudden and permanent change in sales due to the changes in taxes, where ω is the level of change parameter; y_t is the filtered series; B is the backshift operator used to achieve a stationary mean and variance, and $S_t^{(T)}$ is the binary variable that introduces the 'step' intervention into the series. While $\omega = 592.79$, which indicates an increase in sales after the change in the excise tax, the ARIMA analysis suggests that the excise tax increase in Hawaii has not led to a statistically significant change in beer sales.

Illinois

In recent years, Illinois has been home to over 30 brewpubs and nine microbreweries. With the large urban centre of Chicago, Illinois is much like New York in that it is able to support brewing as an important part of its economy. This state was chosen for analysis because of its amount of craft-breweries and because the state government drastically increased its excise tax on beer in 1999.

Effective 1 July 1999, excise tax rates on beer in Illinois increased from $0.07 to $0.185. As may have happened with New York, the Illinois state government was likely trying to help its economy and the employees of the many breweries. The data shows an increase a peak in beer sales in 1995 and a steady climb back near that level between 1996 and 1999. Perhaps as a result of the tax increase, sales for 2000 peak at a lower level than 1999, and 2000 marks the first decline in sales since 1996.

As occurred with Hawaii, the ARIMA intervention analysis that best fits this data does not support the idea that the sales decline after July 1999 was due to the tax increase. Specifically, the time series was identified as an ARIMA $(0,1,1)(0,1,1)_{12}$. Regular and seasonal differencing achieved stationarity in the series. The MA parameter was estimated without a constant and statistically tested with the following results $\theta = 0.66245$ (t = 5.871) with 80 degrees of freedom. Because the t-value for the excise tax variable is insignificant at t = -0.8870 and p = .3777, this data suggests that the model $Y_t = \omega$ B $S_t^{(T)}$ does not apply. Even though $\omega = -30760.28$, which does suggest a decrease in sales after the change in excise tax, the ARIMA analysis suggests that the excise tax increase has not led to a statistically significant change in beer sales. With data for only 17 months past the increase in tax, perhaps more passage of time is necessary for the ARIMA analysis to apply.

New York

New York was once the brewing centre for a young United States. Before World War II, New York City was big enough to support four separate million-barrel breweries entirely on its own. After Prohibition, and as the likes of Anheuser-Busch and Miller moved nationwide, these large New York breweries did not expand into other markets, and they were eventually squeezed out by the national brands, as shown by the numbers. There were 77 breweries in New York City in 1890, but by 1910 the number had shrunk to 37. By the 1990s, the number had slipped to just a couple. Nonetheless, with the growth of microbreweries and brewpubs over recent years, New York State is home to over 60 brewpubs and over 20 microbreweries. Most recently, and perhaps to support the employees of those breweries, New York state lowered its excise tax on beer.

Effective 1 January 1996 excise tax rates on beer in New York decreased from $0.21 to $0.16. Three years later, the tax was lowered to $0.135, and effective 1 April 2001, the tax rate was lowered to $0.125. The data shows an increase in sales over 1993–95, and a subsequent increase from 1996–99, after a decrease in 1996. The increase between 1996–99 may be attributable to the decrease in the excise tax. Such a decrease may have occurred due to economic conditions within the state and to support the employees of the breweries. The change seems to have been successful for the brewers.

The ARIMA intervention analysis that best fits this data does indeed support the idea that the sales increase after January 1996 was due to the tax decrease. Specifically, the time series was identified as an ARIMA $(1,1,0)(1,1,0)_{12}$. Regular and seasonal differencing achieved stationarity in the series. The AR parameter was estimated without a constant and statistically test-ed with the following results: $\phi = .51233$ (t = 5.317); = .33901 (t = 2.176) with 79 degrees of freedom. This data suggests that the model $Y_t = \omega \, B \, S_t^{(T)}$ is statistically significant (t = 2.6704 and p = 0.00919).

The ARIMA Intervention analysis suggests that the excise tax decrease in New York has led to a statistically significant increase in beer sales. Specifically, that change led to an increase of $\omega = 150,067$ 31/gallon barrels per month, which means that the change in excise tax altered the trend of the previous few years. Policy makers were successful in helping the local economy, as some of the 150,067 barrels per month increase very likely came from New York micro and regional breweries.

The results of this analysis point to the importance of microbreweries and micro-pubs in a state. The existence of these 'socially' acceptable drinking establishments paved the way for excise tax decreases which in turn promoted the sales of these establishments. Note too that these establishments also provide employment effects for the state. In the next section, we will analyse those factors that contribute to the legitimacy of the microbrew industry and in turn the beer industry as a whole.

Determining the Size of a State's Microbrew Industry

This model was designed to test how state-specific information affected the micro-brewery market. It demonstrates how the strength of the microbrewery tradition within the state, the state's excise tax, the state's average temperatures, and a variety of demographic trends affected the demand for craft beer in each US state in 2001. The dependent variable is the number of craft brewers distributing within each state. The multiple regression model is as follows:

$$\text{Brewers} = \alpha + \beta_1(\text{Homes}) + \beta_2(\text{Ex\_Tax}) + \beta_3(\text{July\_Temp}) + \beta_4(\text{Pop\_21}) + \beta_5(\text{Male}) + \beta_6(\text{F\_25-59}) + \varepsilon$$

Thus, every point in the data set represented the number of brewers distributing to a specific state. The variance was explained through each state's geographic, demographic, and economic characteristics that were captured by the various explanatory variables.

The first of the explanatory variables was named *HOMES*. This represented the number of breweries that were based in the state. If a craft brewer had a brewpub, restaurant or a production facility in the state, it was considered to be based in that state. Therefore, any brewer could have been based in multiple states and any given state could have been the home of multiple brewers. In essence, this variable captured the strength of the microbrewery tradition in the particular state. Breweries, like all businesses, tend to base their production facilities close to the areas of highest demand in order to minimise transportation costs. They also open restaurants or brewpubs in the areas of highest demand for their specific brand of craft beer. The hypothesis was that as the number of breweries based in a certain state grows, the craft beer tradition increases in that state, leading to a higher demand. The majority of breweries have established themselves in California, Oregon, Washington and Ohio. Consequently, the demand for craft beer was found to be the highest amongst those four states.

The *Ex_Tax* variable had two variations and represented the state excise tax on craft beer. The regression was run using an excise tax on packaged craft beer (or cases of craft beer) and then it was run a second time using the excise tax on kegs. The results derived from these variables are crucial in determining the extent to which the state government could control the microbrewery market through the means of taxation. The hypothesis was that as the excise taxes rose, the number of brewers distributing in the state would decrease (and so would the consumption of craft beer). A secondary issue here was to determine which tax rate, on cases or on kegs, was a more effective means of controlling the market. The hypothesis was that increases in the excise tax on cases of craft beer would be more detrimental to consumption than increases in the excise tax on kegs of craft beer. This is because cases accounted for most of the sales of the general malt beverage industry at the time and the microbrewery market was predicted to follow the same trend.

The *July_Temp* variable stood for the state's average July temperatures. This was the only seasonal factor in the regression and was meant to capture weather-related effects on the demand for craft beer. The hypothesis was that there would be more brewers distributing in the states with the higher average July temperatures. The demand for beer was predicted to increase because warmer weather encourages people to go to more bars, picnics, and other outings that involve the consumption of beer.

The average annual temperature was excluded from the regression because it failed a Pearson's test with some of the more important explanatory variables. Similarly, the average January temperatures were also highly correlated with other explanatory variables and could not be used in the regression. As a side note, the number of days of precipitation of 1 inch or more and the average annual precipitation for the state were excluded from the model due to multi-collinearity issues. However, all of these variables were found to be statistically insignificant when the regression was adjusted to incorporate them.

The *Pop_21* variable represented the number of residents in the state over 21 years of age. Of course, the hypothesis was that as the legal drinking population of the state increased, so would the demand for craft beer within the state (as represented by more brewers distributing). Under age drinking was not believed to be an issue with the microbrewery market mostly because craft beers are significantly more expensive than regular beers. This meant that the under-age drinker (naturally belonging to the lowest income bracket) could not substitute craft beer for regular beer. Therefore, the model did not have to account for the number of individuals under the age of 21.

The variable *MALE* represented the percentage of the states population that was male. Men account for the majority of consumption in any alcoholic beverage industry and the microbrewery market was predicted to be no different. Consequently, as the percentage of males increased within a state, the demand for craft beer was predicted to increase as well, meaning that more brewers would distribute to the state.

The last demographic variable in the base regression was *F_25–59*. This represented the fraction of a state's population between the ages of 25 and 59 – a general measure of the beer-drinking segment of each state's population. A more general measure would have been to use the fraction of people between the ages of 20 and 59; however, this data was correlated with the *Pop_21* variable (state's population over 21 years of age) at Pearson's 95 per cent interval. The hypothesis was that as this fraction of the population increased (while the population itself was held constant), the demand for craft beer in the state would increase as well (represented by a higher number of brewers distributing in the state).

Results

The regression results had an adjusted R-squared of 0.593, which was very good considering the data that was being used. It included six explanatory variables and a data point for every US state; therefore, there were 44 degrees of freedom. The F statistic was significant, showing that the combination of all the explanatory variables was statistically significant.

As expected, Homes (the measure of the strength of the microbrewery tradition within a state) was significant at the 99 per cent confidence interval and had a positive effect on the demand for craft beer. As the number of brewers owning a restaurant, brewpub, or brewery in a state in-creased, the number of brewers distributing to that state increased by 0.837. This showed that the popularity of craft beer grew as more brewers set up within the state. Consequently, the demand for craft beer grew as well.

The excise tax on cases of craft beer was significant at the 96 per cent confidence interval and had a strong negative effect on the number of brewers distributing within the state. For every dollar increase in the excise tax per gallon of craft beer, three less brewers distributed within the state. This showed that the state government had the capabilities of effectively controlling the microbrewery market by raising or lowering the excise tax on cases. Furthermore, the second base regressing, which involved the excise tax on kegs of craft beer, found that this form of the excise tax was also an effective means of controlling the market, however, it was less powerful than the excise tax on cases. For example, for every dollar increase in the excise tax per gallon of kegs of craft beer, only 0.1 brewers were found to stop distributing in the state (compared to the three-brewer decrease from the same increase in the excise tax on cases). The fact that the excise tax on cases was more critical to the microbrewery market than the excise tax on kegs showed that a much greater proportion of craft beer is sold in cases rather than in kegs. This was not surprising since the same is true for the rest of the malt beverage industry.

The average July temperatures were found significant at the 96 per cent confidence interval with a slightly negative effect on the number of brewers distributing. For every 1°F increase in temperature, the number of brewers distributing would decrease by 0.0075. Therefore, it would take an increase of 133°F in the state's average July temperatures to decrease the number of brewers distributing in the state by one! These results explain why the average precipitation and other weather-related variables were found to have insignificant effects on the demand for craft beer. However, if need, the negative effect could be explained in that people who live in areas with hot summers are more likely to drink more beer. However, since they are buying more, they substitute towards the cheaper brands (a 30-pack of Coors is priced at about the same as a 12-pack of Sam Adams). Therefore, they consume more mainstream beer and less craft beer.

The results from the demographic variables were quite surprising. The regression showed that it would take an increase of 5,000,000 in the state's legal drinking population to increase the number of brewers distributing to that state by one. However, for every 1 per cent increase in the proportion of the state's population that was male, the number of distributors in the state grew by 1.084. Similarly, a 1 per cent increase in the fraction of the state's population between the ages of 25 and 59 increase the number of brewers distributing to the state by 0.628. All three results mentioned were significant well past the 95 per cent confidence interval. The regression demonstrated that the breakdown of a region's demographics, especially in terms of the fraction of males and 25 to 59-year-olds, is one of the most important contributors to the demand for craft beer in the region. Because these findings were in accordance with all previous demand studies on the malt beverage industry, they proved that the model was effective in estimating demand despite the proxy variables that were used to replace sales.

Overall Conclusion

In the first seven months of 2002, nine states raised their cigarette excise taxes and 11 other states have introduced bills to raise the tax. In contrast, only one state has raised the beer excise tax while two other states have actually lowered their beer excise tax. In addition, the federal government is considered lowering the excise tax on beer while it has already raised the cigarette excise tax. What accounts for this drastic difference towards these two 'sin' industries?

As we have seen in our analysis, legislators view these industries as sources of revenue. We have also seen that if legislators are truly interested in decreasing sales, they must be willing to enact very large excise tax increases. However, when they enact this large increase, they are risking competition from neighbouring states as well as an increase in smuggling activity. This is certainly the scenario that has been played out in the cigarette industry.

Yet, as we have just seen, this is certainly not the case with the beer industry. Not only has the industry been able to stop excise tax increases, it has managed to even have excise tax rollbacks enacted. While many reasons can be given for the power of the beer lobby the one striking difference between beer and cigarette is the number of local producers, i.e., the rise of the microbrewer and the micropub. These small brewers and pubs now exist in every state and enable the beer industry to claim that it is an engine of economic development in almost every section of the nation.

The political maxim that 'all politics is local' rings true. The cigarette industry's power base has been confined to the South and Southwest. The oligopolistic cigarette industry has few local supporters outside of the small convenience stores that sell the majority of cigarettes. Meanwhile, even though the vast majority of beer is produced by two producers (Busch and Miller), the rise of the microbrewery and micropub has enabled the beer industry (which is just as concentrated as the cigarette industry) to portray itself as an industry that needs not only less taxation but one that needs to promoted.

While economies of scale are a way of achieving economic efficiency, these results point out that it is very unwise corporate political strategy. It would appear that an industry's corporate political strength is dependent on the depth of local support that it can garner. Just as diversification is wise a strategy for the investor, firms need to diversify their bases of power in playing the political and social game of public policy.

The trade-offs between fiscal and physical health are real and ongoing. When tobacco companies began paying $246 billion in 1998 to offset the costs of treating smoking related illnesses, it was considered a great social victory. The money was supposed to go to smoking prevention programmes—but what happened? According to Scherer (2002):

- North Carolina (the nation's biggest tobacco producing state) has allocated 75% of the money spent to private tobacco producers;
- Virginia gave $2 million to a new cigarette company that used the money to sue the state to overturn the settlement;
- seven (7) states have invested the settlement monies in tobacco company stocks;
- Alabama has devoted millions to build factories for car manufacturers; and
- as the US economy has weakened, 13 (yes 13) states have cashed in all of their future settlement monies (nearly $3 billion) to solve current fiscal problems.

Where is the 'social responsibility' of governments here? Where is the research and analysis that questions governmental social responsibility, and raises it as an issue worthy of research, analysis, and discussion? Although it is presumed that governments act in the social interest, the data here would suggest otherwise. We need to expand our debate and analysis in social responsibility to include considerations of governmental behaviours and actions – why are they not held accountable for their social responsibility?

References

Alcohol, Firearms and Tobacco (AFT), sales data for cigarettes and beer.
American Lung Association (ALA) (2002), 'State Ratings for Smoking', http://www/ala/org, 'Investment in Tobacco Control: State Highlights'.
Association of Brewers (2000), 'Craft-beer Industry Keeps Growing', http://www.aob.org.
Baron, S. (1962), *Brewed in America: A History of Beer in the United States*, Boston: Little, Brown and Company.
Berghoff, Hackett, Hun, Liebwald, Reddinger (1996), *Tapping into the Craft-Brewing Industry*, http://www.sonic.net/brews/articles/mgmtbeer.html.
Brewer's Almanac (1990, 1995–2001), Washington, DC: Beer Institute.
Business Week (1994), 'Are Cigarette Firms Charging Too Much?', 9 February.
Federation of Tax Administrators, ' State Excise Tax Rates', http://www.taxadmin.org.
Irving, C. 'Where It's Brewed: Brewpubs and Microbreweries', *New York City Beer Guide*, New York: http://www.nycbeer.org/brewpubs.cgi.
'Introduction to ARIMA', *Statistical Department of Duke University*, http://www/geocities.com/colosseum/5585/ARIM1.htm.
McGowan, R. (1995), *Business, Politics and Cigarettes*, Westport, CT: Quorum Books.
McGowan, R. (1997), *Government Regulation of the Alcohol Industry*, Westport, CT: Quorum Books.
Harris, J. (1987), 'Break Up the Cigarette Cartel', *New York Times*, 30 January: D1.
Quindlen, A. (1994), 'Who Needs the Stuff?', *New York Times*, 15 October: A15.
Philip Morris, *Annual Reports*, 1996–2000.

Appendix 1: ARIMA Results

Cigarette Excise Tax Hikes and Cigarette Sales

California

The time series of cigarettes sales (1981–2001) for CA was identified as an ARIMA $(1,1,1) (0,1,1)_{12}$. ($p < .05$).

$\Box_1 = -.5329$ ($t = -2.88$) $\Box_1 = -.4658$ ($t = -10.84$) $\Box_{12} = -.7626$ ($t = -2.86$) $Q = 12.8$ with 36 degrees of freedom and so the model's residuals are white noise and the tentative model is accepted.

A model was postulated that corresponds to the third hypothesis:

$$y_t = \{w \, B/ (1 + \Box)\} \, P_t^{(T)} \text{ with the following results:}$$

$w = -9158.9$ ($t = -2.59$) $\square = .33$ ($t = 2.85$).

These results indicate that cigarette sales went down initially in reaction to the excise tax increase and then sales gradually returned to their former rate of decline.

Delaware

The time series of cigarettes sales (1981–2001) for DE was identified as an ARIMA $(0,1,1)(0,1,0)_{12}$ ($p < .05$).

$\square_1 = -.6021$ ($t = -11.11$) and $Q = 18$ with 36 degrees of freedom ($p < .01$).

The second dynamic model postulated was:

$$y_t = \{wB/(1 - \square B)\}S_t(T)$$

where $\square$ is the rate change with $\square = .1$ implying the change is abrupt and $\square = .9$ implying that the change is quite gradual; w is the level of change parameters; y_t is the filtered series; B is the backshift operator used to achieve a stationary mean and variance, and $S_t^{(T)}$ is the binary variable which introduces the 'step' intervention into the series. With this model, it was hypothesised that sales went down gradually after the imposition of the excise tax. The parameter values estimated were:

$\square = -.1619$ ($t = -.38$) and $w = -308$ ($t = -.65$).

These statistics indicate that although the level of sales drop as a result of the excise tax increase, it was not statistically significant. Sales in the long-run were still declining at the same rate that they were before the imposition of this excise tax increase. Therefore, these results indicate that the small rise in the cigarette excise rate had little or no effect on cigarette sales in Delaware.

Florida

The time series for Florida's cigarette sales was identified as an ARIMA $(0,1,1)(0,1,0)_{12}$. ($p < .05$)

$\square_1 = -.7416$ ($t = -9.19$) ; $Q = 17.8$ with 36 degrees of freedom ($p < .01$).

The first dynamic model postulated was: $y_t = w\,B\,S_t^{(T)}$ where $w = -580.2$ ($t = -.64$).

Once again, there was a decrease in sales but it proved to be statistically insignificant.

The second dynamic model postulated was:

$$y_t = \{w \, B/ (1 - d \, B)\} \, S_t^{(T)}$$

This model is consistent with the hypothesis that sales went down gradually after the excise tax increase. The parameter values were estimated as:

$\square = -.17$ (t $= -.51$) and w $= -705.6$ (t $= -.62$).

These results, like those of Delaware, show that while sales did continued to fall after the excise tax increase, the rate of change of sales did not change nor was there a one time significant fall in cigarette sales after the cigarette excise tax rise. Once again, the small cigarette excise tax increase seemed to have no effect on cigarette sales.

Kentucky

The time series for Kentucky's sales was identified as an ARIMA $(1,1,0)$ $(0,1,1)_{12}$ (p $< .05$).

$\square_1 = .6163$ (t $= 3.21$) $\square_{12} = .5462$ (t $= 2.83$)

Q $= 21.2$ with 36 degrees of freedom.

These results indicate that Kentucky's cigarette sales have a pronounced upward trend and in fact there has been pronounced increase in sales during the period from 1995 to 1999.

New Jersey

The time series of cigarette sales for New Jersey was identified as an ARIMA $(0,1,1)$ $(0,1,1)_{12}$. $\square_1 = -.4821$ (t $= -7.23$); $\square_{12} = -.3529$ (t $= -2.84$) and Q $= 17.3$ with 36 degrees of freedom (p $< .01$)
The first dynamic model postulated was: $y_t = w \, B \, S_t^{(T)}$.
The parameter value was: w $= -9,879$ (t $= -.85$)
The second dynamic model postulated was:

$$y_t = \{w \, B/ (1 - \square B)\} \, S_t^{(T)}$$

This model is consistent with the hypothesis that sales went down gradually after the excise tax increase. The parameter values were estimated as:

d $= -.67$ (t $= -.91$) and w $= -7005.6$ (t $= -.95$).

These results, like those of Delaware, show that while sales did continued to fall after the excise tax increase, the rate of change of sales did not change nor was there a one time significant fall in cigarette sales after the cigarette excise tax rise. Once again, the small cigarette excise tax increase seemed to have no effect on cigarette sales.

Cigarette Excise Taxes and Pricing Strategies

California

An ARIMA model (0,1,1) was employed to describe the relationship between the price of cigarettes and the cigarette excise tax for California. The parameters were estimated and found to be statistically significant at the .01 level with the following results: $\square$ = –.7252 (t = –2.45) with Q = 18.6 with 30 degrees of freedom. Hence, the tentative model was accepted, i.e., the residuals constitute white noise. The dynamic intervention model which was postulated was one which hypotheisised that the excise tax hike resulted in an abrupt increase in the percentage of the retail price which excise taxes made up, followed by a gradual decline to pre-intervention levels. The following model fulfils the above specifications:

$$y_t = \{wB/(I - \square B)\}\ P_t^{(T)}$$

The parameter values were found to be w = 10.6 (t = 3.27) $\square$ = –.1092 (t = –3.31). The dynamic model was found to be significant at the .05 level.

The results indicate that cigarette firms did respond to a large cigarette excise tax increase. Since the percentage of the retail price due to cigarette excise taxes fail to raise as a result of this low increase in the excise tax, cigarette firms were able to get at least their usual yearly price increase. Even more striking is the result that the cigarette firms seem to refrain from raising cigarette prices in the period of time after this large increase in excise taxes. It certainly appears that large cigarette tax increases are quite capable of influencing the pricing policies of cigarette firms for a substantial period of time.

Florida

In order to ascertain the effect of that the 1990 cigarette excise tax increase had on retail prices of cigarettes in Florida, an ARIMA model (0,1,1) was employed. The parameters were estimated and found to be statistically significant at the .01 level with the following results:

$\square$ = –.1092 (t = –.3.52) with Q = 8.9 with 30 degrees of freedom.

Hence, the tentative model was accepted, i.e., the residuals constitute white noise.

The dynamic intervention model which was postulated was one which hypotheisised that the excise tax hike resulted in an abrupt increase in the percentage of the retail price which excise taxes made up, followed by a gradual decline to pre-intervention levels. The following model fulfils the above specifications:

$$y_t = \{wB/(1 - \square B)\} \ P_t^{(T)}.$$

The parameter values were found to be: w = 9.108 (t =.27) d = −.1092 (t = −31). The dynamic model was found to be significant at the .05 level.

The results indicate that cigarette firms fail to respond to a low cigarette excise tax increase. Since the percentage of the retail price due to cigarette excise taxes fail to raise as a result of this low increase in the excise tax, cigarette firms were able to get at least their usual yearly price increase. One might make the case that it actually used the cigarette excise tax increase as an excuse to raise prices more than would have if no excise tax increase had occurred.

Chapter 6

Corporate Social Responsibility: Exploration Inside Experience and Practice at the European Level

Rute Abreu and Fatima David[1]

Introduction

Much has changed in the last 50 years in the area of corporate social responsibility (CSR) since it is largely a product of the twentieth century (Carroll, 1999). Peyró (1997) emphasised that a concern with social responsibility is not a recent phenomenon, having registered its peak in the 1970s in industrialised countries, as a consequence of the serious problems resulting from a society guided by a market economy: the petroleum crisis, a scarcity of mineral resources and acid rain, among others effects, were manifest. At an international level, some public authorities and organisations increasingly consider different aspects of CSR and promote their intent to present them as actions to be undertaken, via public documents and regulations. For example, the United Nations (UN), with Kofi Annan's Global Compact Initiative, analysed CSR in a context of globalisation; the International Labour Organisation produced the *Fundamental Principles and Rights at Work;* the Organisation for Economic Cooperation and Development (OECD) introduced the *Principles of Corporate Governance* (1999) and *Guidelines for Multinational Enterprises* (2000); the EU, and specifically its Commission, presented the Green Paper – *Promoting a European framework for Corporate Social Responsibility* (COM, 2001) and more recently *Corporate Social Responsibility: A Business Contribution to Sustainable Development* (COM, 2002). Other important documents must also be remembered such as the *Universal Declaration of Human Rights,* the *Rio Declaration on Environment and Development* and *Agenda 21.* All these documents, and the principles contained therein, were strongly reaffirmed at the World Summit on Sustainable Development of the UN held, in 2002, in Johannesburg (South Africa).

These examples reflect the growing concerns, developments and challenges that each institution wants, or desires, to face and thereby affect in society. This behaviour

1   The authors are grateful for financial support to Prodep III Programme (European Community, European Social Fund, Concourse 4/5.3/ Prodep/2000, Request ref. 182.004/00-ESTG-IPG). This article represents the opinion of the authors and is our own responsibility.

represents the new age of globalisation. Because resources are scarce while needs are close to infinite, then corporations need to play an important role in fostering social responsibility but, of course, this is not a new concept which should be promoted. Social responsibility involves a host of complex and contradictory needs and competition from within and without the corporation influences its ability to respond to social needs (Mintzberg, 1983). It is important to remember, the Brundtland Commission's (1987: 1)[2] definition of sustainable development that is one of the most accepted with increased attention and use:

> ... development that meets the needs of the present without compromising the ability of future generation to meet their own needs.

This report makes institutional and legal recommendations for change in order to confront common global problems. More and more, there is a growing consensus that firms and governments in partnership should accept moral responsibility for social welfare and for promoting individuals' interest in economic transactions (Amba-Rao, 1993).

The authors agree with Díaz-Zorita and Gonzalo (1996) that to defend the social responsibility of the firm is a logical consequence of the special place that firms have in society. Yet, they considered it unquestionable that firms have an imperative towards social responsibility because their activity depends upon the present and future health and welfare of the society of which the firm is part. Thus, this chapter[3] presents and discusses different definitions of CSR and examines their underlying guidelines and principles. Subsequently, the authors have developed an empirical analysis based upon a survey that supports the link between the experiences and practices at the EU level of CSR, based on the reports of the Observatory of European SMEs (hereafter OE SMEs). Finally, the authors discuss the results and the implications of their study.

Corporate Social Responsibility

Several strands of literature in the management, organisational and accounting areas have devoted attention to CSR. In particular Quazi and O'Brien (2000: 35) argue for:

> ... two-dimensional model of corporate social responsibility ... The model has two axes. The horizontal axis having two extremes: a narrow and a wide responsibility ... The vertical axis of the model represents two extremes in the perceptions of the

2   The World Commission on Environment and Development, chaired then by the Prime Minister of Norway, Mrs Gro Harlem Bruntland produced, in 1987, the Bruntland Report.

3   The authors do not enter into the discussion on appropriate social and legal behaviour, but attempt to support, though an empirical analysis the consequences that proponents of various theories promote and develop an approach to CSR that is really workable.

consequences of social action of businesses ranging from concern with the cost of social commitment to a focus on the benefits of social involvement.

The authors do not intend to debate a complete definition of CSR, but suggest that some researchers with their arguments and definitions have demonstrated that this subject needs further empirical studies applied to actual behaviour in order to understand that a corporation with socially responsible behaviour is a necessary prerequisite of global economic activity and thereby to make this accepted as a different perspective (Abreu, Crowther, David and Magro, 2003).

The authors deliberately do not provide just one definition of the CSR, since there are many factors that are involved in this concept. Consequently they consider some aspects that are incorporated within the concept to show that its origins that are within the activities of the firm (Peyró, 1997). As an adaptation from the proposed concepts of CSR made by Joyner and Payne (2002), it can be shown to involve several of these, which have been considered by authors in the period from 1938 until 2002. These concepts emphasise aspects of social responsibility and show the growing recognition that values, ethics and behaviour of firms can have (positive and/or negative) impacts upon society. For example:

- Barnard (1938),[4] '... analyse economic, legal, moral, social and physical aspects of environment ...';
- Simon (1945),[5] '... organizations must be responsible to community values ...';
- Drucker (1954),[6] '... management must consider impact of every business policy upon society ... ';
- Selnick (1957),[7] '... enduring enterprise will contribute to maintenance of community stability ...';
- Friedman (1962, 1970: 126), '... there is one and only one social responsibility of business – to use its resources and engage in activities designed to increase its profits so long as it stays within the rules of the game, which is to say, engages in open and free competition without deception or fraud';
- Andrews (1971),[8] '... firm should have explicit strategy for support of community institutions ...';

---

4   See C.I. Barnard (1938), *The Functions of the Executive*, Cambridge, MA: Harvard University Press.

5   See H.A. Simon (1945), *Administrative Behavior*, New York: Free Press.

6   See P.F. Drucker (1954), *The Practice of Management*, New York: Harper and Row Publishers.

7   See P. Selnick, *Leadership in Administration*, New York: Harper and Row Publishers. There was a first version in 1957 and a second with title *Leadership in Administration: A Sociological Perspective* in 1959.

8   See K.R. Andrews, *The Concept of Corporate Strategy*, New York: Richard D. Irwin, Inc. There was a first version in 1987 and a second that is a revision published by Homewood: Dow-Jones-Irwin in 1971.

- Fitch (1976: 45), '... corporations can achieve social responsibility if they attempt to identify and solve those social problems in which they are intimately involved, and when the possibility of profit is available as an incentive';
- Carroll (1979: 500), '... business encompasses the economic, legal, ethical and discretionary expectations that society has of organization at a given point in time';
- Jones (1980: 59–60), '... corporations have an obligation to constituent groups in society other than stockholders and beyond that prescribed by law or union contract';
- Tuzzolino and Armandi (1981: 23), '... socially responsible organization is the self-actualisation organization, having satisfied prepotent needs ... in an envious position of voluntarily contributing to the welfare of all their constituencies';
- Freeman (1984),[9] '... business must satisfy multiple stakeholders ...';
- Drucker (1984: 62), 'Business turns a social problem into economic opportunity and economic benefit, into productive capacity, into human competence, into well-paid jobs, and into wealth';
- Epstein (1987: 30), '... discernment of specific issues, problems, expectations and claims on business organisations and their leaders regarding the consequences of organizational policies and behavior on both internal and external stakeholders. The focus is on products of corporation action';
- Angelidis and Ibrahim (1993: 8), '... corporate social actions whose purpose is to satisfy social needs';
- Balabanis, Phillips and Lyall (1998: 25), 'In the modern commercial area, companies and their managers are subjected to well publicised pressure to play an increasingly active role in [the welfare of] society';
- Com [(2002) 347 final: 5], '... CSR is a concept whereby companies integrate social and environmental concerns in their business operations and in their interaction with their stakeholders on a voluntary basis.'

So a certain element of commonality in such concerns can be seen spanning the decades but Robertson and Nicholson (1996: 1096) state that:

> A certain amount of rhetoric may be inevitable in the area of social responsibility. Managers may even believe that making statements about social responsibility insulates the firm from the necessity of taking socially responsible action. However, some firms have moved beyond rhetoric to reports of specific programs and actions ...

but previously Ostlund (1977) noted that managers agree with statements in support of CSR.

According to Gelb and Strawser (2001: 1):

---

9   See R.E. Freeman (1984), *Strategic Management: A Stakeholder Approach*, Marshfield: Pitman Publishing, Inc.

... there is a positive relationship between disclosure level and CSR. That is, firms that engage in socially responsive activities provide more informative and extensive disclosures than do firms that are less focused on advancing social goals.

Thus CSR is one aspect of the global strategy adopted by enterprises. It can be seen therefore within the framework of corporate governance, as explained in a document of OECD (1999: 7):

A good corporate governance regime helps to assure that corporations use their capital efficiently ... take into account the interest of a wide range of constituencies, as well as of the communities within which they operate, and their boards are accountable to the company and the shareholders. This, in turn, helps to assure that corporations operate for the benefit of society as a whole.

This suggests that each enterprise defines for itself an attitude towards society that contributes to the global environment. Consequently, as Jones (1980: 65) states:

Once this concept of corporate social responsibility is accepted, the problem, as before, becomes one of implementation.

This fundamental problem centred in the field of business and society explains the voluntary nature that this socially responsible behaviour should have. This voluntary nature is usually discussed and explained in the document that each institution produces, like the one produced by the European Commission[10] that made one of the central aspects that of partnership.

The Communication is addressed to the European institutions, Member States, Social Partners as well as business and consumer associations, individual enterprises and other concerned parties, as the European strategy to promote CSR can only be further developed and implemented through their joint efforts. The Commission invites enterprises and their stakeholders as well as Social Partners in candidate countries to join this initiative.

This and other pronouncements cause the authors to conclude that the European Commission has firmly rejected a regulatory approach to CSR. And the same point of view is expressed by the OECD (2000: 16):

... Guidelines are recommendations jointly addressed by governments to multinational enterprises. They provide principles and standards of good practice consistent with applicable laws. Observance of the Guidelines is voluntary and not legally enforceable.

This has fundamental importance for the increasing concern for this matter adopted by the European Commission. The aim of the Green Paper was to launch a debate

---

10   In COM (2002) 347 final: 3.

about corporate social responsibility and to identify how to build a partnership for the development of a European framework for its promotion. The Commission received from different authorities, approximately, 266 responses[11] to this document between August 2001 and April 2002, subdivided in 27 different classifications (see appendix A). The authors verified that in relation to the responses of public authorities at the international level, only the OECD answered; at the national level nine EU country's governments [12] (which represents 60 per cent of all of the EU countries) responded. The omission of the government of Portugal did not match with its policy and behaviour. Several conferences[13] were organised in Portugal to discuss this subject. At a local level,[14] only the city of London answered. However the most representative group to answer was individual companies (50 answers) and academic responses were much fewer (10 answers). In relation to organisational responses at an international level there were only the International Organisation for Standardisation (ISO)[15] and Social Accountability International (SAI). In a social responsibility context, after an analysis of each response, it can be argued that most proposals, commentaries, articles and opinions show important conflicts of interest.

The authors agree with Crowther (2002a, 2002b) that the activities of corporations' impact upon the external environment and, indeed, the same actions can be viewed as beneficial by some people and detrimental by others. Probable causes of current excesses, which might lead to future ones, include such factors as the link between rights and duties, ethics and responsibilities that have been severed and forgotten. In response to growing awareness it has been suggested that accounting should develop an important role in the reporting of the impact of an organisation in this respect. Indeed, as Joyner et al. (2002: 113) consider:

> ... the behavior of a firm with respect to its ethics and social responsibility is important to society in general, it behoves us to understand how firms develop their ethical stances and the values that are the foundation of their decision-making frameworks.

11　In responses to the consultation on the Green Paper on CSR (available online at http://europa.eu.int/comm/employment_social/soc-dial/csr/csr_responses.htm).

12　The country's governments which did not answer were Denmark, Greece, Italy, Luxembourg, Portugal and Spain.

13　In March of 2000 in Lisbon, the Economic and Social Committee supported the European Commission to realise the strategic goal which *the most competitive and dynamic knowledge-based economy in the world, capable of sustainable economic growth with more and better jobs and greater social cohesion.* In May of 2000 in Lisbon, it was compelled by the Directorate-General for Employment and Social Affairs to organise the first European conference on Triple Bottom Line Investing that promotes socially responsible investment (available online at http://europa.eu.int/comm/dgs/employment_social/lisbonconf.htm).

14　The Eurostat statistics express the existence in 1999 of 800,000 local authorities in the EU field.

15　The International Organisation for Standardisation (i.e., ISO as short form) is a non-governmental organization established, in 1947, that represents a worldwide federation of national standards bodies from more than 140 countries, one from each country.

Experiences and Practices at the European Level

The methodological axioms of research projects should have reliability, validity and representativeness and generalisability (McNeil, 1990). Yet the renewed interest in CSR does not generate much in the way of empirical studies. One aspect to detail is that the authors did not participate in or influence the survey, so they were outsiders. The axioms like the reliability and the validity of the survey cannot be measured directly. Nevertheless, some information is missing, but the authors believe that with the available data they can express an independent opinion. Nevertheless, on balance, the authors defend the maxim that *we must not let the perfect be the enemy of the good.*[16]

The European Commission created in 1992 the Observatory of European SMEs that developed various research projects to provide an overview of the current situation in SMEs. Over the last 11 years, the number of countries analysed has increased from the initial 12 states to the actual 19 states (OE SMEs, 2000). This Observatory was made by establishing a consortium with the European Network for SMEs Research (ENSR) and EIM Business and Policy Research (Netherlands) and was led by KPMG Special Services (Netherlands). It developed each year an annual survey that (OE SMEs, 2002a: 7):

> ... should contribute to the knowledge of the actual state of affairs in the business sector in Europe and foster understanding of development taking place in various fields.

and as Riley et al. (2001: 20) states:

> Facts, research methods and research data do not speak for themselves; they are interpreted by researchers and others.

Following this opinion, the authors analysed the 2001 ENSR survey[17] collected from managers and entrepreneurs within SMEs. It considers the way that the basic concepts, rules and knowledge and the domain of corporate governance seem to 'manipulate' a new image that changes CSR. This concept and methodology and its development, has led the authors to search for explanations of the phenomenon at a European level.

Before considering the results of the survey, it is important to specify the concept[18] of SMEs in the framework of EU, which is that an enterprise has to satisfy the criteria for the number of employees being less than 250 and one of the two financial

---

16 With the information available, it seems one of the shortcomings of this survey is the small sample size and the limitations that places on statistical analysis and inferences. Nevertheless, studies like this do not exist so it is better to have imperfect evidence that could be improved than not having any evidence.

17 The survey was carried out from May to August of 2001 and used the system called computer assisted telephone interviewing (CATI) to collect data.

18 In European Commission (1996: 4).

criteria:[19] a maximum of €40 million annual turnover or a maximum of €27 million annual balance-sheet total. If one of these limits is exceeded, in the field of the EU, this company must change its classification and now will be a large-sized firm. In addition, it must be independent, which means less than 25 per cent owned by one enterprise or jointly by several enterprises.

The survey was supported by interviews based on the questionnaire[20] with 59 questions that are subdivided into nine groups (OE SMEs, 2002a, 2002b). Each group or section of the questionnaire has a specific subject: the first is screening questions (five questions); the second is general characteristics (five questions but only three are available); the third is internationalisation (five questions); the fourth is entrepreneurship and management (four questions but only three are available); the fifth is Information and Communication Technologies (ICT) and e-commerce (four questions but only three are available); the sixth is social and environmental responsibility of SMEs (ten questions[21]). The questions from the seventh and eighth group, that are, respectively, administrative burdens when hiring employees (11 questions) and taxation and SME growth (12 questions), are not available. The ninth section is about stock options (three questions). The survey is shown in Appendix B, as an adaptation of the available questions of the survey.

Before the results analysis, the authors decided to study the survey itself. First of all, the main objective is to study the nine specific aspects of business administration. The purpose of the survey is to understand the global strategy of SMEs. In the Green Paper[22] promoting a European framework for CSR point 5 of executive summary explains that the:

> ... corporate social responsibility concept is mainly driven by large companies, even though socially responsible practices exist in all types of enterprises, public and private, including SMEs and co-operatives.

This judgment has no equivalence in the whole survey and especially in section 6 that is concerned with this subject. The Observatory (OE SMEs, 2002b: 36) refers that:

> ... the public's perception of the SMEs contribution to pollution and waste suggests that the effects of individual SMEs on the environment are smaller in comparison to their larger counterparts ... SMEs collective contribution can de very significant, due to the cumulative effect derived from the large amount of existing SMEs. There is very little information on this ...

---

19 The two financial criteria, turnover and total of balancesheet, will be adjusted regularly, to take account of changing economic circumstances in Europe.

20 At this time, the complete questionnaire and data are not available. It is expected to be forthcoming as a European Observatory CD-ROM.

21 A methodological issue is that some questions in the analysis could allow more than one answer. This rule does not allow having a full comparison between firms, because the subsamples values are not available.

22 In COM (2001) 366 final: 3.

In empirical research of this type, it is important to find this evidence. So, probably, this aspect is related to common sense, and means that large companies have a large impact on CSR. It could be true if in the economy there is mostly large companies, but the main problem is that there are thousands and thousands of medium-sized, small and micro companies that really demonstrate CSR behaviour. Thus in a perspective of scale each firm has a specific attitude towards CSR that could influence all of society.

In the survey (OE SMEs, 2002a, 2002b) within this firm classification of SMEs it is subdivided into:

- number of employees or workers size, with less than 250, and three classes can be distinguished as micro (0-9), small (10-49) and medium-sized (50-249);
- economic sectors, bellowing to manufacturing (ES1), construction (ES2), wholesale (ES3), retail (ES4), transport and communication (ES5), business services (ES6) and personal services (ES7);
- country, located in 15 European Union countries[23] plus Iceland (IS), Liechtenstein (LI), Norway (NO) and Switzerland (CH). It generates 19 countries (i.e., Europe-19).

The classification developed therefore generated 399 strata.[24]

The authors do not have access to the methodology used to make the selection of the sample from the population. According to the Observatory (OE SMEs 2002a: 8), the population data, in 2000, for the 19 European countries show that there exists 40,890 (0.2 per cent) enterprises of large-size, 163,560 (0.8 per cent) medium-sized enterprises, 1,226,700 (6 per cent) small enterprises and 19,013,850 (93 per cent) micro enterprises that totalled 20,445,000 enterprises. The analysis of such data was therefore impossible and the results were potentially descriptive, confusing and/or theoretical. The population was therefore restricted to SMEs. The information in the survey report shows that the sample obtained was responses from 7,662 SMEs. Probably, time and cost considerations associated with the collection and treatment of the population have limited the sample.

The enterprises in the sample have a distribution which represents: of the 0–9 workers size nearly 0.02 per cent of the total population; while the 10–49 workers size represents 0.2 per cent of the population and the 50–249 workers size represents 1.2 per cent of its population. The methodology of selection was not a code selection with proportionality from the population. The sample distribution of number of employees, in 2000, was nearly 42 per cent of the representation of micro enterprises, around 32 per cent of small-sized enterprises and nearly 26 per cent of medium-sized enterprises.

---

23 The 15 countries are: Austria, Belgium, Denmark, Finland, France, Germany, Greece, Italy, Ireland, Luxembourg, Netherlands, Portugal, Sweden, Spain and United Kingdom.

24 It was defined by the survey team that each strata should have a minimum number of interviews to allow conclusions when each question is analysed individually and at aggregated level, but this specification it is not available.

At another level, the distribution of SMEs for the seven economic sectors analysed (OE SMEs, 2002a: 8) were 17 per cent in manufacturing, 16 per cent in personal services, 14 per cent in retail, in construction and business services, 13 per cent in wholesale and 12 per cent in transport and communication. Another aspect analysed is the enterprise age. In the sample, the enterprises most represented are those with 'more than ten years' existence which register 61 per cent, with '6–10 years' representing 19 per cent, with '2–5 years' having 17 per cent and 'less than 2 years' only 2 per cent of the total sample. In the highlights from the 2001 survey, it was referred to that the process of selection may be biased, because enterprises 'less than 2 years' of age are selected by addresses from databases that are in the public domain and it takes some time before start-ups find their way to these databases, so they may be under-represented in the sample. This aspect of the selection may be biased not for this type of firms, but for all the firms that change their address for fiscal, economic, cultural, social and other reasons.

Given this perspective of enterprise age (OE SMEs, 2002a: 9), in the sample the results of 'more than 10 years' (i.e., the most important class of the age structure) show that 88 per cent are medium-sized enterprises. It is also interesting, in relationship to the firms of the same age class (OE SMEs, 2002a: 16), to observe that the main focus of business policy was 'growth' (38 per cent) with 'consolidation' (18 per cent) second, and as the last specified focus to 'innovate' and 'struggle to survive' with identical percentages (8 per cent). These firms will become bigger or will disappear from the market in the medium term. Still, with 'more than 10 years' of activity are 81 per cent of small enterprises. The main focus of these small enterprises in their business policy is also 'growth' (30 per cent) and 'consolidation' (21 per cent) in opposition to the policy to 'innovate' (7 per cent). Last, but not least, 59 per cent are micro enterprises with 'more than ten years' existence. This percentage shows that the influence of survival rate in the global market is very much lower when compared with medium-sized and small enterprises. So, probably, micro firms are still concerned about their economic survival. Then, they do not have time to be concerned with socially responsible activities, or to answer surveys. Sometimes, they change location, because of workers, clients, suppliers, markets, fiscal benefits and the sample selection process is thereby affected. Thomas (2001) stated that SMEs will need help from larger companies and organisations, as they will be unlikely in many cases to have the resources of staff or money to meet some of the standards. Survival will remain a crucial goal for many SMEs. But the results of the survey show that medium-sized and small firms are more stable than others and the enterprise age could allow them to be classified as mature firms.

The answers given to the evaluation of corporate social behaviour has always shown different perspectives, so it is analysed for all of the SMEs that did not claim this kind of activity. Jones (1980: 66) reports two fundamental situations, which are:

> ... voluntarily adopted process changes could well result in sincere efforts to incorporate more diverse inputs into corporate decisions ... and ... process changes will not necessarily result in changed corporate behaviour ...

and:

> ... we must not expect more of our corporations than we do of our other social and political institutions.

The survey results show a different perspective that generally (Frankental, 2001: 20):

> No corporation affairs manager will admit that their company is not socially responsible.

The question that has been asked of SMEs in the 2001 ENSR survey was to express the single most important reason for not performing any of external social actions and, indirectly, to give a reason that could be connected to CSR behaviour.

The results show that (OE SMEs, 2002b: 31) significant reasons for not performing any external social activities are 'never thought about it' (24 per cent), 'lack of time' (19 per cent), 'not related to the activities of my enterprise' (17 per cent), 'lack of money' (16 per cent) and 'no benefits expected' (8 per cent). In contrast, only 1 per cent of SMEs argue that the reason is 'lack of public support'. Another point of view shows that 25 per cent of micro enterprises answered 'never thought about it'. Another perspective demonstrates that 21 per cent of small and 21 per cent of medium-sized said it was the 'lack of time'. In medium-sized firms none answered 'lack of public support'. Therefore it is crucial that this concept (i.e., CSR) should be used and developed in the most beneficial way. As Weston (2003) and the authors argue, it is not just about technology, because the process, the people and culture come before that. As shown by the available data, the enterprises did not adopt social external activities due to limited resources because 2 per cent of these SMEs 'plan to start participation', 10 per cent 'consider participation' while 82 per cent stated 'no participation foreseen' (OE SMEs, 2002b: 33).

A positive perspective of this empirical study is the good result about social external activities developed by SMEs (OE SMEs, 2002b: 20) which shows that 48 per cent of micro, 65 per cent of small and 70 per cent of medium-sized firms are involved in social activities. But, it presents different degrees between them. For example, in Portugal there are 65 per cent of micro, 79 per cent of small and 78 per cent of medium-sized enterprises in this category. Of course, it is important to notice higher percentages of involvement of the firms in external social activities. The authors agree that these answers are like that, because as Deegan (2002: 283) said:

> ... public disclosure of social and environmental information, in media such as the annual report, is undertaken for legitimising purposes.

The main aspect is that a higher percentage of firms demonstrate this behaviour and they attempt not to cause damage to the global environment. It is readily observed that an organisation can have a very significant effect upon its external environment and actually change that environment through its activities.

The authors discuss a biased overview presented in the report by the Observatory (OE SMEs 2002b: 20) when:

> ... it is possible to identify a direct relationship between enterprise size and percentage of enterprise involved in external social activities in nearly all countries ... The only exceptions to this are given by Sweden and Finland, as well as ... Greece, Italy, Portugal and Spain ... where the ... small enterprises have got a higher percentage in comparison to their medium-sized counterparts.

This reference is hard to understand because:

• in Luxembourg, Iceland and Liechtenstein the number of medium-sized firms is too small to be computed as per thousand. So, to develop a comparison it should refer to all of the 19 countries, in order to have an equal basis of analysis. Nevertheless, supposing that each country sample is representative from its population then if three of them were left out it will reduce the heterogeneity of all samples;
• the sample number of small and medium-sized firms of each country is different in this analysis and consequently the results are different.

As shown in Figure 6.1,[25] the lower proportion of SMEs involved in external social activities is represented by France, Greece, Spain, United Kingdom and Italy with a bigger proportion in Finland, Denmark, Iceland and Liechtenstein.

Also, interestingly from the 2001 ENRS survey (OE SMEs, 2002b: 20), was the higher involvement of small-sized firms in Finland. Notice that in France the same firms were less represented in the same category. Also in France, the micro firms were less concerned about external social responsible activities, while in Finland it seems the opposite. In this case the French government policy is concerned with different objectives than CSR and firms could concentrate on other operational aspects. In the preceding analysis, there are very important differences between France and Finland that should be identified to understand CSR behaviour. But the discussion does not end, because Broberg (1996: 618) argues that:

> ... Scandinavian countries are all so called welfare states. Thus the State provides an extensive safety net and a whole range of benefits. This means that to the Scandinavians it is only natural that the State interferes in more or less all aspects of life – in particular in the economic life.

With an increase in the number of workers an enterprise is more likely to be concerned about socially responsible activities. A smaller sample than the initial, that is the SMEs that have external social activities, was asked[26] which have been the

---

25 The figure presents different degrees because the individual percentage of each country is not comparable, due to methodological procedure used; for example, the sub-samples are not known.

26 The result of this question presents another problem because the percentage is not weighted and each respondent was allowed to answer with several reasons.

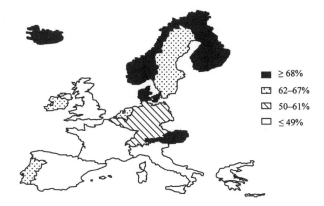

Figure 6.1   Distribution of the SMEs surveyed by external social responsible activities

Source: OE SMEs (2002b).

major reasons or motivations for contributing to these activities. In this line, the main answers were 'ethical reasons (mainly altruistic)' (31 per cent), 'improve relations with the community and public authorities' (19 per cent), 'improve customer loyalty' (15 per cent), 'improve relations with business partners and investors' (8 per cent), 'improve employees' job satisfaction' (8 per cent). The small percentage of the last aspect is because it is easier to retain or attract employees. It is important to notice that a smaller percentage (2 per cent) explains the reason as 'pressure from third parties' and also the 'use existing public incentives', both demonstrating the voluntary nature of these activities (OE SMEs, 2002b: 28).

Data disaggregated by country shows that 'improve customer loyalty' and 'employees' job satisfaction' were the main reasons in Finland, Iceland, Ireland, Italy and Netherlands. They are under the median values in other reasons, except in 'Other', so it is not possible to analyse. Portugal is above the median in all aspects with the exception of 'ethical reasons' which is under. Spain only has two important main reasons which are 'ethical reasons' and 'improve relations with the community and public authorities' and others almost do not matter. This behaviour seems to denote that the enterprises know the reason for their behaviour. But more important is to notice that this question presents behaviours which show that the culture and values of each country very much affect the results. As Gray et al. (2001: 332) states:

> ... it is increasingly clear that social and environmental disclosure varies according to country. Not only is mandatory disclosure different between countries but the volume and subject of voluntary disclosure also varies ...

From normal business activities, the organisations that contribute/participate in external social objectives or activities, were asked to say if the enterprise did this in one of several ways in 2000. All the enterprises that develop external social activities point out that their actions, with equal distribution of the answers in all size distributions, relate to 'sporting activities' (28 per cent), 'cultural activities' (19 per cent), 'health and welfare activities' (19 per cent), 'education and training activities' (12 per cent), 'environmental activities' (7 per cent), 'contribute in other way' (6 per cent), 'participate in public affairs or political process on behalf of the enterprise' (5 per cent) and lastly 'give preference to personnel from socially deprived groups when recruiting' (4 per cent). But in this analysis the degree of importance of each category is too large, because these activities are not all possible ones. For example, where the objective is to affect the employees of enterprises is excluded from the possible categories. Also, Observatory (OE SMEs, 2002b: 21) states that:

> ... there is a positive relationship between the size of the enterprises and their degree of involvement in the different types of external social activities.

From a geographical perspective[27] (OE SMEs, 2002b: 22), Liechtenstein, Norway, Portugal and Greece are more concerned about cultural activities. In Portugal, activity results from a special law – *Lei do Mecenato*[28] – that reduces the income tax payable for each enterprise in a particular year. All these expenses of the firm in different social activities are classified as Social Responsible Investment (SRI). For example, in 2001 the Association of British Insurers (ABI) established new guidelines for socially responsible investment (Simms, 2002). Accounting remains focused upon the actions of the organisation and ignores the effects of the organisation upon its external environment.[29] However, a growing number of researchers have recognised that the activities of an organisation influence the external environment and have suggested that one of the roles of accounting should be to report upon the impact of an organisation in this respect.

The Observatory (OE SMEs, 2002b: 22) was concerned about the SMEs' main ways of involvement in external social activities and from the available data suggest that 40 per cent of the answers show actions as 'donations (ad hoc or once only in cash or kind)', 32 per cent as 'sponsorships (regular or continuing)', 11 per cent in 'cause related marketing and campaigning' (i.e., advertisements dealing with social issues), 8 per cent in 'employer involvement in community activities (on behalf of the enterprise)' and 6 per cent with 'employee involvement in community activities (on behalf of the enterprise)'. The results show a clear policy of support for external social activities with 'donations', because this only happens occasionally. But medium-sized enterprises also made 'sponsorships', which could mean a strategy of support for social activities like professional sports on a regular basis. From a country perspective, in

27 This commentary is only related to SMEs involved in external social activities.

28 Regulated by the *Decreto-Lei nº 74/99* from 16 March published *in Diário da Republica, nº 63, Iª Série* A. Several changes have been made like in *Lei nº 160/99* of 14 September, *Lei nº 176–A/99* of 30 December, *Lei nº 3-B/00* of 4 April and *Lei nº 30–C/00* of 29 December.

29 Indeed this is consistent with financial accounting theory, its concern with the boundary of the organisation and with generally accepted accounting principles (GAAP).

Portugal, Liechtenstein, Greece, Iceland, Spain, Austria, as in the UK, 'donations' are more common than 'sponsorships'; an example could be support to marathon events as opposed to football teams. By way of contrast, Belgium, Ireland, Denmark and Sweden have more 'sponsorships' than 'donations'. And Finland, Luxembourg and Switzerland have both ways very similar in popularity. The 'cause related marketing and campaigning' (i.e., advertisements dealing with social issues) is important for Norway and Austria while 'employee involvement in community activities (on behalf of the enterprise)' show the greatest percentage in Liechtenstein, Austria and Switzerland. Once more, cultural and social differences between countries are very important and should be to related specific laws or rules that could cause benefits to the enterprises. The authors suggest that there exists a connection here with the different activities that people in each country spend their free time engaging in. All these results agree with McGuire et al. (1988: 854) that:

> ... explicit costs of corporate social responsibility are minimal and that firms may actually benefit from socially responsible actions in terms of employee morale and productivity.[30]

Gelb and Strawser (2001: 1) express this that:

> ... socially responsible firms are more likely to provide this increased disclosure through better investor relations practices.

It was asked of SMEs involved in external social activities to state, in practice, which have been the major benefits for the enterprise. The responses show that 24 per cent say that 'improved customer loyalty' (i.e., better image), 19 per cent 'improved relations with the community and public authorities', 12 per cent 'improved employees' job satisfaction' (easier to retain or attract employees), 11 per cent 'improved relations with business partners and investors' and 10 per cent 'improved economic performance' (reduce costs and/or increase sales) were the benefits. There is a very interesting result as 18 per cent of the answers of SMEs involved in external social activities say that there are 'no perceived benefits' (OE SMEs, 2002b: 30). This could show that after the decision is adopted, the enterprise does not monitor the activity, because the result indicates that customer loyalty is the only important aspect that needs to be confirmed. As Joyner and Payne (2002: 309) conclude:

> ... the firm is engaging in philanthropic activities they have no legal or even moral obligation to do: however, in fulfilling the firm's discretionary responsibilities, the firm may certainly act to benefit of society.

---

30 McGuire et al. (1988: 854) suggest more opinions like those expressed by: M. Moskowitz (1972), 'Choosing Socially Responsible Stocks', *Business and Society*, 1: 71–5; R, Parket and H. Eibert (1975), 'Social Responsibility: The Underlying Factors', *Business Horizons*, 18: 5–10 and R. Soloman and K. Hansen (1985), *It's Good Business*, New York: Atheneum.

From a national view (OE SMEs, 2002b: 30) in Italy and Finland, enterprises have lower proportions in the option of 'no perceived benefits'. In opposition are Sweden, Iceland and Spain. Portugal has the most important category as 'relations with the community and public authorities' which is the opposite in Sweden and Denmark. The 'customer loyalty' reason is very important in Finland and the enterprises know very well the benefit (with not so high degree of importance) but as the main benefit it appears in all the other countries. Weston (2003: 19) states:

> It is the smart businesses that invest in their customers all the time – not just when times are good!

So, the organisation should recognise the importance of customers (internal and external). From a Portuguese perspective, the authors know that SMEs are involved in community causes and projects that focus their activities and interest at a local level. It is important to explain that each time a Portuguese SME contributes to social external activities the organisation, association or people involved always provide information and publish it to the general public. Additionally, only a small number of SMEs would themselves publish such information except that fiscal law that permits a decrease in the income tax payable due to such activity.

When SMEs answer that they participate in social activities, then it is necessary to understand the main characteristics of these activities. The question asked was *Is your involvement in these social activities occasional or regular? And is it related to your business strategy or not?* And the survey shows that 37 per cent of answers have 'occasional activities, unrelated to business strategy', 31 per cent have 'regular activities, unrelated to business strategy' and with equal value of answers (14 per cent) appears the 'occasional activities' and 'regular activities' but that are related to business strategy (OE SMEs, 2002b: 23). An increase in size of the enterprise increases the regular basis of such activities and the concern for it to be related to the business.

On a national basis (OE SMEs, 2002b: 25), the results show differences like:

- in Switzerland (30 per cent) and Greece (29 per cent) enterprises have the most regular activities that are related to the strategy. In opposition are Norway (4 per cent) and Italy (3 per cent);
- Spain (45 per cent), Portugal (44 per cent), Belgium (41 per cent) and Iceland (40 per cent) have the most regular activities which are unrelated to the strategy. In opposition are Finland (8 per cent), Denmark (16 per cent) and Greece (17 per cent);
- the least representative group of answers is occasional activities which are related to the strategy. In this group, Austria (29 per cent), Denmark (24 per cent) and Iceland (24 per cent) have more responses than Italy (5 per cent) and Sweden (5 per cent).

The full analysis shows that the 'unrelated to the business strategy' and 'occasional' bases for contribution are the most chosen responses for all countries; in this matter there are no differences. This analysis identifies, among the SMEs surveyed, that this involvement in social external activities is based principally on short-term decisions, because it is occasional and unrelated to the general business strategy. When the SMEs strategic planning is analysed, for example by Stonehouse and Pemberton (2002), they focus on short-term horizons for business planning and they explain that:

> ... managers either appear unconvinced or unaware of the practical benefits of using frameworks for strategic planning.

However, Peel and Bridge (1998) report a strong positive relationship between the success of SMEs and the degree of long-term planning. In this respect, we find evidence to show that the increase in number of workers in firms seems to affect the involvement of firms in social external activities on a regular basis and related to the general business strategy.

The Observatory (OE SMEs, 2002b: 25) finds that:

> ... a positive and statistically significant relationship between involvement in external social activities and age of the enterprise, in the sense that the percentage of SMEs involved in these activities increases with the number of years in business operations.

This commentary is based on 52 per cent of SMEs having more than ten years in operation, 51 per cent having six to ten years, 40 per cent between two and five years and 37 per cent less than two years.

In any case, the Green Paper (COM, 2001) suggests the voluntary nature of corporate social responsibility, but these activities are already bound to some extent by directives and/or legislation in a national and European framework; examples include environmental rules and laws, health and safety legislation, specific employment legislation, amongst other social aspects. The last chapter of the survey is about environmental responsibility of SMEs. Before the analysis of the questions, the Observatory (OE SMEs, 2002b: 36) explains:

> There is little statistical information on this ... or ... there is very limited empirical information on the degree of involvement of SMEs in environmental practices ....

In this sense, the results of the survey could not be compared with other sources of information, which represents a difficulty in understanding CSR in SMEs. As Amba-Rao (1993: 562) states:

> ... socio-economic, legal and cultural differences among nations make it difficult to follow uniform practices. Hence, multilateral agreements may have limited effectiveness in enforcing the practices.

Indeed L'Etang (1995: 125) argues that:

> ... difficulties arise from conflicting interests and priorities. Pressures may be both internal and external and corporate social responsibility programmes usually evolve

from a combination of proactive and reactive policies.

The model of ISO,[31] specifically ISO 14000, is intended as a worldwide approach to management systems that encourage environmental protection. ISO 14001 and 14004 govern the policies, procedures and organisational structure for a company's environmental management system. Additional standards address auditing (ISO 14010, 14011 and 14012) and environmental labelling (ISO 14024), while, as of 2000, standards for life-cycle assessment are contained in ISO 14040. The environmental performance evaluations expressed in ISO 14003 remain under development. This analysis is about the number of certified sites by the International Organisation for Standardisation, promoted by the ISO 14001[32] series in December 2000. The European Commission developed the Environmental Management and Audit System (EMAS) at validated sites in January 2002. The results show the number of certified sites by each of the mentioned procedures and the information was collected in two different periods of time. In Austria (362 *versus* 203) and Germany (2,662 *versus* 1,260) the EMAS system is more accepted by enterprises than ISO (OE SMEs, 2002b). Because the number of certified sites is small and in several countries (Iceland, Luxembourg, Liechtenstein, Greece and Portugal), the promoting of this kind of measure is not popular then firms actually need to seek out certification.

The analysis and results discussed are not supported in this study. It shows that these are new measures that are becoming available to SMEs, because first they need to have internet access to make a certification of their sites. The Observatory (OE SMEs 2002b: 37) included two more pieces of information concerning the relative presence of certified firms per thousand enterprises and has concluded that:

> ... the countries with the higher presence of certified enterprises are the Nordic countries of Denmark, Sweden and Finland, as well as Liechtenstein and Switzerland. By way of contrast, the opposite is true in the case of the Southern European countries of Spain, Italy, Portugal and Greece.

But, the authors do not agree with this kind of analysis which is biased because the total number of enterprises is very small and different in each country. The relative presence per thousand means that the countries with fewer enterprises will lose importance while others will gain.

In a complementary analysis based upon ISO (2002), the distribution of firms certified by the ISO 14000 model between 1995 and June 2002, all over the world, are 40,970 enterprises in 112 countries. An EU sample (of the 19 countries of Europe) of the survey represents[33] 64 per cent of the total and 69 per cent of world value,

---

31 See ISO (2002).

32 In the framework of ISO certification, and strictly speaking, ISO 14001 is the only one in this series that has a certification standard.

33 This analysis is made on a basis of six complete years 1995–2001. The main reason is that not all the countries have complete available information for the same period.

respectively. In the EU, the most representative countries are Germany (3,380), United Kingdom (2,722) and Sweden (2,070). The fewest representatives are in Portugal (88), Greece (66) and Luxembourg (9). There are two extraordinary examples of growth, between 2000 and 2001:

- Spain with 1464 enterprises; this value is bigger than all the represented firms from France (1,092) and Italy (1,295) and more than the other 13 countries. Only the most represented in the EU have more enterprises certified;
- Italy with 774 firms; this value is bigger than all the represented enterprises from 11 countries.

A reverse approach, in spite of growing between 1999–2001, is that Portugal is the last country of the distribution of SMEs by the Europe-19 to have access to the internet, in the both years (OE SMEs, 2002a). The growth of the Portuguese rate is well above (114 per cent) the average (69 per cent), as are the Greek (225 per cent) and United Kingdom (105 per cent) rates. From the author's experience one reason could be that access to the internet is too expensive, as well as computers, software and security. But the survey shows that for 43 per cent of non-user SMEs of the internet the reason is because it 'does not apply to the type enterprise/product'; 18 per cent per cent non-user SMEs cited the reason as 'it would not pay off' and the third reason is 'no skilled personnel' with 17 per cent per cent of non-user SMEs. It is interesting to note that Sweden (16 per cent) and Iceland (14 per cent) show the lowest growth rates of SMEs that have access to the internet. But they have, too, the biggest percentages of SMEs in 1999 and 2001, nearly 70 per cent and 80 per cent, respectively. In a statistical analysis which did not express development, the total percentage is lower than others, because they probably do not need to, nor could, grow more.

It was asked of the SMEs that do not use the internet, *what is the single most important reason for not using the internet to sell products or services?* In an SME's strategy and its decision-making process this new concept of suitability of the internet is not important. Like its connection to size it seems this did not have any influence. This view puts the organisation at the centre of its world and the only interfaces with the external world take place at the beginning and end of its value chain, in the physical business environment. The perspective of Holmes and Grieco (1999) states that, based upon an expectation that Internet Based Reporting (IBR)[34] and the technology, the web will have a beneficial impact upon the way in which society operates. However, Friedman's (1970) argument that the corporation, as an economic

---

34 It is possible to see reports in several institutions like: 'Firms' (available online at http://www.corporateregister.com); 'Global Reporting Initiative' (available online at http://www.globalreporting.org); 'Accountability 1000' (available online at http://www.accountability.org.uk); UK social investment forum (available online at http://www.uksif.org); 'Sustainable Investment Research International Group' (available online at http://www.sirigroup.org).

institution, should thus specialise in its economic sphere, could be acceptable if there is no small-market, otherwise the corporation is losing opportunities. Ackerman (1975) argued that big business was recognising the need to adapt to a new social climate of community accountability but that the orientation of business to financial results was inhibiting social responsiveness. The authors suggest that the Ackerman argument is the same for SMEs when facing the use of the internet, because they want an expected profitability. Thus social responsibility will lead to enhanced financial performance (Pava and Krausz, 1997) and consequently firms will have a good social reputation which implies a correlation with stock price (Bernhut, 2002).

Portuguese CSR faces problems like urbanisation, with the subsequent desertification of the rural environment and growth in the population density in the six major cities, which has resulted in a number of urgent social problems. For example, in Portugal, large foreign corporations[35] announce, almost every day, that they will be laying off all their workforce and closing factories. Some of them explain that they will move to other countries with lower wage rates, but in Portugal, in 2003, the minimum wage, per month, is €357. Note that these actions are legal. The authors think that they are made with the purpose of improving profits and maximising shareholder value. Another very interesting perspective, is the commentary made by Schlusberg (1969: 66) that '... certain types of decisions can be generally accepted as having significant public consequences. Some obvious examples: whether to relocate a factory, and where ....'

The authors agree with Reich's (1998) opinion that the importance of CSR behaviour is not whether companies should be responsible to society, but rather how they should be responsible. So, these firms know that the public opinion and the media discussion would be intense if these firms were acting unethically, with the Portuguese society in particular and with the European Union in general. Because most of them received European financial support to develop in countries like Portugal, should they not therefore be socially responsible? Between countries in the Europe field when they relocate why are firms not being deprived of the resources provided? Could the financial support be used to develop important measures? Reich (1998: 15) suggested that:

> ... if we want companies to take on the responsibilities of finding new jobs for employees who are no longer needed, and of retraining them of such jobs, perhaps government should offer these companies tax deductions or credits for doing so.

Some of these questions do not have answers, but the authors agree with the perspective proposed by Vogel (1996: 146–60) that:

---

35 April 2001 saw the latest series of announcements of job losses in Portugal, following the restructuring of multinational companies involving closures and relocation. These policies have affected sectors such as textiles and clothing (C&J Clark), electronics (Siemens) and motor manufacturing (Autoeuropa-Volkswagen). The job losses, often hitting especially women and poor regions, have prompted much criticism and debate in local and national society.

... management textbooks and journals ignored politics and public policy ... What is need is an analysis that links both perspectives, one that shows the interrelationship between the role of politics in shaping management decision making and the role of business in influencing governmental decision making.

This perspective should be very important because if politics defends the free market and the relationship between government and firms is not doing this in the best way, all of society unfortunately loses. Smaller Portuguese towns have shown the ability to solve these problems through a strong sense of social responsibility in the actions of the various local bodies (companies, governmental institutions and social solidarity institutions) (BNCSR, 2001: 13).

Corporate citizenship has arrived and charity no longer makes sense. Cause-related marketing is invading the retail sector like Swatch[36] in Portugal. Those consumers who value CSR are willing to pay a higher price for a product or service with an additional social characteristic than for an identical product without this characteristic (McWilliams and Siegel, 2001). Thus managers see the opportunity to differentiate their product as part of the firm's interest (Windsor, 2001a). In that case, Swatch donated €6.75 from each watch sold for the reconstruction of a school in East Timor. The advertising played an important part in the promotion of this to all the stakeholders. In Swatch's case the promotions in television, newspapers and radio were made with images of actors, music and television presenters that decided to help this cause. There are enterprises, for example, Norvartis and SmithKline Beecham, which have employees volunteering and helping local communities (Anonymous, 2000).

The authors and the Observatory (OE SMEs, 2002b: 52) argue that:

... the analysis of the CSR issue in SMEs has received little attention from researchers in comparison to the CSR issue in large enterprises ... especially true as far as the social domain is concerned.

Probably, there is a lot of unreported corporate social responsibility behaviour for any particular business, because there are no clear differences between SMEs and large-sized enterprises. In this sense, CSR needs improvements not concerned with the size of the enterprise, or the country, but, for example, because what constitutes legitimate CSR activities has not always been clearly defined (Pava and Krausz, 1996). And as Freer (2002: 4), in the Millennium survey carried out by PriceWaterhouseCoopers, Inc. reports, the survey:

---

36 On 15 June 2000, Swatch released in Portugal a benefit special called 'A Escola' (school in Portuguese). There were two versions, one regular in a paper box and one special edition in a brick. Another one has been made on May 28 2002: Swatch Fraldinhas (nappies in Portuguese), give financial support to a non-governmental institution 'Ajuda de Berço'. This institution helps babies to three years of age in a dangerous situation. These watches are only sold in Portugal.

... interviewed 25,000 citizens in 23 countries. It showed that two-thirds of respondents want companies to go beyond their historical role of making money. They want them to contribute towards the broader societal goals as well.

The authors agree with the commentary made that CSR:

... is not just about managing, reducing and avoiding risk. It is about creating opportunities, generating improved performance, making money and leaving the risks far behind.

The findings could provide a cautionary message to SMEs that CSR can offer an opportunity for firms to review the critical aspects of their operations and to identify the actions necessary for effective operations and greater competitive advantage. Thus a full-scale CSR needs a full-scale social audit which examines, as Miles (2000, 43–4) states:

... the records, systems procedures and performance measures of an organization to provide assurance about the organization's social, environmental and ethical performance claims. In designing an audit to measure the ... firm's ... compliance with its ethical policy, citizens took a significant first step towards a comprehensive social audit.

Prado (1994) and Díaz-Zorita and Gonzalo (1996) agree that the auditors' social responsibility is equal to attributing a social function to auditing.

Discussion

For a long time, CSR has been undertaken by firms. But, in the past, it was purely voluntary and generally centred in civic responsibility. Nowadays, the authors believe that in an area where social responsibility is, or should be, an operative cliché, the theory and empirical analyses to prove it, might facilitate improved corporate governance (Tuzzolino and Armandi, 1981). So, experiences and examples of (worst and best) practices could support technical knowledge. The authors agree that CSR is not a geographic problem or dependant upon the location of countries, but it is a subject of behaviour and ethics and specific studies applied to this research line are needed to connect these aspects. According to Kok et al. (2001: 286):

A quality management framework should require consistency in ethical behaviour throughout the organisation.

Portugal's accession to the European Economic Community, in 1986, forced the country to develop. Ever since, the Portuguese economic model has been based on SMEs. These enterprises are an integral part of the local community and their success is related to the capability to obtain legitimacy and consensus among the local stakeholders, like: customers, potential clients, suppliers, employees, competitors, financial institutions, public authorities, citizens, and others. These local networks are based on responsible business practices, informal and tacit relationships, whose results are often not communicated, or simply, can not be measured. These stakeholders now expect management to participate in the debate on societal problems and proactively think about the effects of their business on society at large (Kok et al., 2001).

The study of CSR behaviour of firms cannot simply be done as an abstraction; its influence needs to be empirically demonstrated. But, the policy adopted by the Observatory of European SMEs of making less information available does not allow researchers to discuss the results properly. Beyond this, the survey could show some evidence. It will be possible to search for government strategies on the external environment in the area of the European Union as a composite society without differences of classification between countries. One aspect that should be studied is an understanding of the practice of social reporting of SMEs. As Adams (2002) discusses, corporate characteristics, and general and internal contextual factors, are important influences upon the extent and nature of ethical, social and environmental reports and the interrelation between these variables and the report itself.

The analysis of this survey shows the diversity with which a concern for CSR is manifest and that there is no single definition. For further research, the authors propose specific questions to be introduced into the survey such as: age of respondent which could be connected with psychological attitude and sociological behaviour; years in operation that allows the analysis of the life cycle of the firm; annual turnover so it is possible to understand the level of economic influence of the respondent of the survey; annual balance-sheet total which could be connected to the investment and depreciation policy of the firm. And more questions could be revised, like the work by Deegan (2002), that over the years develop an empirical analysis that presents different questions such as: company report and its disclosure; attributes of performance (economic performance); identification of factors (industry membership, country, culture, size); reactions of stakeholders and shareholders to disclosure; accountants' and auditors' attitudes and formal education; correspondence between different reports; role of taxation or laws in CSR; practical financial and management accounting aspects; behaviour and motivation of managers and agency theory. Another proposal of the authors is to develop a longitudinal study using a time frame of ten years or more with a large sample of SME firms. This proposition allows the discovery of direct and indirect influences of economic, legal, cultural, moral, social and physical aspects of the society.

The authors agree with Schlusberg (1969) about solving one remaining question, which is that if the European Commission substitutes the voluntary nature of CSR behaviour with laws and specific regulation in this field then it will play an important role in determining the extent of corporate social responsibility and in solving the crisis of firm legitimacy. Moneva and Llena (1996) consider that the growth of social practices which create an important demand for information for shareholders, also provides an imperative to know the ethical behaviour of the firm. Thus, reports, particularly of the Observatory of European SMEs, constitute an important form of communication about external social activities, and consequentially about ethical behaviour practised by enterprises.

As final discussion, the authors aim is that this European village should be transformed into a large-scale inclusive village providing all its members with a better place to live and enjoy. Corporate socially responsible behaviour should lead enterprises throughout the world to recognise this and adjust their actions accordingly. As Moir (2001: 17) states:

> Whether or not business should undertake CSR, and the forms that responsibility should take, depends upon the economic perspective of the firm that is adopted.

Windsor (2001b) defends three emerging alternatives to CSR: an economic conception of responsibility, a global corporate citizenship and stakeholder management practices. The authors know that it has been and it will be a long way to travel, but to stop trying is not the solution.

References

Abreu, R., Crowther, D., David, F. and Magro, F. (2003), *A European Perspective of Corporate Social Responsibility*, paper presented at 7th Interdisciplinary Perspectives on Accounting Conference, Madrid.

Ackerman, R.W. (1975), *The Social Challenge to Business*, Cambridge: Harvard University Press.

Adams, C.A. (2002), 'Internal Organisational Factors Influencing Corporate Social and ethical Reporting. Beyond Current Theorising', *Accounting, Auditing and Accountability Journal*, Vol. 15, No. 2: 223–50.

Amba-Rao, S.C. (1993), 'Multinational Corporate Social Responsibility, Ethics, Interactions and Third World Governments: An Agenda for the 1990s', *Journal of Business Ethics*, Vol. 12: 553–72.

Angelidis, J.P. and Ibrahim, N.A. (1993), 'Social Demand and Corporate Supply: A Corporate Social Responsibility Model', *Review of Business*, Vol. 15, No. 1, Summer/Fall: 7–10.

Anonymous (2000), 'Ajudar para Ganhar', *Fortunas e Negócios*, November: 12.

Balabanis, G., Phillips, H. and Lyall, J. (1998), 'Corporate Social Responsibility and Economic Performance in the Top British Companies: Are They Linked?', *European Business Review*, Vol. 98, No. 1: 25–44.

Bernhut, S. with Pratima Bansal (2002), 'Corporate Social Responsibility', *Business Journal,* March/April: 18–19.

Broberg, M.P. (1996), 'Corporate Social Responsibility in the European Communities – The Scandinavian Viewpoint', *Journal of Business Ethics*, Vol. 15: 615–22.

Brundtland Commission (1987), *Our Common Future*, The World Commission on Environment and Development, Oxford: University Press (available online at http://geneva-international.org/GVA/WelcomeKit/environnement/chap_5.E.htm).

Business Network for Corporate Social Responsibility (2001), 'Inside Europe: Portugal – Focus on Portugal', *CSR Magazine*, 2/1: 12–13 (available online at http://www.csreurope.org/uploadstore/cms/docs/CSRE_mag_PDF_May2001.pdf).

Carroll, A.B. (1979), 'A Three-dimensional Conceptual Model of Corporate Performance', *Academic of Management Review*, Vol. 4, No. 4: 497–505.

Carroll, A.B. (1999), 'Corporate Social Responsibility', *Business and Society*, Vol. 38, No. 3: 268–95.

Crowther, D. (2002a), *A Social Critique of Corporate Reporting*, Aldershot: Ashgate.

Crowther, D. (2002b), 'The Importance of Corporate Social Responsibility', *Estudos e Documentos de Trabalho, EDT–05/2002*, Guarda: Escola Superior de Tecnologia e Gestão.

Decreto-Lei No. 74, 16 March 1999.

Deegan, C. (2002), 'The Legitimising Effect of Social and environmental Disclosures – A Theoretical Foundation', *Accounting, Auditing and Accountability Journal*, Vol. 15, No. 3: 282–311.

Díaz-Zorita, A.L. and Gonzalo, J.A. (1996), *Las responsabilidades del Auditor: Responsabilidad social*, paper presented to XI Congreso de Auditores-Censores Jurados de Cuentas, Instituto de Auditores-Censores Jurados de Cuentas de España, October: 3–40.

Drucker, P.F. (1984), 'The New Meaning of Corporate Social Responsibility', *California Management Review*, Vol. 26, No. 2, Winter: 53–63.

Epstein, E.M. (1987), 'Business Ethics and Corporate Social Policy. Reflections on an Intellectual Journey, 1964–1996, and Beyond', *Business and Society*, Vol. 37, No. 1, March: 7–39.

European Commission (1996), *Recommendations from 3 April concerning the Definition of Small and Medium-sized Enterprises (SME)*, Brussels: Official Publications of the European Commission, 30 April.

European Commission (2001), *Green Paper – Promoting a European framework for Corporate Social Responsibility*, COM (2001) 366 final, Brussels: Official Publications of the European Commission, 18 July.

European Commission (2002), *Corporate Social Responsibility: A Business Contribution to Sustainable Development*, COM (2002) 347 final, Brussels: Official Publications of the European Commission, 2 July.

Fitch, H.G. (1976), 'Achieving Corporate Social Responsibility', *Academy of Management Review*, Vol. 1, No. 1, January: 38–47.

Frankental, P. (2001), 'Corporate Social Responsibility – A PR Invention?', *Corporate Communications*, Vol. 6, No. 1: 18–23.

Freer, S. (2002), 'Reaping the Benefits of Responsibility: The Need to Address Social and Environmental Risk Issues is Rising on the Corporate Agenda', *Financial Times,* London edn, 20 November: 4.

Friedman, M. (1962), *Capitalism and Freedom*, Chicago: University of Chicago Press.

Friedman, M. (1970), 'A Friedman Doctrine – The Social Responsibility of Business is to Increase its Profits', *The New York Times Magazine*, 13 September: 32–3.

Gamble, G.O., Hsu, K., Jackson, C. and Tollerson, C.D. (1996), 'Environmental Disclosure in Annual Reports: An International Perspective', *International Journal of Accounting*, Vol. 31, No. 3: 293–331.

Gelb, D.S. and Strawser, J.A. (2001), 'Corporate Social Responsibility and Financial Disclosures: An Alternative Explanation for Increased Disclosure', *Journal of Business Ethics*, Vol. 33: 1–13.

Gray, R. (2002), 'The Social Accounting Project and *Accounting, Organizations and Society*: Privileging Engagement, Imaginings, New Accountings and Pragmatism over Critique?', *Accounting, Organizations and Society*, Vol. 27, No. 2: 687–708.

Gray, R., Javad, M. Power, D.M. and Sinclair, C.D. (2001), 'Social and Environmental Disclosure and Corporate Characteristics: A Research Note and Extension', *Journal of Business Finance and Accounting*, Vol. 28, Nos 3/4, April/May: 327–56.

Guthrie, J. and Parker, L.D. (1989), 'Corporate Social Disclosure Practice: A Comparative International Analysis', *Advances in Public Interest Accounting*, Vol. 3: 159–76.

Holmes, L. and Grieco, M. (1999), *The Power of Transparency: The Internet, E-mail and the Malaysian Political Crisis*, paper presented to Asian Management in Crisis Conference, Association of South East Asian Studies, UNL, June.

Hopkins, M. (1999), *The Planetary Bargain: Corporate Social Responsibility Comes of Age*, Basingstoke: Macmillan.

International Organization of Standards (2002), 'The ISO Survey of ISO 9000 and 14000 Certification', Geneva: Official Publications of the ISO (available online at http://www.iso14000.com/Community/RegisteredList.htm).

Jones, T.M. (1980), 'Corporate Social Responsibility: Revisited, Redefined', *California Management Review*, Vol. 23, No. 2, Spring: 59–67.

Joyner, B. and Payne, D. (2002), 'Evolution and Implementation: A Study of Values, Business Ethics and Corporate Social Responsibility', *Journal of Business Ethics*, Vol. 41: 297–311.

Joyner, B.E., Payne, D. and Raiborn, C.A. (2002), 'Building Values, Business Ethics and Corporate Social Responsibility into the Developing Organization', *Journal of Developmental Entrepreneurship*, Vol. 7, No. 1, April: 113–31.

Kok, P., Wiele, T., McKenna, R. and Brown, A. (2001), 'A Corporate Social Responsibility Audit within a Quality Management Framework', *Journal of Business Ethics*, Vol. 31: 285–97.

Law no. 160, 14 September 1999.

Law no. 176-A, 30 December 1999.

Law no. 3-B, 4 April 2000.

Law no. 30-C, 29 December 2000.

L'Etang, J. (1995), 'Ethical Corporate Social Responsibility: A Framework for Managers', *Journal of Business Ethics*, Vol. 14: 125–32.

Mathews, M.R. (1997), 'Twenty–five Years of Social and Environmental Accounting: Is There a Silver Jubilee to Celebrate?', *Accounting, Auditing and Accountability Journal*, Vol. 10, No. 4: 481–531.

McGuire, J.B., Sundgren, A. and Schneeweis, T. (1988), 'Corporate Social Responsibility and Firm Financial Performance', *Academy of Management Journal*, Vol. 31, No. 4: 854–72.

McNeil, P. (1990), *Research Methods*, London: Routledge.

McWilliams, A. and Siegel, D. (2001), 'Corporate Social Responsibility: A Theory of Firm Perspective', *Academic Management Review*, Vol. 26, No. 1: 117–27.

Miles, V. (2000), 'Auditing Promises: One Bank's Story', *CMA Management*, Vol. 74, No. 5: 42–6.

Mintzberg, H. (1983), 'The Case for Corporate Social Responsibility', *Journal of Business Strategy*, Vol. 4, No. 2, Fall: 3–15.

Moir, L. (2001), 'What do we Mean by Corporate Social Responsibility?', *Corporate Governance*, Vol. 1, No. 2: 16–22.

Moneva, J.M. and Llena, F. (1996), 'Análisis de la información sobre responsabilidad social en las empresas industriales que cotizan en Bolsa', *Revista Española de Financiación y Contabilidad*, Vol. 25, No. 87: 361–402.

Observatory of European SMEs (2000), *Sixth Report, Executive Summary*, Luxembourg: Official Publications of the European Communities.

Observatory of European SMEs (2002a), *Highlights from the 2001 Survey*, Luxembourg: Official Publications of the European Communities.

Observatory of European SMEs (2002b), *European SMEs and Social and Environmental Responsibility*, Luxembourg: Official Publications of the European Communities.

Organisation for Economic Cooperation and Development (1999), *OECD Principles of Corporate Governance*, Paris: OECD Publications.

Organisation for Economic Cooperation and Development (2000), *The OECD Guidelines for Multinational Enterprises-Revision*, Paris: OECD Publications.

Ostlund, L.E. (1977), 'Attitudes of Managers Toward Corporate Social Responsibility', *California Management Review*, Vol. 19, No. 4, Summer: 35–49.

Pava, M.L. and Krausz, J. (1996), 'The Association Between Corporate Social Responsibility and Financial Performance: The Paradox of Social Cost', *Journal of Business Ethics*, Vol. 15, No. 3: 321–57.

Pava, M.L. and Krausz, J. (1997), 'Criteria for Evaluating the Legitimacy of Corporate Social Responsibility', *Journal of Business Ethics*, Vol. 16: 337–47.

Peel, M.J. and Bridge, J. (1998), 'How Planning and Capital Budgeting Improve SME Performance', *Long Range Planning*, Vol. 31, No. 6: 848–56.

Peyró, E. (1997), *Información social y ambiental en España: un estudio empírico,* paper presented at the IX Congreso AECA, Asociación Española de Contabilidad y Administración de Empresas, September: 681–703.

Prado, J.M. (1994), 'La responsabilidad en auditoria', *Técnica Contable*, Vol. 46, No. 544, April: 225–42.

Quazi, A.M. and O'Brien, D. (2000), 'An Empirical Test of a Cross-national Model of Corporate Social Responsibility', *Journal of Business Ethics*, Vol. 25, No. 1: 33–51.

Reich, R.B. (1998), 'The New Meaning of Corporate Social Responsibility', *California Management Review*, Vol. 40, No. 2, Winter: 8–17.

Riley, M., Wood, R., Clark, M., Wilkie, E. and Szivas, E. (2001), *Researching and Writing Dissertations in Business and Management*, London: Thomson Learning.

Robertson, D.C. and Nicholson, N. (1996), 'Expressions of Corporate Social Responsibility in UK Firms', *Journal of Business Ethics*, Vol. 15, No. 10: 1095–106.

Schlusberg, M. (1969), 'Corporate Legitimacy and Social Responsibility: The Role of Law', *California Management Review*, Vol. 12, No. 1, Fall: 65–76.

Simms, J. (2002), 'Corporate Social Responsibility – You Know it Makes Sense', *Accountancy*, Vol. 130, No. 1311, November: 48–50.

Stonehouse, G. and Pemberton, J. (2002), 'Strategic Planning in SMEs – Some Empirical Findings', *Management Decision*, Vol. 40, No. 9: 853–61.

Thomas, R. (2001), 'Response to the Consultation of the European Commission on Green Paper Promoting a European Framework for Corporate Social Responsibility', Brussels: Official Publications of the European Commission (available online at http://europa.eu.int/comm/employment_social/soc-dial/csr/pdf2/098-ACA_Rosamun-Thomas_UK_011208_en.htm).

Tuzzolino, F. and Armandi, B.R. (1981), 'A Need-hierarchy Framework for Assessing Corporate Social Responsibility', *Academic Management Review*, Vol. 6, No. 1: 21–8.

Vogel, D.J. (1996), 'The Study of Business and Politics', *California Management Review*, Vol. 38, No. 3, Spring: 146–65.

Watts, T. (1999), '"Social Auditing" the KPMG UK Experience', *Australian CPA*, Vol. 69, No. 8: 46–7.

Weston, T. (2003), 'Cutting Costs Through Better Customer Service', *Management Services*, Vol. 47, No. 1, January: 19–29.

Windsor, D. (2001a), '"Corporate Social Responsibility: A Theory of Firm Perspective" – Some Comments', *Academic Management Review*, Vol. 26, No. 10: 502–4.

Windsor, D. (2001b), 'The Future of Corporate Social Responsibility', *International Journal of Organizational Analysis*, Vol. 9, No. 3: 225–56.

Appendix A

Responses online to the consultation on the Green Paper on CSR

Public authorities	International level; European level; national level; regional level; local level
Political parties	
Organisations	International level; European level; national level; regional level
Companies	Networks (international level, European level, national level, regional level); individuals companies; consultants; social economy
Social partners	European level; employers (European level, national level); trade unions (European level, national level) International level; European level; national level
Advocacy groups	
Academics	
Other interested individuals	

Appendix B

Adaptation of the Questions Available in the ENSR 2001 Survey (Observatory of European SMEs, 2002a: 26 and 2002b: 33–4, 53–6)

Section 1 – Screening questions

X1   Is your business an independent enterprise or a subsidiary of another enterprise?

X2   What is your position within the enterprise?

X3   *[Internal: note down gender of respondent]*

X4   What is the main activity of your enterprise in terms of turnover?

X5   How many people did your enterprise employ on average during 2000?

Section 2 – General characteristics

X6 And how many people did your enterprise employ on average during 1999?

X7 *Not available*

X8 How many years has your enterprise been in operation before 2001?

X9 *Not available*

X10 *Not available*

X11 *Which of the following factors* has been the major constraint on your business performance over the last two years?

Section 3 – Internationalisation and growth

X12 Did your enterprise have any exports in 2000?

X13 And could you indicate the percentage of exports to total turnover for the year 2000?

X14 Have you faced an increase or a decrease in competition from **domestic** enterprises over the last 5 years?

X15 Have you faced an increase or a decrease in competition from **foreign** enterprises over the last 5 years?

X16 Do you have more international business contacts than you did 5 years ago?

Section 4 – Entrepreneurship and management

X17 *Not available*

X18 What has been the main focus of your enterprise policy recently?

X19 What does 'growth' mean to your enterprise?

X20 On which factors do you consider your enterprise to be competitive?

Section 5 – ICT and e-commerce

X21 *Which of the following forms* of ICT does your enterprise use?

X22 What is the single most important reason why your enterprise has not used the Internet to sell its products or services?

X23 Not available

X24 For *which of the following* commercial activities does your enterprise use the Internet?

Section 6 – Social and environmental responsibility of SME

X25 Aside from the normal business activities, enterprises may contribute to external social objectives, or participate in external social activities. Did your enterprise do this in one of the following ways in 2000?

Note: 1. *Do not include activities for or support to your own employees.*

2. *Read out; more than one answer are allowed.*

1. Support sport activities (not own employees)
2. Support cultural activities (not own employees)
3. Support health and welfare activities (not own employees)
4. Support education and training activities (not own employees)
5. Support environmental activities (other than directly related to consequences of the firms' own operations)
6. When recruiting workers, giving preference to personnel from socially deprived groups (ethnic minorities)
7. Participate in public affairs or political process on behalf of the enterprise (in local or regional community)
8. Contribute in any other way
9. (Do not read) None

Note: Go to question X33

10. (Do not read) Do not know and/or No answer

Note: Go to question X35

X26   Could you indicate which have been the major reasons or motivations for contributing to external social goals or activities? *Note: Read out; more than one answer is allowed*
1.   Ethical reasons (mainly altruistic)
2.   Improve relations with the community and public authorities
3.   Improve customer loyalty
4.   Improve relations with business partners and investors
5.   Improve employees' job satisfaction (easier to retain or attract employees)
6.   Improve economic performance (reduce costs/increase sales)
7.   Apply code of conduct (standard on socially or environmentally responsible business practices)
8.   Pressure from third parties (ie, clients, competitors, governments)
9.   Use existing public incentives (tax incentives, subsidies, others)
10. (Do not read) Other
11. (Do not read) None
12. (Do not read) Do not know and/or No answer

X27   In practice, which have been the major benefits for your enterprise? *Note: Read out; more than one answer are allowed*
1.   Improved relations with the community/public authorities
2.   Improved customer loyalty (better image)
3.   Improved relations with business partners and investors
4.   Improved employees' job satisfaction (easier to retain or attract employees)
5.   Improved economic performance (reduce costs/increase sales)
6.   Other
7   No perceived benefits
8.   Do not know and/or No answer

X28   **In which way** has your enterprise supported social activities during 2000? *Note: Read out; more than one answer are allowed*
1.   Sponsorships (regular, or continues)
2.   Donations (ad-hoc or once only in cash or kind)
3.   Cause related marketing/campaigning (ie, advertisements dealing with social issues)
4.   Employee involvement in community activities (on behalf of the enterprise)
5.   Employer involvement in community activities (on behalf of the enterprise)
6.   Other
7.   (Do not read) None
8.   (Do not read) Do not know and/or No answer

X29   **Did you receive** any public support or encouragement to participate in social activities during the last three years?
1   Yes
2.   No
Note: Go to question X31
3.   Do not know and/or No answer
Note: Go to question X31

X30   **What type of public support** did you receive to participate in social activities during the last three years? *Note: Read out; more than one answer are allowed*
1.   Tax reduction
2.   Subsidies
3.   Provision of information
4.   Other

5.   (Do not read) None
6.   (Do not read) Do not know and/or No answer
X31   Is your involvement in these social activities occasional or regular? And is it related to your business strategy or not?
1.   Occasional activities, unrelated to business strategy
2.   Occasional activities, related to business strategy
3.   Regular activities, unrelated to business strategy
4.   Regular activities, related to business strategy
5.   Do not know and/or No answer
X32   Are you planning to decrease or to increase the firm's participation in social activities over the next three years?
1.   To decrease participation
2.   To continue as it is
3.   To increase participation
4.   Do not know and/or No answer
Note: Go to question X35
X33   What is the single most important reason for not performing any of these actions? *Note: Only one answer allowed*
1.   Never thought about it
2.   Not related to the activities of my enterprise
3.   No benefits expected
4.   Lack of time
5.   Lack of money
6.   Lack of public support
7.   Other reason
8.   Do not know and/or No answer
X34   Do you have plans to participate in external social activities over the next three years?
1.   Yes (*Note: Go to question X341*)
2.   No (*Note: Go to question X342*)
3.   Do not know and/or No answer (*Note: Go to question X342*)
X341   Yes, in what way?
1.   To decrease participation
2.   To continue as it is
3.   To increase participation
4.   Do not know and/or No answer
X342   No, Why not?
1.   No participation foreseen
2.   Consider participating
3.   Plan to start participation
4.   Do not know and/or No answer
Section 7 – Administrative burdens when hiring employees
Not available
Section 8 – Taxation and SME growth
Not available
Section 9 – Stock options
X58   Do you use or plan to use employee stock options as a remuneration instrument?
X59   What is your main motivation to use stock options for remuneration?
X60   What is your main motivation not to use stock options for remuneration?

Chapter 7

Corporate Social Reporting: Genuine Action or Window Dressing?

David Crowther

Introduction

As socially responsible behaviour moves up the agenda of corporate activity these corporations can been seen to be active in the reporting of their activities in this respect. On corporate websites this is very evident and is becoming more evident also in the annual reporting of these organisations. For many however this is represented by a separate social and/or environmental report rather than the embedding of this activity in the annual report itself (Crowther, 2002).

Although there is no legislation requiring any social or environmental accounting or reporting there (at least in the UK) have been a number of recommendations from the EC, based upon their Fifth Action Programme on the Environment. Thus in a 1992 report entitled 'Towards Sustainability' the EC calls for organisations to:

- disclose in their annual reports details of their environmental policy and activities, and the effects thereof;
- detail in their accounts the expenses on environmental programmes (this recommendation requires a clear definition of such expenses);
- make provision in their accounts for environmental risks and future environmental expenses.

The EC also produced an Environmental Management and Audit Scheme (EMAS) in 1993 which encouraged companies to:

- set their own objectives for environmental performance and develop management systems which would achieve those objectives;
- initiate a pattern of eco-auditing to assess their environmental performance and to provide the information needed to develop environmental management systems;
- show commitment to externally validated assessment of their progress in meeting these objectives and make such information available to the public in a concise and comprehensible form;

• produce an environmental statement which would be available to the public and which would contain:
  • a description of the company's activities;
  • an assessment of the significant environmental issues of relevance to these activities;
  • a presentation of the company's environmental policy, programme and management system implemented;
  • a deadline for the submission of the next statement;
  • a summary of the figures on pollutant emissions, waste generation, consumption of raw material, energy, water and noise;
  • other significant environmental aspects as appropriate as well as other factors regarding environmental performance;
  • the name of an accredited environmental verifier.

This has been followed by such initiatives as the Green Paper – *Promoting a European Framework for Corporate Social Responsibility* (COM, 2001) and more recently *Corporate Social Responsibility: A Business Contribution to Sustainable Development* (COM, 2002).

Although this does not have the force of law it provides recommendations with respect to best practice. Some countries within the European Union have gone further and made mandatory requirements with respect to environmental reporting.

If socially responsible behaviour is being undertaken within organisations then it seems appropriate that these organisations should report it and increased disclosure in this respect is to be expected. It has been suggested by Schaltegger et al. (1996) that one of the driving forces in the development of social and environmental accounting was the need to placate, through the production of appropriate information, those members of society who could be classified as environmental activists. They further suggest that the such accounting information developed for this purpose has now been adopted into the repertoire of organisational accounting and forms an important part of the internal management control information of the organisation.

Of course it is equally true that, in the current environment, corporations have an incentive to present their activity as socially responsible whether or not they are particularly addressing this kind of activity. In this case such reporting becomes little more than window dressing rather than a reporting of activity. The purpose of this chapter is to explore the extent to which either of these motives apply.

Reporting Socially Responsible Activity

Although topical at the present time, social accounting can be seen to be a relatively recent phenomenon. As such it has by no means met with universal acceptance as an aspect of the activities of a firm which is of importance and worthy of involvement in by members of the firm, as far as accounting in this manner is concerned. The perceived benefits of such accounting to organisations has not been demonstrated to such an extent that all organisations consider such measurement and reporting would benefit them, although this view is being modified over time. Increasingly organisations are seeking to measure environmental impact and to report upon it both internally and externally. Indeed there is an increasing acceptance that environmental issues have a direct relationship with the economic success of an organisation. This view of the perceived irrelevance of environmental information however is particularly prevalent amongst accountants. Thus Frost and Wilmhurst (1996) report the findings of a survey among practising accountants in which they found that not only were the majority of accountants not involved in environmental management issues but a only minority believed that such environmental information was important to users of annual reports. Equally Quellette (1996) reported that traditional accounting used by firms provided inadequate information on environmental impact and costs and this resulted in ill-informed management decisions.

Equally it has been argued that ethical behaviour, corporate governance and environmental accounting are inextricably intertwined in determining the performance of a firm. Indeed these arguments are slowly becoming embedded into professional practice. Thus the ICAEW (1993) have produced guidelines which recommend that organisations publish their environmental objectives in ways which are open to the measurement of performance and give details of expenditure on specific objectives.

Exactly how such environmental information can be quantified and incorporated into traditional company accounting is a matter of some debate. Even if accounting in such a manner were to be promoted in practice then the problems of how to quantify environmental impact would become of significance. In this respect Hooks (1996) argues that the accounting profession has a responsibility to address this issue and to develop a means of accounting which establishes a balance between accounting for profit and accounting for environmental impact. She argues that this accounting would be wider than the current practises regarding disclosure, which appear to be linked to a desire to create an appropriately environmentally conscious image rather than any true concern with environmental impact. Similarly Howard (1996) concurs and argues that ethical behaviour, corporate governance and environmental accounting are inextricably intertwined in determining the performance of a firm.

There have been many claims that the quantification of social and environmental costs[1] and the inclusion of such costs into business strategies can significantly reduce operating costs by firms; indeed this was one of the main themes of the 1996 Global Environmental Management Initiative Conference. Little evidence exists that this is the case but Pava and Krausz (1996) demonstrate empirically that companies which they define as 'socially responsible' perform in financial terms at least as well as

---

1   Social and environmental tend to be treated as synonymous and interchangeable terms in corporate reporting, and this approach has been adopted in this chapter.

companies which are not socially responsible.[2] Similarly in other countries efforts are being made to provide a framework for certification of accountants who wish to be considered as environmental practitioners and auditors. For example the Canadian Institute of Chartered Accountants is heavily involved in the creation of such a national framework. Azzone, Manzini and Noci (1996) however suggest that despite the lack of any regulatory framework in this area a degree of standardisation, at least as far as reporting is concerned, is beginning to emerge at an international level. If this is the case then it can be expected to become reflected in the regulatory frameworks at national levels in due course. It can equally be considered that firms which regard themselves as successful can afford to devote more effort towards being socially responsible as they progress upwards through a form of Maslow's hierarchy.

Bailey and Soyka (1996) claim that environmental accounting provides a firm with a set of tools which can help the firm with both improving the quality of the environment and with improving business performance and hence profitability. They significantly however fail to address the problems of quantification which beset attempts to account for environmental impact suggesting, by implication, that environmental engineers and the techniques of TQM have already solved these problems. This is perhaps a reflection of the engineering background of the authors and the implicit certainty embedded within the discourse of TQM, rather than a genuine suggestion that the problems besetting the accounting community in this respect have been solved elsewhere. Milne (1996) suggests that management accounting is deficient in that it ignores the impact of the firm upon the biophysical environment. He argues that the making of decisions affecting the environment requires a multidisciplinary approach which needs the inclusion of non-accounting information as well as the development of new accounting techniques. He suggests as examples social cost – benefit analysis and non-market valuation techniques. Birkin (1996) on the other hand argues in favour of the adoption of environmental management accounting, which he defines as a set of techniques concerned with the provision and interpretation of information to aid managerial decision making and which takes into account effects upon the external environment. While both writers argue for their individual preferred techniques both again significantly fail to explain such techniques in a way which can be applied in practise by firms concerned with the effects of their actions upon the external environment. Jones (1996) suggests that any method of accounting for biodiversity should be based upon the concept of stewardship rather than ownership.

Similarly Ranganathan and Ditz (1996) state that when environmental issues are quantified they are more likely to be included in the business decision making process and can therefore help to improve the performance of firms, when measured by traditional accounting means. They recognise however that existing management accounting systems are deficient in this respect but argue that incorporating

2   It is accepted however that different definitions of socially responsible organisations exist and that different definitions lead to different evaluations of performance between those deemed responsible and others.

environmental accounting information into existing accounting information systems need not necessitate a major overhaul of such systems. Again such statements are made without any evidence and without the kind of detail needed to allow such changes to be made to the systems of other firms.

As well as a concern with environmental accounting from the point of view of the internal use of such information for decision making purposes, of equal concern is the use of environmental accounting information for external reporting purposes. In this respect it can be seen that the incorporation of environmental information into the annual reports of firms reflects the concern of the evaluators of such information for investment purposes with the wider scope of organisational activity. Such concern can be seen to be reflected in the discourse concerning environmental issues which is taking place in society at large and is reflected in the media. Equally however it can be argued that the inclusion of such information into the corporate reporting system, as manifest in the annual reports, is a reflection of the desire of firms, and their managers, to address a wider audience through their reports than merely the traditional investors in the firm, either actual or potential. This wider audience can be considered to be those members of society at large who are concerned with the environment and with environmental issues. This will include environmental pressure groups and their individual members as well as other individual members of society. At one level it can be argued that this reflects a recognition by the firm and its managers that the wider external stakeholder community has an interest in the firm and the effect of its actions upon the environment.

At another level however it can be argued that these individual members of society, whether members of environmental pressure groups or not, also may be stakeholders in the firm in other roles; for example they may well be customers, or potential customers, or suppliers or employees. As stakeholders may well have multiple roles in their interaction with an organisation it becomes impossible to separate out the reasons for an organisation desiring to increase the extent of its environmental reporting, except in terms of the creation of a semiotic for the maintenance of managerial hegemony. It is also impossible to ascertain whether or not the firm is seeking to address a different audience, or merely seeking to address differing concerns of the same traditional audience, its owners or potential investors. Nevertheless, as Jones (1996) reports, the extent of environmental reporting, in terms of the number of firms engaged in such reporting, has grown rapidly since 1990 and continues to grow. Similarly KPMG (Management Accounting, 1996) confirm this growth in environmental reporting but state that it differs considerably in terms of just what is reported. They argue that a lack of standards, coupled with an uncertainty as to whom such reporting is directed, has led to this wide variation in environmental reporting. This issue of the target audience of such reporting will be the subject of further consideration later. Gamble, Hsu, Jackson and Tollerson (1996) on the other hand argue, based upon empirical research, that environmental reporting is not increasing in coverage but that there are national differences. Beaver (1989) however has identified some changing trends in reporting and highlights a rapid growth in reporting requirements and changes in existing requirements, with less emphasis on earnings and more on soft data and a greater emphasis on disclosure. He claims that there has been a shift from an economic view of income to an informational perspective with a recognition of the social implications of an organisation's activities. Eccles (1991) concurs and states that there has been a shift from treating financial figures as the foundation of performance measurement to treating them as part of a broader range of measures.

Purdy (1983) identifies that not only is there pressure for a general review of corporate reporting but that there have been new types of accounting responding to this pressure, and he mentions among others the treatment of cash flow accounting, the distribution to different groups, and the reporting of organisational activity in terms of value added. He discerns two worrying trends however in the subordination of shareholders rights to the needs of the company and its survival, and in the tendency for this to lead to short term satisficing and risk reduction rather than to profit maximisation. This implicit assumption that profit maximisation is, or should be, the aim of a firm is a return to economic theory and it is worth remembering that Clark (1957: 218) pointed out that profit maximisation is a difficult concept leaving room for good citizenship when he stated:

> Corporate business must still consider profits, and it has an obligation to do as well by its equity investors as it reasonably can. But when economic theorists describe business as 'maximising profits' they are indulging in an impossible and unrealistic degree of precision. The further a firm's policies extend into the future, the less certain can it be just what policy will precisely 'maximise profits'. The company is more likely to be consciously concerned with reasonably assured survival as a paramount aim, and beyond this, to formulate its governing policies in terms of some such concept as 'sound business', usually contributing to healthy growth ...
>
> Where there is this margin of uncertainty as to precisely what policy would 'maximise profits', there is room for management to give the benefit of the doubt to policies that represent good economic citizenship. And it seems that an increasing number of managements are giving increasing weight to this kind of consideration.

As far as reporting is concerned Bell (1984) found by using an experimental methodology that the form of presentation does affect the confidence that decision makers have in their judgement of company performance and that quantification adds weight to their confidence, thereby demonstrating that while soft issues might be increasing in importance there is still a need for hard accounting data. Bhaskar and McNamee (1983) suggest that organisations have multiple objectives in performance evaluation and reporting and that these are fundamentally irreconcilable and so proxy goals and measures are used as surrogates, but suggest that these multiple objectives are reflected in the new information needs of users of information thereby leading to changes in the types of data collected and analytical tools used. Changing information needs and the use of surrogate measures and goals were found to be a feature of non-profit organisations by Greenberg and Nunamaker (1987: 332) who state:

> Without a doubt, the use of multiple performance measures in evaluating and controlling non-profit activities is commonplace. These multiple measures can be viewed as short-run objectives in themselves, or as surrogates for more ill-defined non-measurable goals.

Kimberley, Norling and Weiss (1983: 251) also make this point and argue that traditional measures do not necessarily even measure some aspects of performance and can certainly lead to inadequate and misleading evaluations of performance. They state that:

> Traditional perspectives on performance tend to ignore the fact that organisations also perform in other, less observable arenas. Their performance in these arenas may in some cases be more powerful shapers of future possibilities than how they measure up on traditional criteria. And, paradoxically competence in the less observable arenas may be interpreted as incompetence by those whose judgements are based solely on traditional criteria. Particularly in the case of organisations serving the interests of more than one group where power is not highly skewed and orientations diverge, the ability to develop and maintain a variety of relationships in the context of diverse and perhaps contradictory pressure is critical yet not necessarily visible to the external observer.

An examination of the external reporting of organisations does however demonstrate an increasing recognition of the need to include environmental information and an increasing number of annual reports of companies includes some information in this respect, as we will consider later in this chapter. This trend is gathering momentum as more organisations perceive the importance of providing such information to external stakeholders. One trend which is also apparent however is the tendency of companies to produce separate environmental reports. While these reports tend to contain much more detailed environmental information than is contained in the annual report the implication of this trend is that such information is required by a separate constituency of stakeholders than the information contained in the annual report. This suggests an impression therefore that environmental information is not necessary for the owners and investors in a business but is needed by other stakeholders. This suggests therefore that organisations view environmental issues as separate from the economic performance of the business rather than as integral to it. This conflicts with the findings considered above which suggest the need for the integration of environmental and economic performance within the accounting needs of a business for the sake on continuing future performance.

Disclosure in Corporate Reporting

An examination of the external reporting of organisations does however demonstrate an increasing recognition of the need to include environmental information and an increasing number of annual reports of companies include some information in this respect. This trend is gathering momentum as more organisations perceive the importance of providing such information to external stakeholders. It has been suggested however (Till and Symes, 1999) that the inclusion of such information does not demonstrate an increasing concern with the environment but rather some benefits to the company itself.[3] One trend which is also apparent however is the tendency of companies to produce separate environmental reports. In this context such reports, which will be considered later in this chapter, are generally termed environmental reports although in reality they include both reporting upon environmental impact and upon social impact. Thus the terms social accounting and environmental accounting tend to have been conflated within the practice of corporate reporting and the two terms used interchangeably for the form of performance measurement and reporting which recognises and reports upon the effects of the organisation's actions upon its external environment.

While these reports tend to contain much more detailed environmental information than is contained in the annual report the implication of this trend is that such information is required by a separate constituency of stakeholders than the information contained in the annual report. This suggests an impression therefore that environmental information is not necessary for the owners and investors in a business but is needed by other stakeholders. This therefore leads to a further suggestion that organisations view environmental issues as separate from the economic performance of the business rather than as integral to it. This conflicts with some of the arguments and findings considered above, which suggest the need for the integration of environmental and economic performance within the accounting needs of a business for the sake of continuing future performance. It does however highlight the problematic nature of environmental accounting and some of the problems associated with environmental impact measurement which have been considered.

There appears to have been a resurgence of public interest and concern about the environment in recent years and this is being reflected in corporate reporting. Adams (1992: 106–7) explains this resurgence of interest as follows:

> In Britain during the last four decades, within a market economy driven by consumer preference and purchasing capacity, greater economic leisure has provided the opportunity to both analyse and reflect on the underlying nature and direction of a demand led economic system. There is an increasing requirement for information on the social and environmental impact of corporate policy and appraisal effects. The movements for healthy eating, ethical investment and, above all environmental concern have played a big part in awakening the consumer's social awareness …. The very process by which the majority in the West have become affluent is increasingly being questioned by some of its beneficiaries. Can we go on like this? Is it sustainable? Is the whole system flawed and ultimately self destructive? These questions are being asked not just by pressure groups but also by individuals, by business, by governments and global institutions.

---

3   Till and Symes consider Australian companies where there are tax effects of environmental actions and disclosure benefit companies with increased disclosure. The cultural and legal environments differ from country to country and in the UK such benefits do not accrue. Nevertheless the lack of altruism, or concern for stakeholders, needs to be borne in mind when considering such increased environmental reporting.

These concerns have led to the general opinion that there is something different about environmental information which deserves reporting in its own right rather than being subsumed within the general corporate reporting and lost in the organisation-centric norm of corporate reporting. This opinion is based upon a recognition that:

> The environment (which is a free resource to individual businesses) is increasingly being turned into a factor that does carry costs. Primarily as a result of requirements imposed by current or probable future government regulation on pollution control, but also to some extent because of the wider concern of the public, who can affect a business's profitability by their behaviour as consumers, employees, and investors, there is a financial impact that needs to be accounted for. (Butler, Frost and Macve, 1992: 60)

These kinds of argument support the practice of corporate reporting in suggesting a general agreement that environmental accounting is distinct from traditional accounting.

The Perceived Incompatibility of Corporate Financial and Environmental Performance

The discourse of corporate performance measurement suggests that social performance measurement and reporting (including environmental reporting) is very different from traditional performance reporting, and that the use of accounting in such measurement and reporting is therefore very different. Furthermore it seems to be generally accepted that the concerns of the two forms of reporting are very different. Thus traditional corporate reporting is assumed to be for shareholders and be concerned only with the internal effects of the organisation's activities. Environmental reporting on the other hand is assumed to be for other stakeholders and to be concerned primarily, if not exclusively, with the effects of the organisation's activities on its external environment.

Moreover, by implication, the concerns of one must be at the expense of the concerns of the other as the two are assumed to be mutually exclusive. Thus the managers of an organisation must manage two conflicting dimensions of corporate performance in order to satisfy the needs of different stakeholders. Thus these two forms of accounting are presented as being radically different from each other. The differences can be summarised as follows:

- Traditional accounting is basically the conventional method of accounting which measures activities and performance from the perspective of the organisation itself without any attempt to measure and report upon externalities and the effect of the organisation's activities upon those externalities. As such this form of accounting can be considered to be principally from the perspective of the owners of the business, i.e. the shareholders, and the managers of the business. Consequently this form of accounting is referred to in this thesis as shareholder accounting or the internal accounting perspective.

- Social accounting and environmental accounting are similar in concept, although their differences will be explored later. Both of these forms of accounting recognise that the organisation exists and operates in a wider external environment and therefore affects that environment through its activities. This accounting incorporates the effects of the organisation which are external to itself and attempts to measure organisational activity from an external perspective of society at large, recognising that externalities are affected by organisational activity both in a spatial and a temporal sense.

The fact that these two forms of accounting are perceived to be different from each other also extends to an acceptance that they measure two different dimensions of performance. Moreover these two dimensions of performance are assumed to be incompatible so that good performance, when measured traditionally, cannot be achieved at the same time as good environmental performance, as measured through environmental accounting. Research however demonstrates this to be untrue and, in general terms, if a company performs well then it performs well for both these aspects of performance. Moreover this good performance is reflected in the reporting of such organisations. It is to this that we now turn.

Performance Reporting in the Annual Report

Although the annual report is produced to satisfy statutory requirements, and this requires the production of the accounting information contained in the text, it can be seen that this is only one purpose of producing the annual report. This report is actually produced for the whole audience who might read the text. One of the main parts of that audience consists of shareholders of the business, either actual or potential. For this audience the actual accounting information required for statutory purposes has some importance, but so too has the rest of the information contained in the report, and is given prominence. This other part of the report includes the social and environmental performance detail. Thus the accounting information required in order to satisfy statutory requirements has in all cases been relegated to the back of the corporate report. Moreover the font used for the annual accounts is often smaller, and certainly never larger, than the font used in the rest of the text. Equally the use of colour is prevalent throughout the rest of the text but the accounting information is presented in single colour or at most two colours. The only financial information which is highlighted is that which is deemed important to the particular audience which the authors believe themselves to be addressing.

This information is generally presented both numerically and graphically, presumably in the belief that the graphical depiction will aid communication and reinforce the message, even to the financially illiterate. Indeed graphics can be a powerful method of presenting financial information regarding progress to both the literate and the illiterate. Thus for example the information highlighted in a selection of annual reports is as follows:

Thames Water Annual Report and Accounts 1996:
* pre-tax profit;
* post-tax profit;
* earnings per ordinary share;
* dividend per ordinary share.

Asda Group plc Report and Accounts 1996:
* turnover;
* operating profit;
* profit on ordinary activities before taxation;
* earnings per share;
* dividends per ordinary share.

Cadbury Schweppes Annual Report 1993:
* sales;
* trading profit;
* earnings per ordinary share;
* net dividend per ordinary share;
* capital expenditure;
* marketing expenditure.

The financial figures highlighted in this way always compare the year being reported on with the preceding year in order to illustrate the way in which performance has improved. The graphical illustrations of these financial highlights however always compare the results for several years, thereby reinforcing this message of continual improvement. The implication of this message of continual improvement is that next year will be even better. The number of years selected for graphical illustration does however vary from one company to another. Thus while most companies select five years for comparative purposes, others select two and 11 years for different indicators in different years.

It is perhaps also significant that many annual reports are not even titled 'annual report and accounts' on the basis that the accounting part of the report is of less importance than other parts of the report. Thus, for example, Tate & Lyle, Hazlewood Foods plc, United Biscuits and Cadbury Schweppes merely entitle their production as the 'annual report' while Unilever produce two documents, one titled the 'annual review' and the other titled the 'annual accounts'.[4] Needless to say the annual review is despatched automatically while the annual accounts are despatched on request.

---

4   Similarly the Rank Group produce two documents entitled 'Directors Report and Accounts' and 'Review and Financial Summary' while Pilkington entitle their two documents 'Directors Report and Accounts' and 'Annual Review and Summary Financial Statement'.

The non-accounting part of the text makes use of both language and non-linguistic devices such as pictures, graphs and charts. Moreover the language part of the text makes use of different colours, different font sizes and different layouts, as well as including a few key accounting numbers. This part of the text is always at the beginning of the report with the accounting information relegated to the end. Over time this part of the script has gradually increased in size, largely through the inclusion of non-linguistic devices. Indeed arguably the linguistic part of this has reduced in terms of word count through the greater use of highlighted text and bullet points to reinforce the message. The image, sought by the authors to be portrayed, is that of an interesting script and consequently an interesting company – one to be involved with! Social and environmental issues are mentioned in the annual report but not in any great detail. Instead such aspects of performance tend to be detailed in a separate document, the Environmental Report, and it is to this that we now turn.

Performance Reporting in the Environmental Report

Although social and environmental issues are considered in the annual report, full details of environmental concern and performance of the organisation requires a more elaborate report. Thus the corporate report has been divided into the financial report, known as the Annual Report or the Annual Report and Accounts, and the environmental report, known as the Environmental Report.

The production of environmental reports is a recent phenomenon of corporate reporting. Even those companies which, in their annual report, mention their annual environmental report have only in fact produced a few such annual reports, even though the impression intended is of an extensive temporal sequence. Other organisation produce periodic environmental reports which tend not to be tied into the annual statutory reporting cycle sequence which gives added authenticity to such reporting. Thus, for example, B & Q in 1995 produced an environmental report titled 'How Green is My Front Door?' which is quite plainly addressed to customers of the company. Increasingly however organisations are tending to produce environmental reports alongside the traditional annual report.

It appears however not to be universally accepted that an environmental report is actually required and research has shown that a minority although increasing in number) actually produce an environmental report. This appears to differ from one industry to another. Thus for example the need for the production of an environmental report is accepted by water companies, as all of them produce such a report. Amongst other manufacturers such as food manufacturers and retailers however the production of such a report is the exception rather than the norm.

One approach taken by other companies however is the production of a short environmental statement of between one and six pages in length. For example companies such as Iceland, Northern Foods, Tate & Lyle and Unigate each produce such statements. These short environmental statements are not reports upon environmental performance but rather an outline of policy and a reinforcement of the message contained in the annual reports to the effect that these companies are environmentally conscious and responsible. Such a document seems to be concerned with image creation rather than any evaluation of, or reporting upon, performance. It is however unclear who this image creation is being addressed to as such a statement is not referred to in the annual report and is not automatically distributed to anyone but rather is available upon demand. It must be presumed therefore that the production of such a statement is a defensive measure to respond to any environmentalist who may wish to make enquiry regarding the company's environmental position.

The environmental reports which are produced range in length between approximately 20 and 60 pages but this appears to be largely determined by the choice of layout and use of non-linguistic imagery rather than the textual content of the report. Some, such as Unilever and Wessex Water, are in the same format as the annual report and are clearly meant to be part of the same reporting. Others, such as Northumbrian Water, appear to be deliberately different through the use of unnecessarily poor quality recycled paper, presumably to reinforce the message about concern for the environment being translated into action. Still others such as Severn Trent and Anglian Water are different in form from the annual report without any discernible reason for this difference.

When looking at the actual content of the environmental reports themselves, these contain both image building messages and actual reported measures of performance. It is considered however that these reported measures are not designed to enable an evaluation to take place but rather to create an impression of a rigorous scientific control and measurement of performance. This is because the measures actually selected for reporting have little meaning to anyone without the necessary detailed technical background in the area being reported upon for each specific measure. Thus when considering such environmental reports, it is not unusual to find:

- scene setting images;
- images of activity;
- graphical depiction of continuous improvement in areas such as distribution leakage (South West Water Environmental Report, 1996) and number of sewer collapses (Northumbrian Water Group's Second Environmental Performance Report, 1994/95);
- textual messages of action taken such as:

> We aim continually to reduce our impact upon the environment.
> To achieve this aim we have:
> - established a uniform methodology to identify and quantify the environmental impact of our manufacturing operations;
> - developed a database to measure the contribution our packaging makes to the waste stream;
> - identified a number of potentially controversial materials and drawn up plans for their reduction or elimination;

- worked with our operating companies to set reduction targets for these parameters and to integrate environmental measurement and targets into our management reporting structure. (Unilever Environmental Report)

We have developed an extensive environmental information system which enables us to understand the scientific aspects of our environmental performance. We recognise that for a complete business assessment we need to translate this into financial terms. We are working with accounting and educational organisations to make progress in this respect. (Severn Trent Environmental Report, 1996)

Our environmental performance throughout this year is described in detail in this Environmental Review. The following are key achievements of which we are particularly proud.
- Best ever compliance with drinking water quality standards at 98.9%[5]
- Avoided a hosepipe ban and maintained drinking water supplies to customers despite extreme summer drought and harsh winter
- Certificate of Endorsement for contribution to improvements in the quality of the River Thames
- Significant improvement in sewage effluent consent compliance, rising to 98.5%
- Best ever compliance with sewage biosolids recycling to agricultural land
- 100% compliance with sewage biosolids dispersal at sea
- Won eight environmental awards
- Achieved and exceeded policy target to improve energy efficiency by 10% by 1996, against projected levels from 1992 baseline. (Thames Water Environmental Review, 1996)

An evaluation of performance is always comparative, either temporally with previous periods or spatially with comparable organisations. The temporal evaluation is undertaken within the company using the measures which each company decides itself are the most appropriate. It is perhaps unsurprising that all the measures used by all companies show an improvement over past periods.

Thus Thames Water (1996) reports upon measures such as:

- abatement notices served;
- renewable energy generated through combined heat and power;
- fuel use;
- waste recycling.

Severn Trent (1996) reports upon the following measures:

- production of methane;
- nitrogen oxide emissions;

---

5   It is interesting to note that statutory regulation requires 100 per cent compliance and in this case a failure to conform has been represented as a success.

- biochemical oxygen discharged to rivers after treatment;
- type of fuel used;
- trees planted;
- properties flooded by sewage.

Southern Water (1995/96) reports upon such measures as:

- drinking water microbiological compliance;
- bathing water compliance;
- leisure use of reservoirs.

Anglian Water (1996) reports upon such measures as:

- number of sewage samples tested;
- classification of water quality samples;
- sewage sludge disposal;
- number of capital schemes assessed for environmental impact.

Thus each company (these are all from the same industry) is able to select measures which show social concern and environmental responsibility and of continual progress, through the selective use of measures which support this. As a consequence of the individual selection of measures to be reported upon, a comparative evaluation of performance, through a comparison of the performance with other water companies, is not possible and the temporal evaluation is all that remains. It is true however that any measure of environmental performance does not have universal acceptance as a measurement tool, and so each company must determine its own priorities for environmental performance and develop appropriate measures for reporting upon impact.

The use of titles to the reports for some of the companies is also used to help create the desired image of responsibility. Thus the following titles are used:

- Environmental Protection and Stewardship (Yorkshire Water, 1996);
- Safeguarding the Environment (North West Water, 1995);
- Enhancing the Environment (South West Water, 1996);
- Stewardship (Severn Trent, 1996);
- Conservation and the Environment (Southern Water, 1994/95, 1995/96).

Financial Performance v Environmental Performance

Although environmental performance is a separate topic in accounting and has developed its own body of literature, it can also be considered to be subsumed within the broader considerations of social performance. This is taken to be the case and that both social accounting and environmental accounting are manifestations of an attempt to account for, and report upon, the impact of an organisation upon its wider environment.[6] The discourse of corporate reporting, as manifest in corporate reports, tends to classify this external perspective as environmental reporting, as evidenced by the production of environmental reports rather than social reports.

Financial performance and environmental performance can be considered to be different dimensions of performance, each responding to different pressures from different stakeholders of the organisation. Implicit within the discourse and practice of corporate reporting is an assumption that a focus upon one must be at the expense of the other. One outcome of such an assumption is that only one of these two dimensions of performance can be adequately met, and good performance in terms of the one selected to be met necessitates the sacrificing of performance along the other dimension. The actuality is of course that neither of these two dimensions of performance is maximised,[7] and cannot be maximised because of other pressures upon corporate operational performance originating from other stakeholders of the organisation. Thus financial performance, from the point of view of shareholders, is sacrificed for the needs of other stakeholders such as employees and society at large. The extent to which environmental performance is sacrificed is however more problematical as it is unclear what exactly constitutes good environmental performance.

Adopting the view that good environmental behaviour is concerned with sustainability and with negating the effect of the activities of the organisation upon choices available for future generations does not make the position any clearer. Environmental activity normally represents a trade off between one environmental effect and another.[8] Evaluating the net effect of such activity depends upon the perspective of the person undertaking the evaluation as different weightings would be attached to each effect depending upon their respective utility to the person undertaking that evaluation. Moreover it is impractical to determine the environmental impact of any corporate activity merely by the summation of the impact upon all individuals. Thus the net environmental impact of many corporate activities is impossible to assess and evaluate. It is accepted however that the general ethical position of society at large determines that some types of performance are environmentally bad, such as

---

6 Indeed, the two are conflated into a single issue as far as corporate reporting is concerned.

7 This is recognised by the press. See for example *The Times* series of company profiles which attempts to evaluate performance along a variety of dimensions. In most of these profiles (see for example J Sainsbury, 24 August 1998) the companies score similarly along both the financial and environmental dimensions. It is of course recognised that the dimensions used in these profiles do not exactly correspond with the dimensions of the dialectic in this thesis. Thus the environmental aspect of performance is subsumed in this series within the ethical aspect of performance.

8 For example the building of a new reservoir by a water company provides not just water but also leisure facilities both in the present and in the future. At the same time however this reservoir may damage wildlife habitat for some species (albeit maybe also improving the habitat of other species) and limiting other leisure activities.

poisoning the local environment through emissions from the organisation as a result of its activities, while some are good, such as landscaping the local environment of the organisation's location. Any such assessment is however temporally determined depending upon the mores of the time; an evaluation undertaken in the nineteenth century, for example, would give a very different evaluation of environmental performance to one undertaken in the present. Similarly the activities of the present will most likely be evaluated differently in the future on the basis of the knowledge and attitudes prevailing at that time.

Given the difficulties of evaluating environmental performance it might be expected that the organisations studied would make reference to this difficulty as a means of obviating the need to report upon such environmental performance. This is not however the case and all organisations which produce environmental reports actually comment, to a greater or lesser extent, upon environmental issues surrounding the organisational performance. This reporting of environmental performance does not segregate environmental performance from social performance, which tends to be subsumed within the reporting of environmental performance, and both together are considered to be aspects of environmental performance.

It must be recognised that no measures of environmental performance exist which have gained universal acceptability, as good environmental performance is subjectively based upon the perspective of the evaluator and the mores of the temporal horizon of reporting. Consequently any messages concerning environmental performance cannot easily be made which allow a comparative evaluation to be undertaken. This is helpful to the image creation activity of the corporate reporting as the authors of the script are able to create an image which cannot be refuted through quantificatory comparative evaluation. Instead such images can be created through the use of linguistic and non-linguistic means. The non-linguistic mechanisms employed are mostly the use of pictures.

Such images are part of the creation of an impression of environmentally friendly organisations. In most cases the illustrations are only of peripheral relevance to the actual activities of the organisation. Thus the relationship of these images to the actual activities of the organisations concerned is sometimes tenuous, as far as their normal activities are concerned, but the relationship of the images to the message desired to be portrayed through the script is more direct. Comfortable and picturesque images of friendly environmental and social matters convey the image of environmental concern by the organisations and an image of an organisation taking steps to conserve, and even improve, the environment. In this respect the images are symbolic.

The actual language used in the reports to convey environmental activity is much more direct and is used to make statements of what the organisation has actually done, and moreover is going to do in the future, to protect the environment. Examples include:

> Our strategy is to support community activities in the immediate vicinity of our operations. Overseas we have recently made donations to two education charities in

Belize to mark the transfer of the majority of shares in Belize Sugar to its employees. In the Philippines, we support an important conservation project on an island in the south of the island group. Like the earlier Programme for Belize (a rainforest conservation project), it enables supporters to 'own' a parcel of the land being conserved. (Tate & Lyle Annual Report, 1995)

Kwik Save's commitment to the environment remains firm. As retailers we are well aware of our responsibilities to protect and maintain our environment and external recycling facilities available at a number of our larger stores include units for glass and bottles, paper, cans and textiles. In conjunction with Whizz – Kidz, Kwik Save participated in the Blue Peter Paperchain Appeal which resulted in over 200 tonnes of quality waste paper being collected through our stores. There are still 160 collecting skips in situ, continuing the appeal for the benefit of Whizz – Kidz and the environment. (Kwik Save Annual Report and Accounts, 1995/96)

Every part of our business is concerned with protecting and improving the environment. For many companies this is only a peripheral part of their responsibility; for us, it is a core one. Each year we publish an objective assessment of our environmental performance to highlight our 'green' credentials. Anglian Water is the largest investor in environmental improvement in the region with a ten year £4bn programme aimed at improving the quality of drinking water, bathing waters, and waste water treatment systems. (Anglian Water Annual Report, 1994)

We have continued to reduce the environmental impact of our operations and increase energy efficiency.
Water: We have increased efforts to conserve water and improve effluent treatment. McVitie's Halifax factory is recycling 70% of its water and has installed fat separators to reduce effluent pollution ...
Packaging: We have made an important contribution to industry proposals for recovering waste and continue to reduce our own use of materials.
At Ashby, McVitie's reduced cardboard use by 20% while KP cut multipack film usage by 15%. More companies in the UK and Continental Europe are using recycled materials, reducing the volume of packaging and recycling waste. (United Biscuits Annual Report, 1995)

Southern Water is an environmentally responsible company and the regulated business is committed to ensuring that domestic and industrial wastes are treated safely and effectively; this requires extreme care and environmental sensitivity. The Company's seven – point policy, published in its annual Conservation and Environmental Report makes clear its determination to minimise the impact of its activities on the environment, conserve natural resources, comply with statutory standards and ensure the health and safety of its employees. Environmental responsibility extends well beyond the Company's statutory obligations and there are numerous areas where support is offered for environmental projects. These range from creating new wildlife habitats to preserving heritage sites and practical help aimed at improving town and village environments. A good example is 'Pond Week', Southern Water's joint scheme with the British Trust for Conservation Volunteers which goes from strength to strength. The 1995 event involved more that 1,000 volunteers cleaning out or creating some 90 ponds – the UK's biggest wetlands conservation project. (Southern Water plc Annual Report, 1996)

As a major public company operating over some 8,000 square miles in the centre of England, the company is conscious of its responsibilities to the communities it serves. Much of its community affairs programme is completely altruistic. (Severn Trent plc Annual report and accounts, 1994/95)

Large mining operations across the globe are properly accompanied by environmental and social obligations. Full acceptance of these responsibilities is essential to the well being of your company. The fact that we are a welcome partner to governments and other companies in various development areas across the world bears witness to our responsible approach. (RTZ Annual Report and Accounts, 1992)

The need to demonstrate environmental concern and activity is manifest in the annual reports of all companies and seems to be an essential part of the report. Thus the image created is that of responsible behaviour and continual improvement towards a better future. Some statements are rather nebulous however, such as Severn Trent's reference to altruism. Equally some of the companies are making a virtue out of necessity by depicting their meeting of statutory obligations as environmental concern. This is particularly obvious in the cases of Southern Water, with its focus on waste treatment, and Anglian Water, with its focus on investment. Other companies have presented activities which will benefit themselves through reduced operational costs as being a concern for the environment. This applies in particular to United Biscuits whose recycling and cardboard reduction operations can clearly be seen to lead to reduced operational costs. For shareholders the effect of this activity is embedded within the reporting of increased profitability, without being separately explicit.

In the annual reports of companies however environmental reporting tends to be restricted to the creation of images of the companies being active in the area of environmental concern, supported by actions which are essentially trivial in terms of the scale of the companies' activities. In none of the reports is there any attempt at quantification of environmental performance or any reporting thereon. Several of the quotations used in illustration however make reference to separate environmental reports and a large number of companies actually do produce such reports, either annually or periodically.

Conclusions

All companies tend to make some reference to their social and environmental activities and performance in their annual report, although details are not made explicit. When such details are made explicit this tends to be through the production of a separate environmental report. Such reports contain many details of social and environmental performance but because of the voluntary nature of such reporting the details reported upon vary greatly from one organisation to another. This is to some extent inevitable as the environmental concerns of different organisations will be different as will the approaches adopted to dealing with them. This however has the disadvantage of eliminating the comparability aspect of studying such reports. What seems clear however is that an increasing number of companies recognise the importance of this aspect of performance and wish to report upon their actions in this respect. Equally such companies wish not just to report upon their activities but to manage the impression given concerning their activities. Thus the image of concern for the environment is important to companies and this is evidence of a general belief that this aspect of performance is important not just to the companies themselves but also to their investors. This is a reflection of the general belief that a concern for environmental activity and performance actually reflects in the bottom line profitability of the company, albeit possibly only in the longer term.

References

Adams, R. (1992), 'Green Reporting and the Consumer Movement', in D. Owens (ed), *Green Reporting*, London: Chapman and Hall.

Azzone, G., Manzini, R. and Noci, G. (1996), 'Evolutionary Trends in Environmental Reporting', *Business Strategy and Environment*, Vol. 5, No. 4: 219–30.

Bailey, P.E. and Soyka, P.A. (1996), 'Making Sense of Environmental Accounting', *Total Quality Environmental Management*, Vol. 5, No. 3: 1–15.

Beaver, W. (1989), *Financial Reporting: an Accounting Revolution*, Englewood Cliffs, NJ: Prentice-Hall.

Bell, J. (1984), 'The Effect of Presentation Form on Judgement Confidence in Performance Evaluation', *Journal of Business Finance and Accounting*, Vol. 11, No. 3: 327–46.

Bhaskar, K. and McNamee, P. (1983), 'Multiple Objectives in Accounting and Finance', *Journal of Business Finance and Accounting*, Vol. 10, No. 4, 595–621.

Birkin, F. (1996), 'Environmental Management Accounting', *Management Accounting*, Vol. 74, No. 2: 34–7.

Butler, D., Frost, C. and Macve, R. (1992), 'Environmental Reporting', in L.C.L. Skerratt and D.J. Tonkins (eds), *A Guide to UK Reporting Practice for Accountancy Students*, London: Wiley.

Clark, J.M. (1957), *Economic Institutions and Human Welfare*, New York: Alfred A Knopf.

Crowther, D. (2002), *A Social Critique of Corporate Reporting*, Aldershot: Ashgate.

Eccles, R.G. (1991), 'The Performance Evaluation Manifesto', *Harvard Business Review*, Vol. 69, No. 1: 131–7.

Frost, G. and Wilmhurst, T. (1996), 'Going Green ... But Not Yet', *Australian Accountant*, Vol. 66, No. 8: 36–7.

Gamble, G.O., Hsu, K., Jackson, C. and Tollerson, C.D. (1996), 'Environmental Disclosure in Annual Reports: An International Perspective', *International Journal of Accounting*, Vol. 31, No. 3: 293–331.

Greenberg, R. and Nunamaker, T. (1987), 'A Generalised Multiple Criteria Model for Control and Evaluation of Nonprofit Organisations', *Financial Accountability and Management*, Vol. 3, No. 4: 331–42.

Hooks, J. (1996), 'Degradation – The Role of Accounting', *Chartered Accountants Journal of New Zealand*, Vol. 75, No. 3: 63–4.

Howard, K. (1996), 'Should Management Accounting Turn Soft?', *Management Accounting*, Vol. 74, No. 4: 58–9.

ICAEW (1993), *Business, Accountancy and the Environment: A Policy and Research Agenda*, London: ICAEW.

Jones, B. (1996), 'Going for Green', *Management Review*, Vol. 85, No. 10: 54.

Kimberley, J., Norling, R. and Weiss, J.A. (1983), 'Pondering the Performance Puzzle: Effectiveness in Interorganisational Settings', in R.H. Hall and R.E. Quinn (eds), *Organisational Theory and Public Practice*, Beverly Hills: Sage: 249–64.

Milne, M.J. (1996), 'On Sustainability: The Environment and Management Accounting', *Management Accounting Research*, Vol. 7, No. 1: 135–61.

Pava, M.L. and Krausz, J. (1996), 'The Association between Corporate Social Responsibility and Financial Performance: The Paradox of Social Cost', *Journal of Business Ethics*, Vol. 15, No. 3: 321–57.

Purdy, D.E. (1983), 'The Enterprise Theory: An Extension', *Journal of Business Finance and Accounting*, Vol. 10, No. 4: 531–41.

Quellette, J. (1996), 'Environmental Accounting', *Chemical Reporter*, Vol. 250, No. 3: S16.

Ranagnathan, J. and Ditz, D. (1996), 'Environmental Accounting: A Tool for Better Management', *Management Accounting*, Vol. 74, No. 2: 38–40.

Schaltegger, S., Muller, K. and Hindrichsen, H. (1996), *Corporate Environmental Accounting*, Chichester: John Wiley and Sons.

Till, C.A. and Symes, C.F. (1999), 'Environmental Disclosure by Australian Mining Companies: Environmental Conscience or Commercial Reality?', *Accounting Forum*, Vol. 28, No. 3: 137–54.

Chapter 8

The Impact of Socially Responsible Investment upon Corporate Social Responsibility

Thomas Clarke and Marie de la Rama

Introduction

In recent years, interest in socially responsible investing has grown around the world. The European Commission helped launch the European Sustainable and Responsible Investment Forum (Eurosif) in 2001. Eurosif unites existing forums in the UK, France, Italy, The Netherlands, Germany, Luxembourg, and Switzerland, and aims to encourage shareholder action on Corporate Social Responsibility (CSR) policies and publish reports on socially responsible investment issues to influence public policy.

Socially responsible investment (SRI) according to the UK Social Investment Forum (2001) 'combines investors' financial objectives with their commitment to social concerns such as social justice, economic development, peace or a healthy environment'. In an influential Green Paper entitled *Promoting a European Framework for Corporate Social Responsibility* (2001: 4), the European Commission states simply: 'Corporate social responsibility is essentially a concept whereby companies decide voluntarily to contribute to a better society and a cleaner environment.'

In France AFG-ASFFI the association of professional fund managers has requested that corporate boards consider the concept of sustainable development, social responsibility and the environment. French corporate law was amended to require listed companies to disclose in their annual reports how they take the social and environmental consequences of their activities into account in May 2001.

Meanwhile in the UK the Modern Company Law Review (2000) introduced the concept of an extended Operating and Financial Review (OFR) to include environmental policies and performance, and policies and performance on community, social, ethical and reputational issues. In 2000 the UK government passed regulations requiring pension funds to disclose the extent to which social, environmental, and ethical issues are taken into account in their investment decisions.

Responding to the new legislation in 2001 the Association of British Insurers (ABI) announced that it expected companies to assess and disclose the risks and opportunities in social, environmental and ethical matters (Gregory and Pollack, 2002). As a result of these changes Sparkes (2002) calculates the total assets involved in SRI in the UK leapt from £22.7bn in 1997 to £224.5bn in 2001 (Table 8.1).

Table 8.1   Growth of SRI investment assets in the UK 1997–2001

	1997 £bn	1999 £bn	2001 £bn
Church investors	12.5	14	13
SRI unit trusts	2.2	3.1	3.5
Charities	8.0	10.0	25.0
Pension funds	0.0	25.0	80.0
Insurance companies	0.0	0.0	103.0
TOTAL	£22.7bn	£52.2bn	£224.5bn

Source: Sparkes (2002).

The first ethical investment fund, Asahi Life Socially Responsible Investment, was formed in Japan in 2001. At the end of October 2001 the Nikko Fund designed by Nikko Asset Management and Nikko Securities to serve the new interest in corporate responsibility had raised assets of US$1 billion. From small beginnings in investment funds managed by religious organisations, according to the Ethical Investment Association's (EIA, 2002) figures SRI in Australia has grown dramatically rising to A$13.9 billion in 2002, an increase of 31 per cent over the previous year while managed funds as a whole declined by 0.1 per cent (Table 8.2).

Table 8.2   Growth of SRI investment assets in Australia 2001–2002

	2001 A$m	2002 A$m
Total ethical managed funds	1,347.72	1,760.34
Total private SRI portfolios	78.52	123.72
Total religious organisations	6,283.20	6,704.50
Superannuation funds	0.0	5,000.00
Total charitable trusts	5.07	115.81
Total community finance	129.87	163.80
Total shareholder resolutions	2,623.50	0.00
TOTAL	10,467.88	13,868.12

Source: EIA (2002).

Finally in the US socially responsible investing (SRI) is becoming firmly established. According to the biennial report of the Social Investment Forum, of the overall investment through professional managers amounting to US$19.9 trillion in December 2000, over 11 per cent or $2.3 trillion dollars is invested in a socially responsible manner. The Social Investment Forum (SIF) breaks down these figures into $1.4 trillion employing screening only on social or environmental criteria; $601 billion in screening and shareholder advocacy funds; $305 billion in shareholder advocacy only funds; and $8 billion in community investment funds (Table 8.3) (http://www.socialfunds.com/news/article.cgi?sfArticleId=724).

Table 8.3   Growth of SRI investment assets in the United States 1999–2001

Socially responsible investing embraces three strategies: screening, shareholder advocacy and community investing

	1999 (\$billions)	2001 (\$billions)	% change 1999–2001
Total screening	1, 497	2,030	+36
Total shareholder advocacy	922	903	–2
Both screening and shareholder*	(265)	(601)	+127
Community investing	5.4	7.6	+41
Total	2,159	2,340	+8

*   Some social investment portfolios conduct both screening and shareholder advocacy. These assets are subtracted out of the total to avoid double counting.

Source: Social Investment Forum (2001).

As the stockmarkets of New York, London and much of Europe collapsed in 2002 and 2003 the SRI funds seemed to offer the safer haven of sustainable growth rather than the reckless gamble of massive booms followed by apparently inevitable appalling busts (Figure 8.1). Socially and environmentally responsible mutual funds in the US continued their strong performance during the first quarter of 2003, according to data released by the Social Investment Forum. For the first three months of the year, 13 of the 18 (72 per cent) forum-tracked screened mutual funds with $100 million or more in assets received top marks for performance from either or both rating agencies Morningstar and Lipper for the one- or three-year periods ended March 31, 2003. Socially responsible mutual funds continued to grow on a net basis during the first quarter of 2003 while the rest of the mutual fund industry contracted. According to Lipper, socially responsible mutual funds saw net inflows of $185.3 million during the first quarter of 2003. Over the same time, US diversified equity funds posted outflows of nearly $13.2 billion (http://www.socialinvest.org/areas/news/2003-Q1performance.htm).

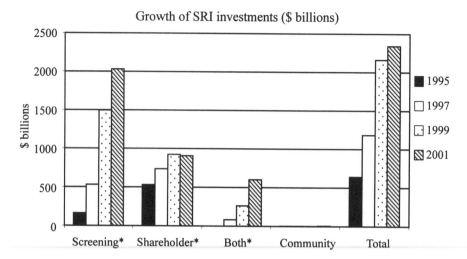

Figure 8.1   Growth of SRI investments in the United States

*   'Screening' and 'Shareholder' both include $84 billion of assets in 1997, $275 billion in
     1999, and $601 billion in portfolios that both screen and conduct shareholder advocacy.
     The calculation for the total is: total = screening + shareholder + community − both. This
     category is not applicable in 1995.

Source: Social Investment Forum (2001).

Reflecting this trend towards SRI, and in all likelihood massively compounding it,
is the advent of social and environmental reporting indices, such as the FTSE4Good
Index and the Dow Jones Sustainability Index. The existence of these indices will
attract more investors, fund managers and institutions to concentrate their minds
on the potential benefits of socially and environmentally responsible investing. In
turn this will lead more companies to both develop and to disclose their social and
environmental policies and performance. At first appearing or not in the SRI indices
may be a matter of corporate pride, but soon enough it will be a matter of access to
an important and growing part of the investment market, and a part of the market
prepared to invest for the longer term if the right corporate policies and practices are
in place. If companies are not attracted to this prospect there is always the possibility
of being compelled, for example in April 2001 the UK fund manager Morley, part
of CGNU the UK's largest insurer, announced that it would not vote for FTSE 100
managements that did not disclose comprehensive reports on environmental issues.
This assertiveness of investment institutions is set to grow, rather than diminish, and
will require positive responses rather than clever evasion.

Corporate social responsibility is no longer the purview of just a handful of
managers concerned with the social or environmental impact of their firm's operations
and increasingly has become part of overall business strategy. Widespread economic

and political concerns are at the heart of this movement, and a number of factors explain the growing interest in corporate social responsibility:

- new concerns and expectations of citizens, consumers, public authorities, and investors in times of globalisation and industrial change;
- the increasing influence of social criteria on the investment decisions of individuals and institutions, as investors or consumers;
- growing concern about environmental degradation;
- the impact of new information and communication technologies on the transparency and circulation of information on business activity.

In the financial and corporate world, corporate social responsibility is increasingly accepted as a given with a positive impact on performance. An indication of this acceptance is the proliferation of voluntary code of conduct. The majority of international businesses now would state that they take ethical issues into consideration in managing their risk, however only a minority of them methodically and regularly evaluate their performance (Committee on Public Finance, 2002).

This chapter will examine some of the investment strategies of the SRI funds, seek to demonstrate the principles and character of the developing different social and environmental investment indices, and investigate the potential impact upon corporate environmental and social reporting. But first it is relevant to review briefly the urgent context in which these developments are taking place. There is mounting evidence that corporations, industries, markets, economies and ecologies are all in serious jeopardy in the foreseeable future, if social and environmental commitments are not fully engaged.

Tomorrow's Markets

The economies of the world are on an unsustainable development path. Trends identified in *Tomorrow's Markets – Global Trends and Their Implications for Business* (2002) a joint publication of the World Resources Institute (WRI), United Nations Environment Programme (UNEP), and the World Business Council for Sustainable Development (WBCSD) illustrate the diversity, severity and complexity of the challenges society and business face to survive and discover new sources of value.

People

- Population – expanding population in developing regions will create large markets dominated by the young with questionable access to the developed world's standard of living (2.4 billion of today's total population of 6.2 billion people are children and teenagers). More than 80 per cent of the world's population live in developing countries and 85 per cent will live in developing countries by 2025.

- Wealth – global wealth is rising but the income gap grows wider threatening civil society. The world is 78 per cent poor, 11 per cent middle income and 11 per cent rich.
- Nutrition – millions of people are malnourished amidst an abundance of food, thousands die of hunger every day. In 1998, 791 million of the 826 million undernourished people lived in the developing world.
- Health – life expectancy rises, yet preventable disease continues to limit development, and epidemics threaten the viability of entire geographic regions.
- Education – primary education is widespread, but opportunities for learning elude many. 113 million children are not in school, 97 per cent of them in developing countries, and 60 per cent of them female. One in every five adults – a total of 880 million adults – is functionally illiterate. This is a dramatic improvement over 1970 when one in three was illiterate.

Innovation

- Consumption – rising consumption creates environmental risks as well as business opportunities for innovation. Consumers in high-income countries spent $15.4 trillion of the $19.3 trillion (80 per cent) of total private consumption in 1998. Purchases by consumers in low-income countries represented less than 4 per cent of all private consumption.
- Energy – escalating demand for energy propels economic development but threatens the Earth's climate and eco-system. The 1990s were the warmest decade since the 1880s, and 1998 the warmest year ever. World energy production rose 42 per cent between 1980 and 2000 and will grow 150–230 per cent by 2050.
- Emissions – pollution increases threatens society and the integrity of ecosystems. Between 50–90 per cent of the mass of industrialised country environment outflows goes directly into the atmosphere.
- Efficiency – throughput still grows even as energy efficiency and improves, adding to society's environmental footprint. But recycling is accounting for an increasing share of production, for example paper recycling into paper and fibre products has risen in the past 3 decades to about 40 per cent of total paper production worldwide.

Natural Capital

- Ecosystems – the productive capacity of the planet is in decline threatening biodiversity, clean air provision and natural global temperature balancing. Nearly 26,000 plant species, more than 1,100 mammals and 1,200 birds, 700 freshwater fish, and hundreds of reptiles and amphibians are threatened with extinction.
- Agriculture – food production is the basis of many economies but threatens the ecosystem upon which it depends, threatening fish stocks and productive agricultural output. About 30 per cent of the potential area of temperate,

subtropical, and tropical forests and about 40 per cent of temperate grasslands have been converted to agriculture.

- Water – freshwater is growing scarce amidst competing human needs, millions exist daily without fresh water. Over the past century, world water withdrawals increased almost twice as fast as population growth.

Connections

- Urbanisation – urban growth concentrates business opportunities and societal challenges while undermining the social fabric for many. By 2050 50 per cent of all people will live in urban areas as 60 million people become new urban dwellers yearly, the equivalent of adding the population of Paris, Cairo or Beijing every other month to the urban population.
- Mobility – people are more mobile, accelerating the flow of goods and knowledge and raising the demand for energy and infrastructure. Transport of people and goods is responsible for about one fifth of worldwide energy consumption.
- Communications – access to information and communication technologies enables economic opportunity, although many remain information poor. Over 50 per cent of the world's population has never used a telephone, only 7 per cent have access to a personal computer and only 4 per cent have access to the internet.
- Labour – as economies are becoming service-based, women are a becoming a growing part of the formal labour force. In developed countries the working population will shrink from approximately 750 million to 690 million between 2000 and 2025, whereas in the developing world the working population will increase 43 per cent from 3 billion to 4 billion people.

Roles and Responsibilities

- Democracy – democracy spreads, creating improved conditions for market-based economies. The number of democratic states in the world has grown from 22 democratic states out of 154 total countries in 1950, to 119 democratic states out of 192 total countries in 2000. The number of countries that have ratified the 6 major human rights conventions has grown from 10 per cent to 50 per cent of all countries between 1990 and 2001.
- Accountability – civil society is demanding greater accountability and transparency from government and business as lack of trust threatens the effective operation of market-based economies. Currently 2,091 NGOs hold consultative status at the United Nations, compared to 928 in 1991 and just 41 in 1948.
- Privatisation – private sector development is increasingly financing economic development. Foreign direct investment in developing countries has risen from about US$24 billion in 1990 to US$178 billion in 2000 as official development aid declined from about US$55 billion to US$39 billion (WRI; UNEP; WBCSD 2002).

As Sustainable Asset Management Group (SAM) (2003: 5) argues:

> Understanding the implications of these trends on business is central to sustainability investing as, despite lower interest rates, increased risk-premia have effectively erased the benefits of low costs of capital for business. The implications of environmental degradation and weakened eco-system have been starkly demonstrated by the spiralling costs of environmental catastrophes. Financial losses due to natural disasters have doubled each decade since the 1950s, and UNEP estimates that natural disasters caused by climate change could cost US$ 150 billion a year by 2012. Socio-cultural disruptions have also had severe financial implications recently: insurers had to cover US$40 billion in losses after the September 11th disaster.

This leads SAM (2003:2) to conceiving of a hypothesis of enlightened self-interest:

> Should extreme climactic events such as flooding occur, the civility of society is disrupted and hence the healthy functioning of the economy undermined. This impacts the possibility of a vigorous population of enterprises thriving which, in turn, compromises the possibility of successful investment. Sustainability investing therefore selects companies that contribute to the vibrancy of the socio-economic system and a sustainable planet.

In the past companies did not recognise or acknowledge the environmental and social effects of their operations, such as the impacts of releases to water have on river systems, or the effects of particular emissions upon human health. The United States Environmental Protection Agency (1995: 1) has developed a useful dichotomy – private versus social costs. The term environmental cost has at least two major dimensions: it can refer solely to costs that directly impact a company's bottom line (termed *private costs*) or it can also encompass the costs to individuals, society, and the environment for which a company is not directly accountable (termed *societal costs* by the EPA but typically referred to as externalities). 'Externalities generated by an organisation, although possibly ignored from an accounting perspective, are often recognised as costs by other entities' (ICAA 2003: 19). Consideration of the range of environmental costs an entity might be encouraged to consider widens the scope of accounting systems, though makes measurement more difficult (Table 8.4).

Together the trends indicated provide the context in which business must operate in future suggest the following imperatives which all corporations will face:

- maintaining a licence to operate via transparency and accountability;
- serving society;
- generating more value with less impact;
- preserving the resource base;
- doing business in a networked word.

In summary the challenge is to find means of enduring value creation without social or environmental harm.

Table 8.4   The range of environmental costs

Tier   Description

Tier 1   Conventional costs
Includes the costs of direct raw materials, utilities, labour, supplies, capital equipment and related depreciation.

Tier 2   Hidden costs
Includes the up front environmental costs, such as search costs relating to environmentally conscious suppliers, initial design costs of environmentally preferable products, regulatory costs which are often obscured in overhead costs, future decommissioning or remediation costs.

Tier 3   Contingent costs
Defined in probabilistic terms and includes fines for breaching environmental requirements, clean up costs, law suits relating to unsound products.

Tier 4   Relationship and image costs
These costs are difficult to determine and would seldom be separately identified within an accounting system. However they could be expected to have some influence on the value of some intangible assets, such as goodwill, brand-names and so forth. The sum of the costs in Tiers 1 to 4 can be referred to as *private costs* and they can directly impact on an organisation's reported profits.

Tier 5   Societal costs
These costs are often referred to as externalities and represent costs that an organisation imposes upon others as a result of their operations but which are typically ignored by the organisation. They could include environmental damage caused by the organisation for which they are not held accountable, or adverse health effects caused by organisation-generated emissions for which the organisation is not held responsible. It is difficult and sometimes controversial to put a cost on these effects and with the exception of a few organisations worldwide, most entities ignore these costs when calculating profits. However, physical measures can be developed, and related KPIs can be used to assess performance.

Socially Responsible Investment Strategies

In exploring the development and implementation of SRI strategies, it is proposed to examine the two countries with the largest SRI institutional investment funds, the United States and the United Kingdom, and thirdly to look at Australia, where the potential for SRI remains considerable.

United States

Socially responsible investment in the United States incorporate three strategies that work together to promote socially and environmentally responsible business practices, and encourage improvements in the quality of life throughout society as a result.

• *Screening*
   The practice of including or excluding publicly traded securities from investment portfolios or mutual funds based on social and and/or environmental criteria. Generally investors seek to own profitable companies that make a positive contribution to society. 'Buy lists' include enterprises with outstanding employer-employee relations, excellent environmental practices, products that are safe and useful, and operations that respect human rights around the world. Conversely they avoid investing in companies whose products and business practices are harmful.
• *Shareholder advocacy*
   The actions many socially aware investors take in their role as owners of corporate America. These efforts include entering discussions with companies on issues of concern as well as filing and voting proxy resolutions. Proxy resolutions on social issues are generally aimed at influencing corporate behaviour toward a more responsible level of corporate citizenship, steering management toward action that enhances the well-being of all the company's stakeholders, and improving social performance over time.
• *Community investing*
   Financing that generates resources and opportunities for economically disadvantaged people in urban and rural communities in the US and abroad that are underserved by traditional financial institutions. Community investors make it possible for local organisations to create jobs, provide financial services to low-income individuals, and supply capital for small businesses, affordable housing, and community services such as childcare (Social Investment Forum, 2001: 6).

With regard to the first SRI strategy of screening, in recent years tobacco is the most common screen employed by socially screened portfolio screens in the US (that is companies involved in tobacco are screened out). The environment, human rights, employment/equality, gambling, alcohol and weapons are widely used screens used by 50 per cent or more of screened portfolios (Table 8.5). Other common screens include labour relations, animal testing/rights, community investing and community relations. More specialised screens include executive compensation, birth control, and international labour standards. Over time screened portfolios have consistently broadened the screens employed, including negative screens (screening out companies for their poor environmental and social records), and positive screens (screening in companies that have excellent social and environmental records). In some cases new issues of social and environmental concern, such as international labour standards, emerge first through shareholder advocacy and as quantitative criteria are developed to apply them as portfolio screens.

Table 8.5   Screens used in screened portfolios in the United States

Broadly used screens (50 per cent or more screened portfolios use)	**Commonly used screens (30% to 49% of screened portfolios use)**	**Specialty screens (less than 30% of screened portfolios use)**
Tobacco	Labour relations	Executive compensation
Environment	Animal testing/rights	Abortion/birth control
Human rights	Community investing	International labour standards
Employment/equality	Community relations	
Gambling		
Alcohol		
Weapons		

Source: Social Investment Forum (2001).

The growth of screened portfolios is due to several factors. Socially responsible investment continues to perform financially well in relation to the market for both institutional and individual investors. Anti-tobacco sentiment goes beyond a social concern and has become a financial consideration. Investors are divesting from tobacco stocks due to concerns about public health, and admissions by the tobacco industry that it has marketed cigarettes to children and withheld evidence about the health risks of smoking. Other factors contributing to a growth of socially screened investment options are the increased participation of retirement plans and employees increasingly moving assets into them. There is also a growth of screened religious funds. Investors are now presented with a growing range of products, SRI portfolios offer investors the ability to invest in a wide range of equities and bonds, as well as domestic, international and global options. All this has given increasing prominence to SRI with increasing media coverage, with greater familiarity among the public and investment professionals (Social Investment Forum, 2001: 9–13).

The second SRI strategy of shareholder advocacy is the one that often hits the headlines and leads to set-piece confrontations between major corporates and influential members of the investment lobby. Of course though,

> shareholders have both a right and a responsibility to take an interest in the company's performance, policies, practices and impacts. The shareholder resolution process provides a formal communication channel between shareholders, management, and the board of directors, and with other shareholders, on issues of corporate governance and social responsibility. (Social Investment Forum, 2001: 14)

There were 261 shareholder resolutions introduced in US companies in 2001 of which 156 were voted on receiving on average 8.5 per cent of the votes. This may not seem impressive, but the figures are deceptive for a number of reasons. Firstly corporations are not used to any public display of dissent among their ranks, and are usually deeply concerned when issues that concern them become matters of open controversy. This leads to an increasing inclination on the part of many companies to engage in meaningful dialogue with shareholders or other stakeholders that have an issue to raise, before the issue becomes too controversial, and often this results in some form of settlement. If the matter does come before the AGM and the company wins the vote, this is often only because of the number of institutions that do not vote their proxies, and the management win be default. However where there is a genuine issue and there is a determination among a significant number of shareholders to see it resolved, often these prove pyrrhic management victories, as shareholder campaigns bring more institutions on board.

Analysts categorise shareholder resolutions into two categories: corporate governance and corporate social responsibility:

- corporate governance resolutions address issues such as confidential voting, board of director qualifications, compensation of directors and executives and board performance;
- social responsibility resolutions most often address issues such as company policies and practices on the environment, health and safety, race and gender, tobacco, sweatshops, and other human rights issues.

Illustrative of the issues addressed by shareholders actions in 2002 are compliance on labour standards, human rights, access to prescription drugs, restraint on genetically modified products, employment of people with disabilities, environmental damage and recycling (Table 8.6).

Leading the charge of the shareholders on corporate governance practices in the United States is the Council of Institutional Investors, whose members have over $1.5 trillion invested. Many of the institutions active on corporate governance are also active

Table 8.6   US shareholder actions planned for 2002 including company dialogues and final resolutions (examples)

Companies	Goal of resolution or dialogue
Disney, Federated Department Stores, Gap, Kohl's, McDonald's, Nike, Wal-Mart	Report on compliance mechanisms for vendors and subcontractors to raise labour standards.
ALCOA, Caterpillar, Chiquita, GE, Honeywell, Johnson&Johnson, Lucent Technologies	Amend international operating standards to protect human rights, labour rights, and prohibit child or forced labour.
Abbott Labs, American Home Products, Bristol Myers Squibb, Eli Lilly, Merck, Pharmacia, Schering-Plough	Create price restraints on, and greater access to, prescription drugs.
Albertson's, Anheuser-Busch, Aventis SA, Campbell Soup, Dow Chemical, Hain Celestial Group, Hershey Foods, Kroger, McDonald's, Monsanto, PepsiCo, Starbucks, Sysco, Tricon Global (Taco Bell/KFC)	Label genetically modified products, or end production or marketing of such products until health and safety tests are performed, or report on the risks of continued use of GMOs.
Philip Morris	Allocate at least 50% of philanthropic dollars to patients (and their families) suffering from lung cancer acquired from smoking the company's products.
Eastman Kodak, Whirlpool	Increase employment of persons with disabilities.
BP Amoco, Chevron, ExxonMobil, Phillips Petroleum	Report on environmental damage from drilling for oil and gas in the Arctic National Wildlife Refuge.
PepsiCo, Coca-Cola	Recycling and container recovery.
Apple, Compaq, Dell, HP, Gateway, IBM	Computer recycling.

Source: Social Investment Forum (2001).

on CSR issues, including the pension funds of New York City, the State of Connecticut and State of Minnesota, State of California, and TIAA-CREF (the Teachers Insurance and Annuity Association College Retirement Equities Fund of New York with $259 billion of assets under management one of the largest wealth management companies in the world), seeing both governance and social issues having an impact of corporate performance (Social Investment Forum, 2001: 14–19).

The final SRI strategy in the United States are assets invested locally by community development financial institutions, providing the financing which helps generate resources and opportunities for economically disadvantaged people in urban and rural communities. Community investors make it possible for local organisations to create jobs, provide financial services to low-income individuals, supply capital for small businesses, affordable housing and vital services like childcare. Though a much smaller part of the SRI world at $7.6 billion in 2001, this form of investing is growing rapidly (Social Investment Forum, 2001: 20).

United Kingdom

Demonstrating how SRI is rapidly becoming a global phenomenon, a dramatic catalyst occurred in the UK government's amendment of the Pensions Act in July 2000 to require all occupational pension funds to declare whether and how they integrate social and environmental factors into their investment decisions. While pension funds are free to declare that they do not have any intention of doing so, this new legislation resulted in a new resolve by many pension funds to engage corporations in dialogue on social and environmental issues. A survey conducted by Environmental Resources Management (ERM) in 2000 revealed that 21 of the UK's largest 25 pensions funds intended to implement socially responsible investment principles, representing nearly half of the US$1.2 trillion in UK pension fund assets, which makes up about a third of all investment in the UK stockmarket.

The ERM survey asked pension funds how they anticipated investing against SRI criteria over the next two years. Nearly 90 per cent of the funds surveyed said they would include environmental, social and ethical impacts in their investments at some level, following the new law. 'If pension funds are going to seriously engage industry on issues such as human rights, child labour, and environmental pollution, they face a steep learning curve', said ERM director Tom Wollard. 'Not only are they going to have to decide what questions to ask companies, but also what they are going to do with the answers.' Around 70 per cent of the funds surveyed said they planned to implement active engagement of companies, rather than simply boycotting specific industry sectors such as tobacco and alcohol. While most funds were undecided about the level of social investment, two said they were committed to implementing social investing principles across 100 per cent of their funds, representing at least US$180 billion in UK equities (http://www.ssocialfunds.com/news/print.cgi?sfArticleID=309).

The UK position in SRI was given a further boost when the Association of British Insurers (ABI) whose members accounted for a further 25 per cent of all

London Stockmarket investments launched new guidelines incorporating social responsibility. They called upon companies to establish formal systems to identify risks and opportunities arising from ethical and environmental issues, to disclose which of these issues are significant for business, and to describe the policies and management systems in place to address these risks (www.abi.org.uk). The ABI guidelines state: 'Public interest in corporate social responsibility has grown to the point where it seems helpful for institutional shareholders to set out basic disclosure principles, which will guide them in seeking to engage with companies in which they invest.'

However a survey of pension funds published as *JustPensions* (Coles and Green, 2002) two years after the introduction of the new legislation suggested that though the majority of pension funds had adopted SRI policies, they often did not have the capacity to implement or monitor these policies in practice. The survey consisted of 14 pension funds managing £170 billion about 20 per cent of the total value of the assets held by UK pension funds. The researchers view of SRI best practice was essentially in terms of policies and people:

- *Policies* – a *Statement of Investment Principles* that states why social, environmental and ethical issues should be considered and why this is consistent with achieving satisfactory investment returns. The exercise of *voting rights* and *public disclosure of engagement activities* backs up the principles taken in the statement. The pension fund SRI principles are consistent with the values on social responsibility of the employer the pension fund is based on, where this is compatible with the interests of the scheme.
- *People* – where investments are managed in-house someone is employed to monitor the social, environmental and ethical performance of investor companies. Where investment management is outsourced, as assessment if made of the capability of the investment managers people in monitoring this performance. Appropriate research is carried out into the social, environmental and ethical performance of companies invested in, both directly by reference to published information, and through the utilisation of research organisations. Formal training programmes are established for both trustees and investment managers on critical social, environmental and ethical issues.
- *Implementation* – the assessment of social, environmental and ethical issues is integrated into the investment process and the risk management process. For all markets the assessment is viewed as being an essential part of good corporate governance and good management. Specific measurable goals are set, and good performance is rewarded. Pension funds collaborate in the consideration of particular issues, and within legal constraints, in the exercise of voting rights.
- *Transparency* – information on how pension funds invest and assess social, environmental and ethical issues and good practice is shared with others through the pension funds website (Coles and Green, 2002).

Universities Superannuation Scheme (USS)

Good corporate governance includes the management of the company's impact on society and the environment. The business impacts of companies failing to satisfactorily address these issues can result in higher operating costs, reputational damage and subsequent loss of confidence and subsequent action by shareholders. USS considers that it is the role of the board to:

- assess strategically the impact of social, environmental and ethical matters on the long and short term value of the business;
- have social, environmental and ethical policies with clear objectives, by which the business operations should be managed;
- appoint a named board member or members to be responsible for the policies;
- set benchmark targets, where applicable, as part of the policy;
- ensure the implementation and ongoing compliance with the policies is audited; and
- be fully transparent in disclosure to enable shareholders to evaluate the decisions of the board, such disclosure being made at least once a year.

USS requires FTSE 100 companies and encourages all other companies to report and fully disclose their policies on and management of these and other relevant business issues at least once a year. USS will engage with companies, and not support companies that are unwilling positively to address these issues. (www.usshq.co.uk)

Source: http://www.usshq.co.uk

Examining how well pension funds lived up to this view of best practice the researchers found some examples of best practice in terms of statements of principles, including BP, Hermes, USS and West Midlands (the first three among the largest pension funds in the UK). The Universities Superannuation Scheme (USS) with £22 billion assets managed in 2001, had the most developed policy (Box 8.1). But even funds with good SRI principles did not have a strong policy of backing this up with the use of voting rights and publicity. Furthermore only a small number of pension funds had in-house specialists responsible for this remit, USS has a team of three Socially Responsible and Sustainable professionals. Hermes has added social responsibility to the remit of its specialist Corporate Governance team, and the Local Authority Pension Fund Forum has outsourced this activity to the Pensions Investment Research Consultants (PIRC). Very few pension funds required their investment managers to use an SRI research organisation, and there was little formal training of pension fund trustees in SRI issues.

With regard to implementation some of the leading SRI pension funds do monitor and review the SRI activity of their fund managers, but these are the exceptions and in general there is little evidence this assessment taking place in most pension funds, and no evidence of it relating to rewards. A few pension funds are actively collaborating around issues such as climate change, and some such as Strathclyde and West Midlands are publishing their investment policy on their websites and reports on engagement. The 2002 *JustPensions* survey demonstrates that a lot of the idealism and policy commitments offered by pension funds two years earlier in the UK in response the change in legislation as revealed in the survey of the UK Social Investment Forum (Mathieu 2000) of the UK's largest 500 pension funds remains to be effectively implemented. However even in the more hopeful earlier survey it was clear that different UK funds had different degrees of commitment to SRI (Figure 8.2).

Australia

Australia has great potential for development in SRI firstly because unlike the United States and United Kingdom, the Australian superannuation scheme requires the majority of employees to make compulsory contributions to their pension funds, covering 81 per cent of all employees, that has resulted in superannuation funds managing A$454.7 billion in assets. Secondly Australia has some of the finest natural assets in the world, though being the driest continent on earth, also has the most precarious ecology with drought and salinity constant threats, that might stimulate a heightened sense of environmental awareness. However though SRI increased to A$13.9 billion in 2002, this is a smaller proportion of investment than in the US or UK. Australian investors have been relatively slow to take up SRI, and the market is relatively immature. Environmental disclosure by corporates appears to be driven by regulatory needs rather than investors and analysts requirements. Presently legislation does not enforce disclosure on environmental, social or ethic considerations in investment decisions. There remains doubt whether SRI performance will be in the best interests of superannuation fund members, and some conservative views among trustees whether SRI investments might compromise their fiduciary responsibility. In the insurance sector also sustainability issues have not featured highly, and responses to the issue of environmental impairment are reactive (PwC, 2001). How fragile is the grip of SRI in Australia despite the appearance of a dramatic increase in scale and significance is illustrated by the fact that the record of shareholder resolutions related to social responsibility in 2001 was limited to one resolution introduced at the Rio Tinto AGM, where 17.3 per cent of the votes cast represented A$2.6 billion in share value. In 2002 there was not a single shareholder resolution relating to social responsibility (Table 8.2).

Yet improvement in understanding and acceptance of SRI is rapidly developing in Australia. A significant number of new SRI investment products are being developed,

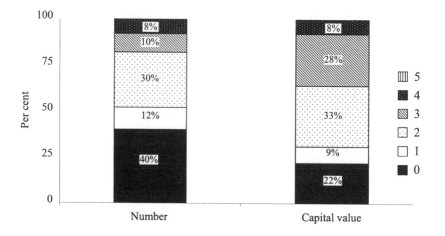

5   The Fund manager is empowered/required to take account of environmental, social and ethical considerations as long as there are no negative financial consequences.

4   The Fund manager is requested to take account of financial implications and trustees associate good environmental, social and ethical performance with positive financial implications.

3   The Fund manager is requested to take account of financial implications of environmental, social and ethical considerations.

2   The Fund will pursue a policy of engagement, but not primarily or necessarily through the fund manager.

1   The Fund delegates the decision to the discretion of the fund manager, with no guidance.

0   There is no statement saying environmental, social and ethical considerations will be taken into account.

Figure 8.2   Proportion of UK funds taking SRI concerns into account to differing degrees

Source: Mathieu (2000).

and superannuation fund Trustees are beginning to appreciate the significance of the SRI alternative. There is an increasing demand for the use of environmental screening as part of the investment process, and superannuation fund members are taking more interest in where their superannuation is invested. Banks are developing environmental risk assessment as part of their lending evaluation processes, and the insurance and re-insurance industry is developing a more comprehensive understanding of environmental risks. Biodiversity and salinity credits are being considered, as the government shows leadership on the issues of climate change, salinity and biodiversity (PwC, 2001). However Australia has some way to go in developing an optimum social and environmental reporting and disclosure regime.

Social and Environmental Investment Indices

The impact of the new Social and Environmental Investment indices will probably hasten all of the developments towards SRI so far observed by highlighting SRI issues, disseminating widely information about corporate social and environmental responsibility performance, and encouraging greater reporting and disclosure by corporations of their CSR. This will help to create a wholly new investment climate in which any sense of SRI being marginal will be divested, as SRI investing moves into the mainstream. The rest of this chapter will review the salient features of the principal SRI Indices.

Calvert

The Calvert Social Index is a broad-based benchmark for measuring the performance of large socially responsible US-based companies. The Calvin index is a product of Calvert which has been in the mutual fund business for 25 years, and manages $25 billion in assets in 27 screened and non-screened portfolios for 220,000 shareholders. It has become a leading provider of SRI mutual funds across equity, bond and money market portfolios. Calvert takes the 1,000 largest companies by market capitalisation in the US listed on the NYSE, and NASDAQ-AMEX. The social research department of Calvert then conducts an audit including product safety, environment, workplace issues, international operations and human rights, community relations and weapons contracting on each company.

The stocks that meet Calvert's social criteria make up the Calvert Social Index, and in September 2002 a total of 637 companies were in the index. Calvert reviews the index on a quarterly basis with companies reviewed for inclusion or exclusion on the basis of their social performance. Calvert states:

> We understand that few companies excel in all these areas and that a portfolio of 'perfect' companies meeting all our ideal standards does not exist. We conduct extensive research on all prospective investments, and our decisions to invest in a particular company are based on both quantitative and qualitative criteria. Calvert's social analysis is a dynamic process. We continually assess our screening analysis to ensure it reflects the evolution of traditional social issues, company best practices, public sentiment, and emerging social issues. (http://www.calvert.com)

KLD BMSI

KLD Research and Analytics Inc provides social investment research, compliance and consulting services to investment institutions, and publishes a series of SRI indices and also SOCRATES a social research database on 650 US corporations. Among the indices KLD offers are:

- *KLD BMSI*: the KLD Broad Market Social Index (BMS Index) consists of all companies in the Russell 3000 that pass KLD's screening criteria. The intent of the index is to give investors a benchmark of socially screened companies against which to compare investment results. Companies involved in alcohol, tobacco, firearms, gambling, nuclear power, and military contracting are excluded from considerations. All remaining companies are then evaluated for employee diversity, product, innovation, and community involvement among other criteria. All Russell 3000 companies passing these screens are included in the index that is reconstituted every June along with the Russell 3000.
- *KLD DSI*: the Domino 400 Social Index (DSI) was launched in 1990 as the first benchmark for equity portfolios subject to multiple screens. The DSI has outperformed the SandP 500 on a total return and on a risk-adjusted basis since its inception.
- *KLD NSI*: the Nasdaq Social Index is the first benchmark for socially and environmentally screened securities traded on the Nasdaq, reflecting the performance of approximately 180 of the largest US corporations in technology, financial, and telecommunications industries.
- *KLD LCSI*: the Large Cap Social Index (LCSI) is a socially screened subset of the Russell 1000 Index. The LCSI represents approximately 92 per cent of available US market capitalisation (http://www.kld.com).

FTSE4Good

FTSE have developed what is likely to become one of the most prominent and influential series of SRI indices, the FTSE4Good Global 100, FTSE4Good US 100, FTSE4Good Europe 50 and FTSE4Good UK 50. In each case the index tracks the performance of the largest socially responsible companies in the relevant part of the world. The companies selected for inclusion in the FTSE4Good index are screened for their performance in three main areas:

- working towards environmental sustainability;
- developing positive relationships with stakeholders;
- upholding and supporting universal human rights.

Companies with operations in the sectors of tobacco production, weapons and nuclear power are currently excluded from the FTSE4Good series. An advisory board of 13 independent experts including members with a professional background in SRI, oversees the screening process and constituent selection.

The FTSE4Good distinguishes between companies that may have a greater impact in a specific area than others:

> In evaluating corporate performance in respect to human rights, stakeholder relationships and environmental sustainability, FTSE4Good is committed to the principle that the more substantial their impacts, the higher the standards that companies should measure up to. For example, in the current FTSE4Good criteria, companies that are expected to have high environmental impacts must meet more demanding criteria for index inclusion than those with low expected impacts. In addition, some industries are 'high impact' due to the nature of their supply chains. Here too, the Committee intends to try and develop suitable criteria for measuring companies efforts.

Also the FTSE4Good plans to adopt significantly higher standards for human rights policies, systems and reporting as these become more common, particularly for those companies with the most significant investments in countries where human rights are most at risk. Because of the high profile of the FTSE4Good already there have been some controversies around the inclusion or exclusion of leading companies from the indices, and it seems inevitable that these controversies will continue if the indices are doing their job (http://www.ftse.com/indices_marketdata/FTSE4Good/index_home.jsp).

DJSI World

The other high profile SRI indices are the Dow Jones Sustainability Indexes (DJSI), established to track the performance of companies that lead the field in terms of corporate sustainability. All indices in the DJSI are assessed according to the same Corporate Sustainability Assessment and respective criteria. The DJSI consist of a global and European set of indices. The DJSI World first published in 1999 consist of a composite index and five narrower, specialised indices excluding companies that generate revenue from alcohol, tobacco, gambling, armaments and firearms or all of these industries. The European indices, the DJSI STOXX were first published in 2001, in combination with the European index provider STOXX Limited.

DJSI emphasise the commercial drivers of SRI:

> Increasingly, investors are diversifying their portfolios by investing in companies that set industry-wide best practices with regard to sustainability. Two factors drive this development. First, the concept of corporate sustainability is attractive to investors because it aims to increase long-term shareholder value. Since corporate sustainability performance can now be financially quantified, they now have an investable corporate sustainability concept. Second, sustainability leaders are increasingly expected to show superior performance and favourable risk/return profiles. A growing number of investors is convinced that sustainability is a catalyst for enlightened and disciplined management, and thus a crucial success factor. (http://www.sustainability-index.com)

ESI Global

The Ethibel Sustainability Index (ESI) set of indices were first published in 2002, developed by Ethibel a leading European screening company in the field of SRI based in Brussels. Ethibel contracted Standard and Poor's to maintain and calculate the indexes. There are four regional indices: ESI Global, ESI Americas, ESI Europe, and ESI Asia Pacific. The ESI applies the same criteria and gives equal weights to company scores on social, environmental and economic criteria, regardless of the type of company or the sector. It is recognised that different sectors and regions are facing different key CSR issues and that the concept of CSR is developing over time, and the methodology reflects these changes.

> The distinctive characteristics of Ethibel's methodology originate from the integration of the two strongest concepts of CSR: sustainable development and stakeholder involvement. Sustainable development focuses on the content of the research. All the aspects of the social responsibility of a company, including its social, environmental and economic-ethical policy, are taken into account: the people-planet-profit approach. A specific aspect of the Ethibel research process is the permanent dialogue with all the stakeholders, including the company, at every stage of the research and evaluation process. (http://www.ethibel.org)

ECP Ethical Global Return

A further series of indices are published by the Italian company E.Capital Partners with a management team drawn from the finance department of SDA Bocconi University, the Ethical Global Return covering the 300 largest capitalisation companies incorporated worldwide which pass an Ethical Screening Methodology. The index invests in all developed stockmarkets, America, Europe, Asia-Pacific, Australia. Ethical Euro Return includes the 150 largest capitalisation companies resident and incorporated in Europe which pass E.Capital's ethical screening. Ethical Global Gov. Bond, includes multi-currency government bonds that have passed the ethical screening test. Finally the Ethical Euro Corp. Bond includes euro-denominated corporate bonds that have passed the ethical screening test. While many SRI funds in the United States exclude government bonds because of the exposure to investment in the Department of Defense, ECP's government bond indexes do not implement such exclusions. E. Capital Partners Analyst Oliviero Gobbi explained:

> We do not want to exclude all governments who support defense because we would have to exclude all government bonds. We prefer a positive approach that considers several points of view because we think it is possible to invest in government bonds in a socially responsible way. We analyze countries under several points of view: respect of human rights; compliance with international treaties; compliance with I.L.O. regulations; respect for the environment; and we exclude countries who have the death penalty … We have excluded all the governments deeply involved in military activities

from our benchmarks. We exclude, for example, the USA, because of the death penalty. (http://www.sri-adviser.com/article.mpl?sfArticleId=989 www.e-cpartners.com)

Conclusions: Impact Upon Corporate Environmental and Social Responsibility

This last comment by Oliviero Gobbi highlights how SRI might have had a remarkable impact in recent years, but there remains a very long way to go. It is deeply ironic that the United States the country that has the largest SRI investment institutions and financial commitment, also has one of the worst human rights records in terms of imprisonment and the death penalty, is one of the world's worst polluters per head of population, and refused to sign the Kyoto agreement on global warming. The US is a market based economy and society, and it is not entirely contradictory that among the most influential opposition to these social and environmental transgressions should be applied through the market system.

How much pressure may be realistically applied through the influence of SRI and the associated indices is still to be ascertained. And of course there will always be insistent pressures in the opposite direction, for example though the work of the World Health Organisation (which estimates that four million people die from smoking-related illnesses every year) and other agencies:

> suggest that tobacco is part of a group of sunset industries where ethical legitimacy has disappeared ... this is not a view shared by FTSE4Good. In January 2002 this index of ethical stocks was reported to be set to lift its ban on companies making tobacco, allowing them to join the listing by the end of the year. The index committee suggesting that it would admit tobacco companies if they were improving their records on issues such as public health, the environment and human rights. (Bendell and Shah 2002: 6)

A more optimistic prognosis would suggest that Socially Responsible Investment will add a huge impetus to the wide stakeholder alliance of customers, employees, managers, suppliers, communities and governments attempting to impress upon the process of value creation ethical, social and environmental concerns.

References

Bendell, J. and Shah, R. (2002), *Lifeworth 2002 Annual Review of Corporate Responsibility*, January–March.

Bennet, M. and James, P. (1998), *The Green Bottom Line: Environmental Accounting for Management – Current Practices and Future Trends*, Sheffield: Greenleaf Publishing.

Blumberg, J., Korsvold, A., and Blum, G. (1996), *Environmental Performance and Shareholder Value*, Geneva: World Business Council for Sustainable Development.

Brill, H., Brill, J.A. and Feigenbaum, C. (2000), *Investing With Your Values: Making Money and Making a Difference*, Princeton, NJ: Bloomberg Press.

Burritt, R., Hahn, T., Schaltegger, S. (2002), 'Towards a Comprehensive Framework for Environmental Management Accounting – Links Between Business Actors and Environmental Management Accounting Tools', *Australian Accounting Review*, Vol. 12, No. 2: 39–50.

Camejo, P. (2002), *The SRI Advantage: Why Socially Responsible Investing Has Outperformed Financially*, Gabriola Island, BC: New Society Publishers.

Canadian Democracy and Corporate Accountability Commission (2001), *An Overview of Issues*.

Canadian Democracy and Corporate Accountability Commission (2002), *The New Balance Sheet: Corporate Profits and Responsibility in the 21st Century*, Final Report, January.

Coles, D. and Green, D. (2002), *Justpensions: Do UK Pension Funds Invest Responsibly?*, http://www.justpensions.org.

Committee on Public Finance (2002), 'Corporate Social Responsibility and Socially Responsible Investment', Consultation Paper, Quebec: Assemblee Nationale, Secrétariat des commissions, May.

Company Law Review Steering Group (2000), *Modern Company Law For A Competitive Economy: Developing the Framework*, London: Department of Trade and Industry.

Dion, M. (1998), *Investissements Ethiques et Régie d'Entreprise, Entre la Mondialisation et la Mythologie*, Montréal: Médiaspaul, Coll. Interpellations.

Dunphy, D., Griffiths, A., and Benn, S. (2003), *Organizational Change for Corporate Sustainability*, London: Routledge.

Environmental Resources Management (2000), *ERM Survey of UK Pension Funds*, June.

Ethical Investment Association (EIA) (2002), *Socially Responsible Investment in Australia – 2002*, http://www.eia.org.au.

European Commission (2001), *Green Paper, Promoting a European Framework for Corporate Social Responsibility*, Brussels: European Commision,18 July.

Fayers, C., Cocklin, C. and Homes, D. (2000), 'Environmental Considerations in the Decisions of Australian Investment Professionals', *Journal of Environmental Assessment Policy Management*, Vol. 2, No. 2.

Feldman, S., Soyka, P., and Ameer, P. (1997), 'Does a Firm's Environmental Performance Result in a Higher Stock Price?', *Journal of Investing*, Winter: 87–97.

Global Reporting Initiative (2000), *Sustainability Reporting Guidelines on Economic, Environmental, and Social Performance*, June.

Gregory, H. and Pollack, J.G. (2002), 'Corporate Social Responsibility', *Global Counsel*, March: 41–55, http://www.practicallaw.com/global.

Guerard, J.B. (1997), 'Is there a Cost to Being Socially Responsible in Investing?', *Journal of Investing*, Summer.

Hamilton, S., Jo, H., and Statman, M. (1993), 'Doing Well While Doing Good? The Investment Performance of Socially Responsible Mutual Funds', *Financial Analysts Journal*, November–December.

Institute of Chartered Accountants in Australia (ICAA) (2003), *Environmental Management Accounting*, Melbourne: ICAA.

Kreander, N., Gray, R., Power, D., and Sinclair, C. (2000), 'Evaluating the Performance of Ethical and Non-Ethical Funds: A Matched Pair Analysis', University of Glasgow, Working Paper, July.

Kurtz, L. (1997), 'The Impact of Social Screening on Growth-oriented Investment Strategies', *The Journal of Performance Measurement*, Spring.

Mathieu, E. (2000), *Response of UK Pension Funds to the SRI Disclosure Regulation*, UK Social Investment Forum, October.

OECD (1999), *OECD Principles of Corporate Governance*, Paris: OECD.

OECD (2001), *Corporate Responsibility: Private Initiatives and Public Goals*, Paris: OECD.

PriceWaterhouseCoopers (PwC) (2001), *The Role of Australia's Financial Sector in Sustainability*, report prepared for Environment Australia.

Russo, M.V. and Fouts, P.A. (1997), 'A Resource-based Perspective on Corporate Environmental Performance and Profitability', *Academy of Management Journal*, June.

Sauer, D.A. (1997), 'The Impact of Social-responsibility Screens on Investment Performance: Evidence from the Domini 400 Social Index and Domini Equity Mutual Fund', *Review of Financial Economics*, Vol. 6, No. 2.

Social Investment Forum (1997), *Report on Responsible Investing Trends in the United States*, Washington, DC: Social Investment Forum Research Program.

Social Investment Forum Industry (2001), *2001 Report on Socially Responsible Investing Trends in the United States*, Washington, DC: Social Investment Forum Research Program.

Sparkes, R. (2002), *Socially Responsible Investment; A Global Revolution*, London: Wiley Europe.

Statman, M. (2000), 'Socially Responsible Mutual Funds', *Financial Analysts Journal*, May–June.

SustainAbility (2001), *Buried Treasure – Uncovering the Business Case for Corporate Sustainability*, UNEP/SustainAbility.

UBS Warburg (2001), *Sustainability Investment*, UBS Warburg, August.

UK Department of Trade and Industry (2001), *Business and Society: Developing Corporate Social Responsibility in the UK*, London: DTI, March.

UK Social Investment Forum (2001), http://www.uksif.org/home/welcome/content.shtml.

United States Environmental Protection Agency (EPA) (1995), *An Introduction to Environmental Accounting as a Business Management Tool: Key Concepts and Terms*, Washington, DC: EPA.

United States Environmental Protection Agency (EPA) (2000), *The Lean and Green Supply Chain: A Practical Guide for Materials and Supply Chain Managers to Reduce Costs and Improve Financial Performance*, Washington, DC: EPA.

World Resources Institute, United Nations Environment Programme, and the World Business Council for Sustainable Development (2002), *Tomorrow's Markets – Global Trends and Their Implications for Business*, Washington, DC: World Resources Institute, United Nations Environment Programme, and the World Business Council for Sustainable Development.

Chapter 9

Bioengineering and Corporate Social Responsibility

R. Seminur Topal and David Crowther

Introduction

It is a recognised feature of the modern world that natural sources are becoming restricted in terms of diversity by exploitative usages which are resulting in both extinctions and a concentration upon only certain strains of plants and animals in order to maximise yields – at least in the short term. Furthermore biotechnology[1] is a current concept and application that regards biological sources as a potential for improving new products or techniques without any seasonal, ecological or other supportable restrictions (Topal, 2000, 2002a, 2002b). Bioengineering is the basic structure of biotechnology. The use of the term implies value neutrality and the adoption of a concomitant scientific paradigm, which in itself disguises the fact of an assumed legitimacy to 'engineer' life in – supposedly for the benefit of humanity but also (coincidentally?) in the pursuit of profit.

The claims of bioengineering are that it seeks to meet various needs of humanity, including meeting of needs for increased consumption as population increases, and hastening advances in practical applications from many different disciplines, such as medicine and genetics, by combining engineering principles with our understanding of biology and applying them to living systems. We have struggled with these processes for over 35 years. Biotechnology claims to consist of 'multidisciplinary' structures, so that the European Federation Biotechnology (EFB) has defined it as:

> Biotechnology is integrated use of biochemistry, microbiology and engineering sciences in order to achieve the technological/industrial application of micro-organisms capabilities, tissue cell cultures and other parts of these. (Wissler, 2000)

With the improvements and scientific practices recently developed, it has become one of the most important technologies, so that the speciality has developed practices

---

1   Biotechnology is the collection of industrial processes that involve the use of biological systems as plants, animals, micro-organisms or any part of these living systems (Government Planning Office (DPT)), 8th Five Annual Developing Plans 'Biotechnology and Biosafety Commission' Report, Ankara (in Turkish).

and process to create many new products. To counter widespread opposition it has been argued that *Traditional Biotechnology* has a long past which coincides with human history, with the clearing of woodland and the breeding of animals for food and work. It is generally accepted that this scientific and technological topic is important for life and includes practice which incorporates many different applications as industrial disciplines. It is related to food, agriculture, health (medicine and pharmacology), textiles, chemistry, mining, energy, environment, social sciences and ethics. Biotechnological studies, which are actualising in fields concerned with variable usages of biological systems, are aimed at creating new sources and products with recombinant DNA techniques. These changes focus on a problem, which directly affects such things as new products, consumers' health, agricultural and environmental safety, with cloning genes or the creating transgenic products (Sanders et al., 1993).

The effects of bioengineering have aroused furious reaction with its proponents claiming it a universal panacea while its opponents regard it as a universal evil. This battle of opinions is both fought out in the media and through direct action on the part of protesters. We do not intend to enter this debate in this paper. Instead we intend to focus upon some of the consequences in the context of a consideration of the socially responsible behaviour of some of the corporations involved. It is our argument that corporate behaviour is more concerned with the short-term creation of profit (conveniently legitimated through the mantra of shareholder value) rather than with the enrichment of the human condition, despite their corporate claims to the contrary. So while we can accept the claim of Monsanto that 'We're excited about the potential for genetically modified food to contribute to a better environment and a sustainable plentiful and healthy food supply',[2] we would contend that they are probably more excited about the profit which these techniques can generate for the corporation over the foreseeable future. Furthermore we contend that these increased profits result in only a part from the creation of the potential for additional food production and in the main result from the expropriation of value form other stakeholders in the food production process.

Biotechnology and Biosafety Relations from the Biodiversity Perspective

With the increased prominence of the debate concerning bioengineering has come a new concept and concern – namely that of biosafety, which has arguably become the most important concept of the moment. Biosafety is the total reflection of a 'risk and safety assessment' which is inherent within the basic strategies of bioengineering. This describes the determination of the possible negative effects, destroying the possible risks or minimising the associated hazards of the problem by continual use of modern biotechnological techniques, practices and products on human health and biodiversity. The basic practices of bioengineering in biotechnology involve a lot of disciplines.

---

2   For this and other claims see http://www.monsanto.co.uk.

These disciplines combine cellular and molecular processes and practices of control. These changes include advancement in the science of public health, changes in how consumers obtain and prepare food, and increased international trade especially in food and harvested products. These improvements, which are apparent in both industrialised and developing nations, are creating enhanced market incentives for producers to improve food safety and enhanced political incentives for public intervention in food markets (Topal, 2002c). Frequently, partnerships between the public and private sectors are needed to respond to incentives for improved consumer safety. At least the public sector has to define the possible negative effects of these techniques and the protection offered to human health, social structure and biodiversity. Also the potential of these require, for living organisms, a structural base, information bank and regulations, which include proceeding-monitoring-control system mechanisms.[3]

Biotechnology certainly changes the existing biodiversity by the creation (engineering) of new strains of plants (products) but we argue that, rather than increasing the extent of biodiversity this actually restricts the available natural resources, which have been used traditionally. This is both because the production methods employed do not include seasonal, ecological, and other potential varieties but also because of the deleterious effect upon other species. Biodiversity in all aspects of life is a complementary part of a big system (Ecimovic, Mulej and Mayur, 2002) and in combination form the Gaia concept of Lovelock (1979). This system includes atmosphere, oceans, water resources, rocks and soil, which are thought as non-living because as humanity we assume ourselves to be the sole significant repository of life. According to the II/15 decision of corresponding parties in FAO's 'Biodiversity Consensus Committee' it was suggested that: 'The possible agricultural biodiversity can affect the natural structure in the future'. Those natural structures which are considered as biological diversity for food and agriculture include crops, genetic resources, wild relatives and harvested wild food plants, animal genetic resources, forests, fish and aquatic life, micro-organisms, soil biota, pollinators and predators.[4]

The cooperation between international trading relations and technological developments has brought about the globalisation concept. So the 'universal market' has spread throughout the world as a new approach to the intercommunity trade platform. By the 'global market' the results of the current combined studies on biotechnology and genetic developments have become actualised within the market and a great deal of discussion has been started by people on 'hope/satisfaction/suspects' as the new dimensions of biodiversity (Barclay, 2000; Gill, 2000a; Pöpping, 2000). This global market is of course predicated on a number of assumptions, one of which is – stemming from the project of modernity – that nature is nothing more than a resource

---

3   See http://www.biodiversity.environment.gov.au/.
4   See Food Security, 'The Role of Biological Diversity in Feeding the World', http://www.fao.org./biodiversity for food and agriculture', 20 August 2001; 'The Role of Biological Diversity in Feeding the World: The Scope of Agricultural Biodiversity', http://www.fao.org/biodiversity/sci/foodsecu2.asp.

to be exploited for human gain in the pursuit of profit. An early manifestation of this in agriculture was the focus upon monoculture and the catastrophic effects of such a focus were dramatically visible in the dustbowl phenomenon of the American Mid-west during the early part of the twentieth century. In the newly engineered environment of the twenty-first century this lesson has not been learned and now – instead of such monoculture – the desirable way to earn profit is by having a single strain of a product (suitably engineered of course) grown on a global basis. Crowther, Carter and Cooper (2001) provide evidence that nothing is learned from past experience in an environment of economics and the pursuit of profit but bioengineering takes this into another dimension.

It is perhaps coincidental that the mutant strains of crops engineered for this global farming are – like all mutants – incapable of reproduction and so seeds harvested cannot be set aside for future planting. Instead a new stock must be purchased afresh each year, enhancing the profits of the bioengineering companies through a redistribution of the profit in their favour. As an oligopolistic industry there is also an element of monopolistic profit attached to these transactions. Given that the future effects of such practices are also unknown then this also demonstrates a powerful use of one of the better known practices of irresponsible behaviour, namely the separation of risk from rewards along a temporal dimension. By this we mean that profits are transferred into the present while the risk, and concomitant costs, are transferred forwards into an unknowable future when the perpetrators of this trick may not be available to be called to account.

The Importance of Biodiversity

Micro-organisms, soil animals, pollen carriers, rodents, etc. and similar living organisms are the basic functions of the agricultural ecosystem. Mostly pesticides and other chemicals are used unconsciously by farmers and their use causes changes on natural biodiversity including micro-organisms (Gill, 2000b; Topal, 2002c). If we are thinking of humans, animals, and micro-organisms with their changes and relations from the genetic, species and ecosystem viewpoints then food production and safety problems become more important from the point of view of agricultural biodiversity. We need to conserve and sustain in use biological diversity, and therefore:

- agricultural diversity should provide enough food and safety for basic needs of human beings;
- the sustainability of components of the ecosystem and the managing of agricultural diversity should be established;
- the agricultural system is related with both cereals and animal potential and the similarities between international food and agricultural procedures (Fresco, 2000).

From the point of diversity the efficiency of widely diverse agricultural species must be protected. The management of priority areas of agricultural diversity is important for the protection of the complete system. The protection of diversity with gene banks or production materials and breeding stations is more important than farming in industrial agricultural systems (Topal, 2002c). Biodiversity, and its agricultural, social, ecological, ethical, medicinal and legal reflections, includes multidimensional discussion and new dimensions of agricultural diversity have gained popularity in recent years. The current dimensions of agricultural biodiversity practices are seen in widespread applications in developed countries at both farming and marketing levels, but also at the consumption level in underdeveloped and Third World countries. The unknown nature of the risk involved and the unusual methods of transmission are highly alarming to many consumers. On the other hand it is important for the sustainability of agricultural production from the side of local varieties. According to the United Nations Millennium Declaration 4.2 from Agenda 21, enabling national and international environments is critical to the potential for achieving sustainable development. National efforts to pursue sustainable development should be supported by an enabling international environment. The international community must lend its full support to national endeavours (Çavdar et al., 2002). Science can provide the basis for understanding and assessing risks, but it cannot always provide answers regarding the degree of certainty that reassures consumers (Unnevehr and Roberts, 2002).

The Usage Areas and Importance of Biodiversity Products in Food and Agriculture

Agricultural biodiversity is a large topic, which includes all related components of food and agriculture. If we think agriculture and ecosystem functions together, from the aspect of sustainability, then animals, plants and micro-organisms have a key function to play at the level of the maintenance of species and diversity within the genetic – application – ecosystem. According to this structural process, it needs the establishment of a 'production/safety' relationship. Controls over this work, now less restrictive than in the past, have been established recently. Genetic resources for food and agriculture are given below:

- genetic resources of plants including forests, pasture, grazing area;
- genetic resources of animals including fishes and other water products;
- microbial genetic resources (bacteria, yeasts, moulds and mushrooms, soil alives, rodents and pollen carriers etc.).

The role of biodiversity in agro-ecosystems and production systems is very important from the perspective of planned agricultural diversity. These are basic units of agriculture, production and selection. All of them have been cultivated/protected and domesticated genus and species are described as 'planned agricultural diversity'.

Biodiversity is important for species and genetics and it is advised, by modern biotechnologists, to widely use these sources as a source of advantage (Topal, 2002c). In this environment the temporal displacement of profit and risk is not responsible behaviour and what is actually needed is more research into the effects of current practice. A semiotic of responsible behaviour (see Crowther, 2002) through corporate websites, even coupled with donations to various charitable causes, will not suffice.

Important Species for Food and Agriculture

The components of agricultural biodiversity have ecological support and they can be divided into two subcategories as *connected agricultural biodiversity*:

1. functional biodiversity:
    * functional biodiversity which must be supported with some organisms (symbiotic soil bacteria, other micro-organisms, worms, termites etc. and a combined usage of these);
    * 'natural combatants' which are restricted and controlled with GM against illnesses and harmful life (insects, plant parasites and other organisms);
    * 'pollen and breed carriers' (bees, insects, birds, bats, etc.);
2. biodiversity that has ecologic advantage in large scale application.

In large-scale applications, biodiversity has very important effects on living conditions. The most important having functions as given below, are those that can be considered as harmless on agricultural biodiversity:

* quality control and improvements of water domain, clarification, natural atmospheric water cycle, protection and management of discharges units, prevention and management of floods/erosions/water-soil, climatic organisation, natural carbon balances, habitat, protection of natural life etc.;
* having non-biological effect functions (technological, industrial practices and improvements) which harm the above summarised coverage.

Bioengineering resources are concerned with and affect many sectors and disciplines. Modern biotechnology is at a point that – especially when considering transgenic plants – is harmful for the traditional agricultural economies (Pimentel et al., 1997). Conversely, the medicinal applications of modern biotechnology are very precious and cannot be measured solely in economic value. The second product group, which goes through the national borders of many different countries, is transgenic animals. Again transgenic micro-organisms are important as *cellular plants* and an important war vehicle against environment (Anon, 2000a).

The Traditional – Regional – Ethical Information of Agricultural Diversity

Cultural factors and associated processes and regional practices are parts of the *traditional biodiversity of agriculture*. *Socioeconomic factors*, trading, marketing practices and property law/regulations are also effective in speeding the spread of the results of biodiversity. Modern biotechnology can advance and increase the economic, agricultural and industrial productivities for developed countries. But at the same time they increase the dependence upon outside factors for underdeveloped and developing countries (Fielder, 2000), again demonstrating a redistribution of profit.

Instead of the rapid and radical solutions, stable and irreversible solutions must be found through experience gained from technological and industrial developments. So problems can be solved which erase from the global effects the potential problems and risks which arise. Many possible risks for future generations can also be controlled by this way. This is another important point from the *ethical perspective* of this subject.[5]

There is not yet enough data about defined harmful/undetermined effects on human health of genetically-modified organisms (GMOs) and products (GMPs). These applications have not yet existed for a sufficiently long period for observation of their effects to reach any firm conclusions. Accordingly GMOs and GMPs are suspected currently, as 'widening the dimensions of consumer and product risks and resultant more horrible realities'. GMO and GMPs are still discussed, with widely differing views' as to whether they are blessings, a technologic fact or an anathema (Barclay, 2000). Again however they are certainly harming insofar as they result in the loss of biological varieties, or the creation of ecological poverty by biotransformation – thereby possibly increasing risk in the future. GMPs must be examined by scientific and political questioning and judgement about the relationship of these products and biotechnological evolution is needed as soon as possible (Pöpping, 2000). In this case sharing the actual data, protecting agricultural flora and environmental structure, caring for food and consumer's health must be organised from a central net system and developed control system with experts carrying out inspection. Such results must be audited continuously according to completed and validated sensible control methods and limits, created by the national and international authorities.

The question of GMOs and GMPs and their transfer to application in agriculture without discussion is very important, because of the actual and potential future implications, which are desired to be healthy. They must be warranted and taken under assurance as having agricultural and consumer safety. These are the bases of any ethical discussion. In this case there is an ethics committee of the FAO for food and agricultural security. There is a biological organ of transfer in GMP/GMO introduction which brings anonymity in terms of the perception of the next generation. The actual legal situation for GMOs and GMPs according to the 90/220 (EC, 1990) numbered directive of EU has been described as: 'GMOs are biological objects which are created by way of copying or natural matching and transport of genetic

---

5   See Ethics in Food and Agriculture, http://www.fao.org./Ethics/ser_en.htm.

materials while copying them is not suitable'. In the same source, it is determined that 'If DNA cannot be "sliced" into smaller pieces than a single gene size, this material is not living genetically. In this case they are not covered by the 90/220 directive'. This determination is a kind of dilemma (Harland, 2000). In addition to this, *cross-contamination risks* are very important for protecting natural biodiversity. In large scale and open areas of production these results are another important factor for these reflections and also in these applications (Diamand et al., 1999).

Organisational and Rural Improvements: Current State in The World

There are many governmental organisations and non governmental organisations (NGOs) which are working with or considering this new technology and the resulting products' state and safety. Some of their opinions and advice can be summarised as below:[6]

- Environmental Protection Agency (EPA) pointed out that the protection of consumers against GMOs is important;
- American Medicine Agency (AMA) advised that GMs must be labelled and declared if they are suspect in safety terms;
- American Seed Trade Agency (ASTA) stated that what can be tolerated is a GM content of less than 1 per cent of the total ratio in local corn, cotton and oilseeds;
- Canada Crop Commission stated that there must not be any international transport of these products;
- Greenpeace protests actively against these products and highlights that European consumers reject them;
- Canadian Food and Health Union pointed out that the safety of GM soy products has to be guaranteed by the governments concerned;
- New Zealand government shares this anxiety;
- Australian Genetic Modification Advisory Commission (GMAC) mentioned that 'These products should be discussed and become widespread in a social dimension';
- In the EU there has been an increase in the 'speed' of legalisation of GMO at the beginning of 2001 and through to the new version of EU 90/220 directive, the GMO producers have to be registered and every country has to have completed their national legalisation within two years.

In addition to these, research in India and China has proved that the Bt gene transfer showed a decrease in the productivity of rice, but also an increase in resistance to worms

---

6 'Commission Proposes a New Framework Programme for Research and Innovation in Europe', *Biotech International (Bti)*, April/May 2001: 10.

and a decrease in the use of chemicals on cotton (Shiva, 2000). Many researchers shared the same hesitancy and stated their confusion about the consequences. In Spring 1997 there started action which quickly spread as the Day of Global Action against GM foods.[7] EU experts are seriously concerned about situations on labelling, precisely organising and establishing rural structure. So many regular developments have been exposed by these sensitively evaluated approaches. The directive 49/2000/EC on 10 April 2000 on the new labelling practices norm has become an obligation. There is also a directive (50/2000/EC) related to aroma and ingredients and the other components.

It is a matter of fact that the high test and analysis activities of the British government pointed as widely inconvenient the usage of these foods (Diamand et al., 1999). Some of the civic organisations have organised consciousness raising campaigns for consumers and have brought out a series of slogans saying 'ask/say/purposely buy/be a member'. They also listed 15 firms which use transgenic product as *Frenkenfoods* (OCA, 2000). Essentially, at the end of the Hamburg Declaration, plant genomes must be offered as a 'database' for creating public assurance in the longer term (Fresco, 2000). Also regard must be focused on improving control/audit mechanisms and specifications/rural structure/organisation in the entire world (Labuza, 2000). An organisation, Global Biodiversity Information Facility (GBIF), which focused on the expanding of the limited data about livelihoods on the earth, joined 32 countries and international organisations, including the European Commission, together for the establishment studies.[8]

As for the addressing of food safety on an international scale, the Codex Alimentarius Commission (CAC) has signed the 'Cartegena Consensus Protocol', for protecting and having assurance of environment and consumers, from studies of the biodiversity of living organisms at the 'Biodiversity Agreement Party's' Meeting (January 2000, Canada). Also the 'International Plant Protection Consultation and Consensus' studies are still ongoing (Anon, 2000a). OECD signed the 'Montreal Memorandum' in March 2001 and decided upon developing strategies on *improving life quality and consumers' information level*.[9]

In spite of all of these actions the USA is more tolerant on this subject. Coincidentally there are more corporations in this country which are involved in bioengineering and it is well known – or at least commonly argued – that the politics of this country are carried out in the interests of corporate donors to the political party in power at any time. Related organisations in the USA, such as the Food and Drug Administration (FDA), have claimed that these foods are safe GRAS (Safety). FDA, United States Agriculture Department (USDA), and EPA regulated the rules for GM plants. EPA pointed out that these can cause *'genetic pollution'* and object to more than *'genetic legends'*. This may cause harmful effects in the long term, which have

---

7   'GMOs: Food of the Future or Future Fiasco, EU Biomatters', *Bti*, March 2001: 8–10.

8   'Genetic Engineering under Discussion', *Austria Innovative*, special issue (*Biotechnology in Vienna – the Place to Be*): 28–30; 'Food Safety Agency for EU', *Feed International*, February 2000: 38.

9   'Responsible use of biological resources', *Bti*, April/May 2001: 8–9.

negative effects. EPA called farmers' attention to the fact that they should not use them without official permission (Charman, 1999; Pöpping, 2000).

The New Dimensions of Agricultural Diversity Through Activities and Vehicles in Recent Years

In the Offered Policy Document (1996) of the OECD a considerable amount is included, such as support for new technologies, precautions with improvements, and innovative technologies for socioeconomical strategies. Biotechnological and bioengineering research is continuing by adding new topics in research centres, institutes and universities. Especially in the European Union Fifth (1999–2002) and also Sixth (2002–06) Framework Programmes, there is included as priority 'biotechnology as a part of thematic subprogramme with related information and technologies'.[10] The relations of computation are felt in this area and choosing projects in this area is taking precedence (Busquin, 2000), such as:

*   a financial system which is open to the public for protecting social benefits;
*   the specific projects that create the 'European Added Value' and in large scale concerning all of Europe.

According to these criteria projects can generally be put in order as:

*   post-genome research;
*   nanotechnologies;
*   research, which is aimed to generate information society;
*   mega projects;
*   although national but also can effect the European policy projects.

If we concentrate on the general evaluation of EC studies comprising those which were supported relevant to risk assessment of GMO projects then 81 projects, involving over 400 teams, at a cost of €70 million have been conducted over the last 15 years.[11] These researches are reviewed by a project called 'Communication Management on Biosafety Research', and are very important especially at the patent application stage.

In contrast to these, the usage of some active biological ingredients has increased the functional quality of food against illness through the use of GM applications. Research to promote this technological development by research-industry cooperation is focused in Germany. The projects related to these, are (BEO, 2000b):

---

10 'EC-sponsored Research on Safety of GMOs', *Bti*, September 2001: 8–9.
11 'Byre and Fischler call for Political Leadership on GMOs', *EU Biomatters* in *Bti*, October 2001: 7.

- *Napus 2000* – to produce healthy foods from transgenic rapeseeds/oilseed (because of increasing antioxidant affect for having basic and new components, by transforming unsaturated fish oil to rape);
- *Coeliak* – the development of proteins of corn, millet and rye without toxin and using them in the food process (for having diabetic and therapeutic foods, which are free from prolamine genetically, for intestinally sensitive people, because of cereal protein/glutamine);
- *Richness Bio-available Carotinoide* (improving the carotinoide level genetically for having more healthy food).

While the research is ongoing into biotechnology from all over the world, many experts are concentrating upon the health and ethical dimensions and have tried to improve scientific and social insurance and protection. Developing transgenic application studies are ongoing all over the world, focusing upon the sensitive efficiency of the subject, which is preferred primarily for protecting social and scientific insurance. Also improving related specific precautions has became a priority. This is required by regulation, application and establishment rules by national or international organisations such as FDA, EC, etc. From this perspective the increased spreading of suspicions related to consumer safety and public health caused the World Trade Organisation (WTO) and Organisation for Economic Cooperation and Development (OECD) to establish some precautions and rules about free trade relations. After the 'Cartegena' and 'Seattle' Meetings in 1999, these studies have been accelerated and gained speed as taking in a 'risk management' approach (Ritchie, 2000). *Monitoring biosafety* was taken as the most important priority. For example; there are five basic topics in general of 'CEN TC 233 Standards' (December 1999) about biosafety, for Assurance Standards in Biotechnology according to the regulation for EUcountries:[12]

- research laboratories, evolution and analysing and risk standards;
- process and production related in big scale standards;
- GMOs for environmental practices standards;
- application quality control procedures and their related obligations standards;
- laboratory tools and equipment and related safety standards.

As given above, biosafety is the elimination of possible risks, increasing controls of the hazard(s) involved, or the minimisation of possible risks wherever negative effects for human health might occur and biodiversity of modern biotechnological applications, techniques and products. In other words, it is a variation of reflection of risk analysing and managing practice. There is a high degree of attention given to genetically-modified products (GMP) and organisms (GMO) for control and license,

---

12 'Safe Biotechnology 9: Values in Risk Assessment for Environmental Application of Microoganisms', The Safety in Biotechnology Working Party of the European Federation of Biotechnology, TIBTECH, 17 August, 307–11.

because of their ubiquity on the part of commercial culture and daily consumption. The relevant subject must be underpinned with the dimension of control/audit/ permission for health and environment and with specified norms/rules/organisations for GMOs and GMPs, because of these there has to be more research and control. Of course these are all governmental projects while the activities of the corporations involved tend to be concerned with engineering still more sources of profit.

At present evaluaed a lot of safety standards, practices and regulations on *Safety Precautions* have been evaluated by FDA in the USA. From this perspective FAO established 'Commission Genetic Resource Food and Agriculture (CGRFA)' and followed these events from a wide perspective. The activities and missions of this commission can be summarised as below:

* supports the secretariats of committees, with related international consensus about genetic recourses in food and agriculture, with cooperation of 'Legal Office' and related technical units;
* manages the meetings of Commission with cooperation of related units and governmental technique groups;
* determines and combines information and data which are useful for the Commission, reports periodically to the Commission about programs and activities;
* coordinates with FAO and other Commission-related organisations;
* Acts as a focus point in practice and review of decisions and obligations of commissions by related technical, legal and practice units;
* helps the related technique units supporting technical working groups of the Commission;
* cooperates with the secretariat of international organisations of Commission-related fields.

Recently, a major dimension of the medium-term plan preparation process was, in the first instance, to foster the comprehensive application of the new programming approach endorsed by FAO governing bodies, to activities of concerned technical units and associated regional teams. It was imperative to give due attention to needed cooperation across departments, in order to respond adequately to the call for a 'Strategic Framework' for enhanced multi-disciplinary approaches, known as *Priority Areas for Inter-disciplinary Action (PAIAs)*. PAIA aimed at developing the five Corporate Strategies to address its members' needs concerning the ad hoc working groups and existing inter-departmental working groups dealing with substantive areas of common interest. This structure and 16 projects produced strategic work with the evolution of these projects and practice, recognising that several also contribute to other strategies as given below (Topal, 2002c).

A. Contributing to eradication of food insecurity and rural poverty:
* the local institutions building to improve capacity for agricultural sustainable rural livelihoods;

- disaster prevention, mitigation and preparedness and post-emergency relief and rehabilitation.
B. *Promoting, developing and reinforcing policy and regulatory frameworks for food, agriculture, fisheries and forestry*:
- biosecurity for agriculture and food production;
- WTO, multi-lateral trade negotiations in agriculture, fishery, forestry;
- climate change issues in agriculture.
C. *Creating sustainable increases in the supply and availability of food and other products from the crop, livestock, fisheries and forestry sectors*:
- organic agriculture;
- food for cities;
- integrated production systems (SARD/Spec);
- biotechnology applications in agriculture, fisheries and forestry.
D. *Supporting the conservation, improvement and sustainable use of natural resources for food and agriculture*:
- integrated management of biological diversity for food and agriculture;
- strengthening capacity for integrated ecosystem management.
E. *Improving decision-making through the provision of information and assessments and foresting of knowledge management for food and agriculture*:
- definitions, norms, methodologies and quality of information;
- spatial information management and decision support tools;
- global perspective studies.
F. *Related thematic action groups of PAIAs*:
- Gender mainstreaming trends;
- ethics in food and agriculture.

These works are currently ongoing to consider biosafety risks to food, environment and consumers through the use of transgenic products and look to develop the success of their audit system at an international level. Although there are some national and international regulations and risk management researches, people rely on this process in law. In developed countries, negative reactions to practices of modern biotechnology are still large and extreme; this social selectivity will continue until they are deemed to be 'safe'. This subject is very important in the current global approach and market. Biotechnology and related knowledge/data/applications are given precedence in the EU – Sixth Framework Programme. Also 'New Technologies' is a priority in OECD approaches. No political rodeo will be permitted and there is an increasing focus on this subject, especially in the last two years, for having scientific and social safety and protection from hazards. The scientific authorities and experts on the Food Safety Agency of the EU are warning the related commissions to improve recommended decisions. This function is practised in the USA with FDA, in Europe with FAO, and related commissions in EC, OECD and subcommissions of other groups. In the application of GMP and GMO labels, declaration has become an obligation; also serious limitations in consumption have succeeded, firstly in all EU members, as a biosafety precaution. There are other obligations for consumer consciousness work which have also succeeded; such emergency precautions became very important and urgent in the planning of developing countries. At the last count there have been millions of hectares planted with transgenic plants in the USA, Argentina and Canada. All researchers and consumers must be aware of the developments from the worldwide perspective (Wissler, 2000; BEO, 2000a, 2000b; Topal, 2002c). Also in Europe, GMO and GMP producers are legally required to register under EU 90/220 directive.

Conclusions

The negative effects on human health of transgenic plants are not clearly demonstrated and the genes that are transported by modern biotechnological methods from plants, bacteria or virus are uncertain in their effect. We can identify genes in use, which have resistance against antibiotics as a pointer. So all become suspect. Because of this, possibilities like the transfer of illnesses and allergies from other species and of unexpected biochemicals as primary and secondary metabolites mean they should all be treated carefully. Transgenic diversity of natural species on ecosystem and plant sociology, have been discussed for a long period. Natural evolution and gene recourses can be destroyed for wild and local plants because of these transgenic species. These possible results are more important in countries such as Turkey,[13] which has a wide wild ecoflora. So we must be more sensitive to the need for the protection of local species. These kinds of studies must be established and monitored by a central organisation. Biosafety norms and evolutions should be developed. Actual regulations should be integrated with specially developed ones or as an adaptation for agricultural, health, industrial and social safety according to international models. Research background, educated/expert teams, good established laboratories, and research traditions are components of the completed structure and must be strengthened. Young scientists must be motivated and have benefit from expert scientists. A strong central organisation and productive working platform must be established on this area. Culture collections are available for many researchers which can also be a crossroads for their collective research. For this purpose the cultures should be collected and protected as a kind of natural value for scientific and industrial areas. It provides a cultural accumulation and a stage of developing new processes and substrata for the industrial biotechnology. So international connection must be strengthened for improving protection of agricultural ecoflora. From the wide perspective and forecast (Topal, 2002c):

- improved scientific, social responsibilities and regular systems must be aimed as in developed and well-organised countries;
- all biosafety regulations and related control/monitoring programs must be improved;

---

13   The home of one of the authors.

- regular instructions must be established and applied;
- gene banks, techno parks and communication net must be established in related fields.

From the 'human is the first' perspective; social responsibilities must be assumed. The cooperation of non-governmental organisations and media should be established. A state policy, which has regard to the consumers, having information and selection rights, must urgently be improved. Furthermore we would argue strongly that corporate socially responsible behaviour requires the involvement of the corporations which stand to benefit in this research. Socially responsible behaviour is predicated upon a sense of ethics and global citizenship which provides an imperative for this involvement. Merely leaving it to civic authorities provides yet one more example of the externalisation of costs and internalisation of profit, but in this case with the costs being passed to society at large.

References

Barclay, A. (2000), 'Genetically Modified Organisms in Food: Bane and Boon', Lab*Plus International*, September/October: 4.

BEO (2000a), 'Future-oriented Concepts', *Info Biotechnologie*, Germany: Federal Ministry of Education and Research (BMBF), Project Management Org. Biology, Energy, Environment (BEO) Berlin Office Publication.

BEO (2000b), 'Novel Foods Prevent Widespread Diseases', *Info Biotechnologie*, Germany: Federal Ministry of Education and Research (BMBF), Project Management Org. Biology, Energy, Environment (BEO) Berlin Office Publication.

Busquin, P. (2000), 'EU Biomatters; Busquin, Broad Lines and Policy', *Bio Tech International (Bti)*; November/December: 8–25.

Charman, K. (1999), '"Biotechnology will Feed the World' and other Myths', http://www.prwatch.org/prw_issues/1999-Q4/myths.html (Center for Media and Democracy home page: 1–3.

Çavdar, T., Turan, B., Yalgın, Z., Canat, S. and Gültekin, V. (2002), 'Solving Poverty and Sustainable Development', *Mülkiye*, Vol. XXVI, No. 236: 247–320 (in Turkish).

Crowther, D. (2002), *A Social Critique of Corporate Reporting*, Aldershot: Ashgate.

Crowther, D., Carter, C. and Cooper, S. (2001), 'Challenging the Predictive Ability of Accounting Techniques in Modelling Organisational Futures', *Management Decision*, Vol. 39, No. 2: 137–46.

Diamand, E., Riley, P. and Bebb, A. (1999), 'Genetically Modified Foods: Adding to the Debate', *International Biotechnology Laboratory*, August: 8–10.

Ecimovic, T., Mulej, M. and Mayur, R. (2002), *Systems Thinking and Climate Change*, Korte, Slovenia: SEM Insttitute for Climate Change.

FAO (2001d), 'Functional Statement of CGRFA', http://www.fao.org/ag/cgr.

Fielder, R. (2000), 'Ensuring High Quality PCR Testing for Genetically Modified Foods', *International Biotechnology Laboratory*, February: 6.

Fresco, L. (2000), 'Scientific and Ethical Challenges in Agriculture to Meet Human Needs', *Food, Nutrition and Agriculture Alimentation*, Vol. 27, Nos 4–13, Rome: FAO.

Gill, C. (2000a), 'Precautionary Tale Turns on Genetically-enhanced Plot', *Feed International*, July: 4–5.

Gill, C. (2000b), 'The "Worry List" or, of What – Exactly – Should we be Afraid?', *Feed International*, November: 4–5.

Harland, J. (2000), 'More than a Quality Assurance Issue: What is "GMO Free"?', *Feed International*, July: 6–8.

Labuza T.P. (2000), 'Food Safe: Transgenetic Food' (e-mail message:<tplabuza@tc. umn.edu>). From websites:
<htpp://courses.che.umn.edu/Ted Labuza/tpl.html>,
<http://fscn.che.umn.edu/TedLabuza/tpl.html>,
http//www.aes.ucdavis.edu/college/administration/organization/deans osframe.html>,
http://www.lifesciencenz.com.

Lovelock, J. (1979), *Gaia*, Oxford: Oxford University Press.

OCA (2000), 'What Can we do Today to Avoid Genetically Engineered Foods?', Organic Consumer Association/BioDemocracy Campaign, website: http://www.purefood.org; campaign@organicconsumers.org.

Pimentel, D., Wilson, C., McCullum, C., Huang, R., Dwen, P., Flack, J., Tran, Q., Saltman, T. and Cliff, B. (1997), 'Economical and Environmental Benefit of Biodiversity', *Bioscience*, Vol. 47, No. 11: 747–57.

Ritche, M. (2000), 'Abdication of Responsibility for Biosafety in the Name of Free Trade', http://www.208.141.36.73/listarchive/index.cfm?mthd=msg&ID=13082' (accessed 3 August 2000).

Sanders, E.M., Wasserman, B. and Foegeding, E.A. (1993), 'Research Needs in Biotechnology', *Food Technology*, March: 18–20.

Shiva, V. (2000), 'Genetic Engineered Vitamin A Rice: A Blind Approach to Blindness Prevention', from the network of 'BBC Speech' 14 February.

Topal, Ş. (2000), 'Food Unsafety Problems in the World and in Turkey', in *Globalisation Effects on Agriculture and Alternatives, 2002*, 'SOS Environmental Voluntary Platform' Publication, Istanbul: Ecem Printing Office (in Turkish).

Topal, Ş. (2002a) 'Globalisation and Effects on Agriculture', in *Globalisation Effects on Agriculture and Alternatives* (2002), 'SOS Environmental Voluntary Platform' Publication, Istanbul: Ecem Printing Office (in Turkish).

Topal, Ş. (2002b), 'Reflections of Globalisation on Food Unsafety Problems in the World and in Turkey – Solution Offers', *Inzynieria Srodowiska (Journal of Environmental Engineering)*, Vol. 7, No. 1: 119–39.

Topal, Ş. (2002c), 'Biodiversity from Agriculture, Food, Ecosystem Dimension: Social and Rural Echoes, 'SOS Environmental Voluntary Platform' Publication, Istanbul: Ecem Printing Office (in Turkish).

Wissler, D. (2000), German Association of Biotechnology Industries, ICC, 11th Biotechnology – 2000 Congresss Opening Ceremony Speech (3–8 September, Berlin).

Unnevehr, L. and Roberts, T. (2002), 'Food Safety Incentives in Changing World Food System', *Food Control*, Vol. 13, No. 2: 73–6.

PART 3
THE ETHICS OF CORPORATE
SOCIAL RESPONSIBILITY

Social Responsibility is Free – How Good Capitalism can Co-exist with Corporate Social Responsibility

John Peters

Introduction – The Lessons of Quality Management

Philip Crosby (Crosby, 1979) famously made the point that 'quality is free' – whatever the costs of quality assurance, they are *always* less than the cost of failure in terms of lost reputation, loss of repeat custom and rectification of faults or errors. Until corporate managers believed Crosby's mantra – indeed, until they felt it, hard, in lost market share, lost reputation, lost jobs, lost bonuses, collapsing stock prices and business failure – investment in quality remained peripheral. When the messages of quality were heard using the language of capitalism – profits, bonuses, stock prices – then quality became centre-stage. Today, quality management expenditure is not seen as an option. It is not even a differential advantage any more. If you don't have quality assured products and services, you are out of the game. If you do, you are in the game, and you can start playing it.

This chapter discusses corporate social responsibility (CSR) using some of the lessons from the quality assurance movement. It seeks to illustrate that 'nice guys finish first' (Peters, 1997) – but only if CSR is played out against a capitalist imperative, with its messages heard using the language of capital.

This chapter will go on to review some relevant literature, discuss corporate responsibility as it applies to market reward and avoiding market penalisation, and conclude with some recommendations for managers.

We've Never Had it so Good and We've Never Felt so Bad about it

Capitalism works, and works well. It is fair to say that we have, in the capitalist world, never had it so good, whether our governments subscribe politically to socialised or free-market capitalism. Things are, on the whole, good and they keep on getting better. Governments and citizens of the communist world have moved over to capitalism themselves because it works so well. It can reasonably be said to have won the battle to be the dominant ideology of the human race.

But although we have never had it so good, we have probably never felt worse about it. An increasing number of people are anxious about the environment, social order, the kind of world we are creating for future generations to inherit. We have never been so sensitised to social responsibility issues. And although we like the fruits we reap from business and government, we are increasingly concerned about how those fruits are grown.

Part of the problem is the way we are sensitised to social responsibility in our schools and organisations. Our business schools invariably run a 'business ethics' course on MBA and similar programs, but the sense is too often – interesting, but now let's get to the *real* stuff. If ethics and social responsibility are not placed in our socio-economic frame of reference they will be seen as something to be set aside when expediency beckons. But increasingly, organisations are being taken to task about expedient but irresponsible behaviour, by customers, investors and governments. The Enron corporation has become a symbol of the potential excesses of unchecked capitalism. Its spectacular failure, following the discovery of its corporate misdeeds, and the failure of its corporate auditors, the formerly lionised Arthur Andersen firm, has done more to put business ethics, corporate governance and corporate social responsibility centre stage than any amount of good-natured campaigning ever could.

The 'never had it so good but never felt so bad about it' problem is also reflected in some popular sociology and economics books which have made their way onto the best-seller lists in recent years. Naomi Klein's *No Logo* (Klein, 2001), and Eric Schlosser's *Fast Food Nation* (Schlosser, 2002), mercilessly expose some of the less appealing management practices of some of the world's most successful firms – Nike, Gap, McDonalds – and are written for and consumed by the kind of young, intelligent, socially aware people that such firms spend millions in trying to attract as customers and employees.

Being Good in a Bad World

Frankental (2001), an employee of the campaigning charity Amnesty International, classified much CSR activity as 'corporate PR', reminding readers that markets (as they are currently constructed) do not reward ethical businesses (though as Peters (1997) argued, they can under certain conditions, severely punish bad ones). Elkington (1997) argued that the problem of the failure of markets to reward good behaviour could be solved by the adoption of 'triple bottom line' audit regulations – that public corporations should need to show audited accounts on their financial, environmental and social performance, and that measures of social and environmental 'accounting' exist and are being developed which can be as rigorously applied as those for financial accounting. Frankental's rather pessimistic conclusion is that 'without a triple bottom line, corporate social responsibility cannot be reinforced by market mechanisms, which means that it simply cannot happen'.

Lantos (2001) interestingly argues that CSR has three components – ethical, altruistic and strategic; and that while every organisation must practice ethical (avoiding social harms) practices, for-profit publicly quoted businesses should *not* undertake altruistic CSR (good works at the expense of shareholders) unless these are strategically altruistic (good works which are also good for business).

This kind of argument was also put in a more extreme way in a classic paper by Carr (1968) who argued that business operates within an essentially amoral framework (capital markets) whereas society operates under more defined moral standards. That means that business, like a poker game, operates within a more isolated *realpolitik* where deception or 'bluffing' is legitimate, and that the essentially amoral excesses will only be regulated by the law. Zairi and Peters (2002) suggest that it may be left to pressure groups...to force the business community to change its management ethos'; expanding Carr's poker-game analogy, that the business 'players' themselves will not themselves change the game rules unless the environment within which the game takes place itself provokes a change of rules.

Several commentators have argued that a quest for purpose is part of an essential condition for operating. Chappell (1993) described his personal search, as a successful entrepreneur, for the 'soul of a business'. Handy (1999), pointing out that businesses 'don't have to die – a privilege denied to ordinary mortals' argued that this makes their managers 'especially responsible'. Briggs (2003) argues that if capitalism offers itself as a dominant ideology in the world, it carries an intrinsic obligation to the wider community, and if it fails to serve the wider community, it will inevitably (as Marx would argue) carry the seeds of its own destruction.

Why Social Responsibility can be Good Capitalism

In feudal society, the dominant social principle was of *noblesse oblige* – the obligation of the nobility to protect those less fortunate than themselves. In truth, many nobles failed in their obligations, seeing short term gain from maltreatment and exploitation as a more powerful temptation than the fulfilment of their *noblesse oblige* duty.

But it got them in the end. From King John and the Magna Carta at Runnymede to Marie Antoinette and the guillotine in France of 1789, to the aristocrats in the Russian Revolution, to the British in eighteenth century America – the abuse of power by the powerful proved, time and again, in the long term to be bad for the business of nobility. Philanthropy, fairness, tough-but-tender strength of will on the other hand, not only keeps the peasants off your back but also gets you a statue in the town square and a favourable mention in the history books. In the long term, it's good for business as well as feeling good to do.

Today's nobles are our great corporations. They fuel our economy with taxes. They make products people want to buy, which improve our lives. They employ millions of us, and continue to do so long after our working lives are over, via pension funds.

They endow the arts, join in the funding of community halls and swimming pools, support everything from animals in the zoo to computers for schools.

Why? Because of *noblesse oblige*. Because it keeps the peasants off their backs, and because it feels good, too. Big corporations – and we can include governments, and not-for-profits in this definition too – who don't fulfil their obligations, who are consistently bad corporate citizens – will be headed for the Magna Carta or *la guillotine*.

Also, smart corporations are in tune with the current and emergent mores of their publics. Today's consumers know pretty well what's going on. This increase in awareness is matched by an increase in good-neighbour legislation. Governments, both prospective and incumbent, are learning not turn a blind eye to bad behaviour in the neighbourhood. Emissions taxation, polluter-pays legislation, carbon tax, windfall tax on 'excess' profits from privatisation, are all on the political agenda in the Western world. In Britain the landslide 1997 and 2001 victories of the New Labour government were achieved on a 'stakeholder society' platform. Tony Blair's successful ethical capitalism message has been echoed in elections in Italy, France and Germany, meaning that many of the world's major economies espouse an ethical capitalist economic platform. German Chancellor Gerhard Schroder calls this positioning the 'new middle'; British Prime Minister Tony Blair the 'Radical Centre' (Geary, 1998); British economist Anthony Giddens the 'Third Way' (Giddens, 1998). This message translates to business as – get smart, and put your house in order, unless you want the government to do it for you.

Why Quality is Free – and Corporate Social Responsibility can be too

Crosby's famous exhortation that 'quality is free' can only be understood if a wide interpretation of the notion of cost of quality (CoQ) or cost of non-conformance (CoNC) is used. With a narrow interpretation, quality often patently is not free.

In straightforward economic terms, once the cost of preventing defects overtakes the cost of defect replacement, scrap and rework, then quality investment should cease until equilibrium is reached. But when marketing disciplines are applied to CoQ calculations, different pictures emerge, for loss becomes not just the loss of scrap goods, or the loss of direct time and cost in replacing a faulty product or service, but the loss of a repeat customer; the loss of brand reputation; the loss of potential revenue. In such a circumstance, it becomes appropriate to explore the kind of discipline suggested by Reicheld and Sasser in their 'Zero Defections' paper (1990), when they argued that the cost of replacing defecting customers, using a 'Lifetime Value of a Customer' metric, normally outweighed the cost of trying to retain them.

In a capitalist economy, we are normally able to choose between competing alternatives for product or service provision, thus being able to increase the CoQ for a poor-quality supplier by brand-switching to a potentially higher-quality supplier. Such a choice is crucial. With no alternatives, quality assurance is a cost with no real return, so investment in it will be minimised. With alternatives, quality assurance becomes a necessary investment to protect customers, reputation and prevent revenue loss.

In other words, quality is 'free' when the cost of loss (cost of non-conformance plus cost of lost future revenue) is more than the cost of loss prevention. Indeed, it becomes sensible, depending on how long-term the cost of lost future revenue is, to continue to invest in cost of loss prevention until the two halves of the equation reach a notional equilibrium.

Notoriously, in the 1960s, executives in the Ford Motor Company took a narrow economic decision about replacing the fuel tank position on the Ford Pinto, which was known to carry a high risk of explosion in an accident. They calculated that the amount of compensation paid to dead or burned victims of crashes involving the Pinto caused by successful negligence suits against the firm would be less than the cost of recall and redesign (Birsch and Fielder, 1994).

This is an important lesson of CSR in practice. From a narrow economic perspective, the Ford executives were correct. Without triple bottom-line standards imposed (as per Elkington, 1997, and Frankental, 2001, as discussed above), the 'poker game' morality as discussed by Carr (1968, see above) will come into play. Within an essentially amoral system, morality per se will not find a place.

However, applying the wider lessons of Crosby's (1979) mantra, the Ford decision looks foolish from a *capitalist* point of view, not just wrong from a moralistic one. The loss of reputation from such an incident translates through to a loss of potential customer revenue which normally far outweighs any direct losses. It is, we believe, the only way for CSR to be seen as economically sensible, therefore worth investing in, and would therefore suggest a calculation similar to that of the 'quality is free' rationale:

> If the cost of socially responsible actions is less than the cost of loss (costs of legal and other sanctions plus cost of lost reputation (cost of lost potential revenue plus cost of lost potential desirable employees)) then, depending on timescales, it is economically sensible to invest in socially responsible actions until a notional equilibrium is reached.

If We Want To, We Can

The quality revolution taught us a very valuable lesson; *if we want to – we can*. We can build cars good for 100,000 miles and more; pens that don't leak; hamburgers that taste the same the world over. We can build *brands*. We can do all that by:

- understanding consumer and customer product usage and delivering a product which matches those needs ('fitness for purpose');
- drawing detailed specifications and manufacturing carefully to them ('conformance to specification');
- understanding and managing the variables in the manufacturing process which can lead to deviation from specification ('process control');
- keeping detailed records of the process, allowing deviations to be traced and rectified ('quality audit/document control'); and

- underpinning all those actions by training for and incentivising the behaviour we want to create, and not rewarding the behaviour we want to discourage.

We found we could develop the capability to do all that if we only had the will to do it, and the focus which told us it was sensible to do it (Drew and Smith, 1995). Crucially, we only get that combination of will, focus and capability when we are rewarded in the marketplace for so doing – and/or we avoid being penalised in the marketplace.

What a powerful and profound lesson. If we want to – we can. If we want to produce fit-for-purpose goods and services – we can. If we want to, we can quality assure socially responsible behaviour. If we want to, we can quality assure good corporate neighbourliness. All we need to do is what we did for our products:

- understand how and whether we can be rewarded in the marketplace, or avoid being penalised in the marketplace (which creates the corporate will);
- figure out what we mean, for us, for our societies, by 'social responsibility';
- draw up detailed specifications;
- understand and manage the variables which cause deviation from what we want to achieve;
- document and audit the process;
- build desirable behaviour into our training programs and reward structures.

Implications for Managers

We have argued for an economically rational approach to taking socially responsible action, and have situated that argument largely outside any discussion on morality or ethics per se. If a wider loss-prevention calculation is undertaken, following the lessons of the quality assurance movement, and particularly drawing on a wide interpretation of Crosby's 'Quality is Free' mantra, it is legitimate for managers to ask – so what? What should we do with this information, and it is incumbent on those who study, research and practice CSR to provide a measure of prescriptive advice.

Therefore, we present the ten 'C's of CSR as a menu of interventions for managers:

1. *Customers.* Quality assure customer trust. Being honest with customers isn't soft-heartedness or soft-headedness. Relationship marketing tells us that if you can create a trust relationship with your customers, big profits lie ahead (Gronroos, 1992). Being dishonest is not good pragmatic business practice. Businesses do not sustain on duplicity or rip-offs. You will lose in the market long term, and are increasingly likely to also lose short term in the law courts. Audit your promises to customers – in your contracts, in your advertising, in your market positioning – and come down hard on those who break them. What we call customer orientation is good socially responsible practice.

2. *Capability.* Quality assure your capability to deliver your values. Audit your capability and competence, both individual and organisational, and create strategies to fill gaps – by training, by buying in advice and expertise, by changing the way you do things. Customers and employees alike are sensitive to value promises broken, and there is compelling evidence (Porras and Collins, 1994) that organisations who really stick to a set of values survive and prosper. Don't set yourself up for what you are incapable of delivering without a solid plan to create capability.

3. *Consumption.* Quality assure your consumption management. Murray Duffin, CEO of SGS Thomson Microelectronics in France, says that 'ecology is free … almost all our investments in environmental responsibility pay back in less than two years' (Duffin, 1997). Consuming less costs less. Think of it as 'loss prevention' – just as you would protect your organisation from thieves or fraud; protect it from wasteful use of often costly resources such as power and paper. If you want it to happen – manage it. Put someone in charge.

   Many years ago Lord Leverhulme (Lever Brothers, later Unilever) famously was reputed to have said – 'I waste half the money I spend on advertising. The trouble is, I don't know which half.' Wasting resources which could be better used to serve customers, educate workers or go into health care or pension schemes is less of a joke than it used to be. The money you make should be judiciously consumed, just like other resources.

4. *Campaigners.* Quality assure your reputation. Be future-focused. Don't be in the position of having to explain that you didn't know any better – you were just 'obeying orders'. Put your policies on the line with environmental protection groups, student lobby groups – anyone who can give them a good workover and really test their robustness. Ron Hickson of TransAlta Power in Alberta, Canada, takes his staff and policies to vocal and radical green groups to expose them to the latest thinking in challenges by the environmentally aware. Make sure you are not featured on an internet lobbyist site, or in the next *No Logo* or *Fast Food Nation* exposé.

5. *Citizenship.* Quality assure your position in your community. Show you are a good citizen. Community care is good PR. Depending on how powerful and influential you are in your community, you may be able to contribute to safer streets, after school care, local amenity funding and management, help to schools and community businesses – it will be good for your staff and good for the work environment. And that can reasonably be said to positively correlate to productivity and continuity. The author's own firm, Emerald, has its head offices in one of the most socially challenged city districts in the whole of Britain, epicentre of the 'Bradford riots' in summer 2001. Emerald corporately addresses some of the challenges of staying within and participating in our community by encouraging senior managers to join with and lend expertise to community regeneration groups, coach local schoolchildren in reading skills, and funding a local community centre. You can do likewise and encourage your staff to harness some of their creative

power towards community contribution (encouragement meaning funding, time off and resources; not just the occasional notice on the noticeboard).

6. *Core values.* Quality assure your values. Shoddiness is not tolerated in products and services, and shouldn't be tolerated in how values are lived. Shoddiness doesn't belong anywhere in a high-quality organisation. Separate what you do from who you are – what we do being the best way at the time we can think of to actualise why we are here. Porras and Collins in *Built to Last* present clear empirical evidence tracked longitudinally that companies which focus in a very disciplined way on core values outperform similar firms which do not (Porras and Collins, 1994). Make values explicit by tracing clear lines through to strategies, individual behaviours and corporate behaviours. Integrate how well people live up to value behaviours into your reward structures (see Hutt, 1994).

7. *Culture.* Quality assure diversity. In Western society, discrimination is more than a moral issue today, and even more than a legal one. Be found out behaving badly to ethnic minorities, to women, to disabled people – not only might you feel bad; you will surely end up in court; land yourself in an embarrassing and distracting damage limitation exercise; lose customers; and, in some form or another, damage the net worth of your organisation.

Managing diversity doesn't mean indulging blindly in the outer reaches of absurd political correctness, nor the adoption of mindless quota systems. In successful firms it means addressing the issue that to compete effectively for a very scarce commodity – top-notch knowledge workers – you need to be accommodating the needs of a diverse range of workers. A diverse intellectual gene pool of knowledge workers will bring a richer and more lasting position than a monocultural one. In service firms especially it means that the people you are recruiting to run your front-line customer contacts are likely to encompass a full range of diversity issues, from women with children working part-time to immigrants to unskilled young people. And these are the people that touch your customers; the people who say far more about your organisation than all your policy statements and all your executive think-tanks and all your advertising; the people who actualise what your organisation is. They need a strategy, and quite often an education too.

8. *Compassion.* Quality assure your suppliers. The area of supplier management is another example of what Charles Handy describes as 'upside-down thinking'. Hard-headed thinking says that you should screw your suppliers to the wall, put every contract out to lowest price tender, keep them on their toes by shopping around a lot, and fore them if they slip up. That way you maximise your profits and your shareholder value.

But the socially responsible firm may act differently, and not for soft-headed reasons. Strategic partnership was a phrase coined to describe some of the strategies of Japanese firms like Toyota and Sony, who sometimes behaved in an odd way with suppliers. They supported them, worked with them, sometimes invested in them, shared problems with them. Strategic partnering has become well-used in the world's best firms. It's a perfect example of good capitalism being good social responsibility. You don't put people out of business. You share your good fortune. You help others give you good service. You create wealth.

It is interesting to look at the British shipbuilding firm Swan Hunter from both a social responsibility and strategic partnership perspective. After many years acting as a supplier to the British Navy, Swan Hunter closed down in the early 1990s with the loss of thousands of jobs, marking the demise of the last mainstream shipbuilder in the north of England, traditional home of British shipbuilding, because they could not *at the time* produce lowest-price tenders for naval contracts. Toyota, GE or Microsoft probably wouldn't have dumped their suppliers under such circumstances quite so unceremoniously.

Governments and not-for-profits can be socially responsible too.

9. *Compliance.* Quality assure your conformance to regulations and social norms. You would not like it if your staff members thought it was okay to steal wallets from around the office. Or drive too fast where your kids went to school. Or dumped toxic waste in your garden. So you had better just review the behavioural messages you send to them, about what is and isn't right.

The surest way to assure compliance with both spirit and letter of the law is to be transparent. Get rid, as a policy, of confidential memos about anything to do with safety or pollution. Post the minutes of your meetings on environmental management and safety on the Internet, in the public domain. You send the wrong message by evading environmental controls and safety regulations. Get rid of double standards in your business – you'll be found out and you'll look stupid and immoral; you won't be able to get and keep the right kind of staff or the right kind of customers if you are not the right kind of business.

10. *Continuity.* Quality assure your profit stream. Keep your eye on the ball. Stay in business; stay successful. If you haven't got it, you won't be able to give it away. Margaret Thatcher once famously misinterpreted the Good Samaritan story from the New Testament as a defence of capitalism; the Samaritan was only able to help because he had some money.

We don't live so that we can breathe air. We need to breathe air so we can carry on our lives. Profits aren't the reason most of us are in business – we work so we can have fun, so we can travel to interesting places, so we can do good for others, and so we can acquire things which give us self-worth and security. But just as without air we would die, without profits a business will die. Don't forget to keep breathing.

You are an employer, and that puts you in a responsible position in giving or withdrawing work. Work defines most people's lives. Treat the power with respect and don't fail in your business.

Points for Further Research

This chapter has made a number of assertions which, follow a similar line to Philip Crosby's exhortation to invest and then invest some more in quality improvement, because 'quality is free'. Much of the evidence in support of CSR to date is anecdotal and case-based (see for instance Bollier, 1997; Zairi and Peters, 2002) with neither solid empirical or theoretical model underpinnings.

The author is not an economist, and the tentative modelling of cost of quality/cost of non-conformance and, similarly, cost or socially responsible action, and application of potential revenue and reputation loss, all could well be tested by someone with a deeper grasp of economic modelling than I have.

We would encourage further research on both the validity of social responsibility investment by corporations, and also on appropriate interventions (such as the ten 'C's above) and their management in the future.

Conclusion

Good capitalism and social responsibility are not from different universes. If you are a successful business, the chances are that you are being a good corporate citizen already, and your challenges are to address some of the issues above, add some more to the list, and continue to do what you are doing. Just as people describe total quality as a journey, rather than a destination, so too is socially responsible business behaviour. Like the criteria for quality in an organisation, it needs re-addressing and re-defining constantly. In just the same way as quality, continuous improvement is the key issue.

CSR will not sustain unless it has a capitalist imperative – unless it is shown to make good business sense. Capitalism is amoral – it is a system with no owner, no regulatory body, not much, given its increasingly transnational/global nature, legal restraint. Businesses, particularly large ones, operate within a system where capital is owned through pension funds and investment bodies, at many removes from where managers operate. Managers have little opportunity, in public companies, to take a moral stance, even if they choose to. Distant shareholders demand returns, which means that stock values need to appreciate at least as fast as the market average. Otherwise, incumbent managers will be removed and new ones appointed.

This limits CSR interventions to those which can be seen, by markets and customers, to be strategically sensible. And in a curiously pure form of capitalism, markets and stock values, rather than exhortations to be nice or moral, can drive CSR powerfully and inexorably. Customers, potential employees, journalists and writers are becoming increasingly well-informed. The Internet has democratised information. McDonalds may have nominally 'won' their infamous 'McLibel' case, where they sued two British campaigners in a nightmare court case which ran for years, but they have lost catastrophically in terms of reputation (see www.mcspotlight.org/ for example). When bad ethics is seen to deter customers and employees, firms are likely to be penalised by the markets in the same way as poor profit performers – managers will be replaced with new ones who can do the job better. When shoddy practises are exposed by journalists and writers, corporate value tends to decline. When managers get hauled up in front of juries, their employing firms are damaged in the markets.

The moral seems to be – if you want businesses to be socially responsible – educate yourself, use democratised information systems, support the ones which seem to be going in the right direction, shun the ones who do not. Then the 'invisible hand' of capitalism will work to create socially responsible behaviour.

If you are not being a good corporate citizen, you need to stop and think carefully about your markets, your staff, your future, your corporate value, and ask – what messages am I sending? How sustainable is what we are doing, on a micro-economic level as well as a macro-economic one. Many people in organisations have never even thought seriously about it. You can start, just as you would start quality improvement, by measuring and auditing.

If you are in government, in state-funded or state-subsidised business, in any not-for-profit organisation, the challenges offered in this paper apply even more keenly to you. Capitalist corporations, even the unreconstructed amoral ones running sweatshops in industrialising countries, create wealth at least. You, on the other hand, use it up. You have to be doubly sure of your contribution as a corporate good neighbour.

Social responsibility is good capitalism. Or, put the other way, good capitalism is socially responsible. Nice guys, despite the rumours to the contrary, still can and do finish first.

References

Balabanis, G., Phillips, H.C. and Lyall, J. (1998), 'Corporate Social Responsibility and Economic Performance in the Top British Companies: Are They Linked?', *European Business Review*, Vol. 98, No. 1.

Birsch, D. and Fielder, J.H. (1994), *The Ford Pinto Case: A Study in Applied Ethics. Business, and Technology*, New York: State University of New York Press.

Bollier, D. (1997), *Aiming Higher*, New York: Amacom Books.

Briggs, A. (2003), unpublished lecture notes.

Carr, A.Z. (1968), 'Is Business Bluffing Ethical?', *Harvard Business Review*, January.

Chappell, T. (1993), *The Soul of a Business*, New York: Bantam.

Crosby, P. (1979), *Quality is Free*, New York: McGraw Hill.

Drew, S. and Smith, P. (1995), 'Change Proofing and Business Strategy', *Learning Organization Journal*, Vol. 2, No. 2.

Duffin, M. (1997), correspondence with the author, January.

Elkington, J. (1997), *Cannibals with Forks: The Triple Bottom Line of Twenty-first Century Business*, Oxford: Capstone.

Frankental, P. (2001), 'Corporate Social Responsibility – A PR Invention?', *Corporate Communications; An International Journal*, Vol. 6, No. 1.

Geary, J. (1998), 'Now for the Hard Part', *Time Magazine*, 12 October.

Giddens, A. (1998), *The Third Way*, Cambridge: Polity Press.

Gronroos, C. (1994), 'From Marketing Mix to Relationship Marketing', *Management Decision*, Vol. 34, No. 2.

Handy, C. (1989), *The Age of Unreason*, Harmondsworth: Penguin Books.

Handy, C. (1999), *The Hungry Spirit. Beyond Capitalism; A Quest for Purpose in the Modern World*, New York: Doubleday Broadway.

Hickson, R. (1999), conversations with the author, April.

Karake, Z.A. (1998), 'An Examination of the Impact of Organizational Downsizing and Discrimination Activities on Corporate Social Responsibility as Measured by a Company's Reputation Index', *Management Decision*, Vol. 36, No. 3.

Klein, N. (2001), *No Logo*, London: Flamingo.

Micklethwait, J. and Wooldridge, A. (1996), *The Witchdoctors*, New York: Times Business Books.

Peters, V.J. (1996), 'Back to HRD and TQM Basics', *Training for Quality*, Vol. 3, No. 2.

Peters, V.J. (1997), 'Capitalism and Concern', *The TQM Magazine*, Vol. 8, No. 6.

Peters, V.J. (2002), unpublished presentation notes, MCB University Press.

Porras, J. and Collins, M. (1994), *Built to Last*, New York: Century Hutchinson.

Reeves-Ellington, R.H. (1998), 'Leadership for Socially Responsible Organizations', *Leadership and Organization Development Journal*, Vol. 19, No. 2.

Reicheld, F.F. and Sasser, W.E. (1990), 'Zero Defections: Quality Comes to Services', *Harvard Business Review*, September/October.

Schlosser, E. (2002), *Fast Food Nation*, London: Penguin.

Zairi, M. and Peters, J. (2002), 'The Impact of Social Responsibility on Business Performance', *Managerial Auditing Journal*, Vol. 17, No. 4.

http://www.mcspotlight.org/ for reports on the 'McLibel' case of McDonalds vs Helen Steel and Dave Morris, accessed by the author April 2003.

Chapter 11

Management by Love and Kindness and the Consequent Implications

Roger Haw

This chapter was written and compiled based on the writer's experience and research work, to highlight the various management approaches in the present society which should be implemented as well as cultivated in the modern corporate culture and its environment. The input is not intended to be exhaustive in identifying the better or latest approaches available from time to time. This chapter gives many examples, directions, advice on human expectation towards the needs of working life or living together as a team and society at large. This can be achieved with the right approach, solution, planning, concept and implementation process.

Many of us would have been spared many tears only if we had only had the wisdom to take into consideration the pros and cons of the situation before doing anything. Having adopted a course of action without thinking, we find at once too many difficulties, small or big, impeding our progress. This becomes a source of regular worry. Most of us fail to earn a decent livelihood because we have selected an appointment for which we have no inclination or no special bent. Without taking into consideration our means and capabilities for a particular venture we should not run headlong into it. It is always advisable and prudent to examine and study thoroughly the details of a procedure before accepting or rejecting it. Equally it is a mistake to hesitate or delay action when instant action is called for. Foresight and forethought, combined with courage and confidence in taking unavoidable risks are essential. We must rise to the occasion and ensure success.

In the journey of life, everyone is faced with various hardships. These hardships are like onerous burdens laid upon one's shoulder. Therefore, to lead a better and carefree life, the following suggestions should be taken into consideration. Life moves in cycles. Moods of depression will be followed by periods of confidence and optimism like night follows day. Each of us comes into constant contact with different kinds of emotions which will either breakdown or build up our character and our very life. These feelings are mainly expressed as joy or sorrow. All of us delight in joy so much so that we often take it for granted but we dread the thought of sorrow, which is actually a blessing in disguise. Live for the day and fill with worthy deeds. Fill it with activities and constructive efforts.

Substitute hatred and jealousy with love and sympathetic understanding (Kumar, 1967). It is easy to hate and envy others. So, why not try the difficult alternative

– love and understanding. No ingenious man wants a soft life. If you show love and understanding, you will not be surprised to find yourself loved in turn by everyone. Nobody in this world is perfect, but one should have the courage to live near perfection. Thus, always aim for perfection in your life. If you pursue this, your happiest day will come and the meaning of life will be understood.

Many accountants concentrate more on the aspect of accounting and finance. But I have the opinion that an organisation depends much more on its people. If the people were not satisfied with an organisation, all the systems it applies would fail. However good a system may be; whether it be accounting, finance or other, people are still the important assets required to put the system into proper functioning. I feel that the theories of management are not far stretched enough to reach the hearts of the people of an organisation to give them a sense of want, care and kindness so that the people know they are wanted. Many managers or leaders fail to see that love, care and kindness towards their people has a lot to do with their organisation's success and ensures that it continues to grow from strength to strength.

For example, the structured models of the religious leaders like Jesus Christ and others have proven to be so successful that we do actually see today the Catholic empire, Muslim empire and Buddhist empire prosper, demonstrating, as Christ preached, that 'What is for God does not fail'.

Love, care and kindness for people is the key that the religious leaders have taught and have set as examples for us to follow in order to have things function in proper order and not in chaos. But today we see internal politics being so severe in organisations that each tries to outwit the other thereby leading to much wasted energy and battle fatigue and causing the systems of an organisation to run in chaotic conditions.

In a democratic society every person has the right to his own opinions. The freedom of expression is a prerequisite to the promotion of friendship, harmony and all-round satisfaction. A man must have the right to express his own feelings, his thoughts, his ideas, his likes and dislikes, without pressure from external bodies. This is necessary in order to encourage a wealthy contribution of ideas to the reformation and building of a free modern world.

A poor person will not be bullied and suppressed by the rich and powerful, and he will be given as good an opportunity as any to free himself from poverty and help others who are in the same plight as himself. A man too will be able to discard all conceivable superstitions and fears from his mind and so will be able to attain profound knowledge and have peace of mind. But a man who has no chance to express his own opinions often harbours them in his heart, waiting for the earliest opportunity to give them outlet and he often suffers from high blood pressure. Being men of position, they are afraid of losing their tempers and manners in front of every one, so they are forced to keep a smiling face behind a black and poisoned heart.

Religious leaders have, in fact, shown us how to manage our organisations as they managed theirs. What is good and holy does not fail. We can witness this even today because religious organisations have prospered more successfully than others have.

Which organisation dares to say that it beats the philosophy of the religious leaders with empires worldwide never failing century after century? In fact the teaching of love and kindness towards people has seen genuine religious empires growing stronger and stronger. What I feel is that organisations and their managers should adopt the teachings of the worlds like Christ, Buddha and Prophet Muhammad. The teachings of 'love your brothers as yourself', 'the generation of loving kindness' all have an impact on the people and can be reflected in an organisation. I have much confidence that if we practice loving kindness in an organisation it will grow and prosper. Did not Christ build a kingdom on earth? The holy Catholic religion, the Muslim religion and the Buddhist religion have all been so successfully managed by love and kindness that none has fallen while they practice the truth, the way and the light.

I therefore appeal to all managers, directors and top management to adopt a wider scope of management than just a few theories like management by exception, management by walking about (Peters and Waterman, 1982), management by leadership, management by example, etc. They should see that 'management by love, care and kindness' should be as important if not more important than the management philosophies that we practice today. Various writers have failed to explain the term 'duty'. Some have defined it as a moral or legal obligation (e.g. Kant, 1788), while others say that it is the expression of respect for a superior. It is something expected from all despite obstacles, as Emerson (1860) puts it: 'so high is grandeur to our dust, so near is good to man, when duty whispers low, thou must, the youth replies, I can'.

Duty to our parents is important. In early times, filial attachment was respected and cherished by the people. As a result, the younger generation seldom went against their parents' wishes, not even in marriage. Even in the wild lands of early Mongolia, duty was prevalent. A love story ended in tragedy because of duty. Duty, as heir and successor to the throne, duty to her country, people and aged father, deterred a woman from following her lover to his homeland to be married. Next comes duty to our country; many countries expect every man to do his duty. In a time of war it is the duty of the menfolk to get themselves recruited into their country's army. On the other hand, it is the duty of the wives and parents to let their husbands and sons join the army and fight for their country. Nowadays, parents are trying their utmost to give their children the best of everything especially in education. Their philosophy is to teach their children not to do anything disgraceful and so be a curse to society. These are real dutiful parents.

The employee's duty is to have single-minded loyalty to their company. However, the employer's duty is to take care of the employees' welfare. All this requires a kind of management by love, care and kindness to keep the operation going on.

From all these it can be seen that duty is considered by most of us to play an important part in our lives. It is something which governs every action. Whenever we want to venture upon something new, we always think, 'Is it right and dutiful of me to do this?' In fact the Bible, the Dharma and the Koran are there for us to read and use as a guide in our daily lives and to provide us with solutions to many problems that we face today. Yet most of us have ignored these teachings whether on purpose or through our ignorance. To deploy the powerful tools of these holy books provides us with solutions, even in the management of an organisation. Lack of love, care and understanding of the people and the pressure of internal politics coupled with work pressure have caused high absenteeism and, in extreme cases, high staff turnover. People have emotions and I am very sure that love can attract love and lack of love and kindness can attract dislike and dissatisfaction (Gyatso, 1990).

There are many phrases in the Bible, the Koran and the Dharma that we can rely on to build a successful organisation. I find that many chaotic conditions are man made, such as internal politics, high rate of staff turnover, negativism and even the external environmental disasters. Take time to reflect on these and I am sure a better organisation will emerge. No organisation system can function well without people who are satisfied by the care, love, kindness and understanding which the managers and top management as well as people at all levels can radiate.

The Practice Within

Equality for Women

There is no denying that woman is an equal partner with man in all affairs of life. It is, therefore, expected that she will take part in various sectors. Woman will serve to complete the otherwise incomplete picture of man's politics. She has the same political rights and privileges as man and must be allowed to exercise them for the progress of the whole nation.

Cultural Values

In a multiracial society, there is often an intermingling among the various races, hence a mixture of their various cultures. It is imperative in such a society to unite the various races under a common cultural banner. This is not a direct clash with the view held and advocated by many that racial identity must be preserved. Mixed culture not only is a form of national identity but it is also an evidence of the harmonious way of life that is so characteristic of our society and what every right thinking citizen should strive to maintain. After all, we are all going to live with one another, 'under the same roof' and the sooner we understand one another, the better it is for communal harmony. The most important instrument is a common language. This helps in many ways to foster friendly relations among the races as it serves to facilitate communication.

Continuous Motivation

By this I mean that we must practice kindness on a continuous basis. Our temperament must be cool, calm, assuring and consistent. We should constantly meditate on radiating our care and kindness to our fellow brothers and sisters, to the elders our fathers and mothers. We should give what they deserve within our means. Never promise them something we are unable to fulfil. Give people the credits that they deserve. See their potentials and guide them gently to attain it.

Do Not Harbour Grudges

All of us are human. As humans we have faults. Should a person commit faults we should gently correct them and never scold. Tell him 'I understand you but would it be better if we do it this way', for example. Immediately after this we should forget the matter and begin to look for his good points. Tell him that you had also made the mistakes that he now makes.

Stabbing Behind Backs

When an employee comes to tell you bad deeds of other fellow employees or employee you should say to him that 'we are all in a family and we should understand each other'. If the matter cannot be solved then bring him to see the other employee or employees and try to bring them into an amicable settlement. Encourage them to shake hands and expressly let them know we are in a family. We should expressly bring across to all, the principle 'love your neighbour as yourself'.

Have a Motto

Tell your employees that your motto is 'all in one family'. We should enforce the motto by gathering all employees in an open space each morning before we start work and say together with all sincerity 'united we stand and all in a family we shall succeed'.

Make all our Employees Aware that We are on Earth Only Temporarily

Always implant into the minds of all our employees that the world does not belong to us. We are here only temporarily. If we are aware that we are here only temporarily we do not have so much fighting and greed, as when we die we can take nothing with us. But as long as we are here we should do our best and leave behind our good deeds. When the time is up for us to go, we can really say 'rest in peace'.

Share our Knowledge

We fail by our own selfishness. We think that by withholding knowledge for ourselves we can rule. But if we share our knowledge with all employees who would like to know, we can do better. Did not our religious leaders of the past like Jesus, Buddha and Prophet Muhammad share their knowledge with all? Are their successes seen by us today? In fact if our employees know what we know we can delegate our duties and have things done faster and more effectively than done alone. Knowledge should be passed down and the more we pass, the lighter is our burden. A scheme of houses is not built by one man but by many. By sharing we gain respect and loyalty. We should preach and put into practice the principle of sharing. The willingness to share attracts the creation of more knowledge. A country prospers when the people share what they know.

Admit Our Faults

If we are wrong we must admit that we are humans and, as such, we are not perfect, do not try to cover our faults and argue that we are right. We must be willing to apologise and accept and thank those who notice our wrongs. We seek for forgiveness and in turn we also must forgive. Never practice 'an eye for an eye and a tooth for a tooth'. Then we end up with no eyes and no teeth. 'Whoever exalts himself will be humbled, and whoever humbles himself will be exalted' (Matthew). In one instance I entered the examination room to help invigilate the papers I had set and it was our organisation's policy not to allow the person who set the paper to invigilate the examination of his own subject. My superior summoned me and gave me a good lecture. However, I apologised for my wrong and he forgave me.

Do Not Pretend to Know

A great pretender sorrows his heart for he walks in darkness. He has eyes but does not see. He is not humble enough to accept the views of those who can guide him to see light. If he lets others know his ignorance he will see the right path and head towards the right direction. Pride kills one's knowledge. He must not be afraid that others will humiliate him for if he sees others who can lend a helping hand he begins to realise that there are many who understand and can enlighten his mind. His respect for the views of his fellow colleagues can gain their sympathy for him. Humans are kind by nature but corrupted by the surrounding environment. Keep our minds on the right track and we can see that we have love around us.

We Need a Break

Know that our employees are humans and can accumulate frustration. A kettle without any holes will burst when the water boils. See their weaknesses and give them a break. Many illnesses develop because we are enveloped by frustration. An organisation will fail when the people are sick either physically or mentally. We must be kind enough to know them as humans. In fact we should take off to release our tension. The TV advertises that high blood pressure and many related illnesses are caused by mental stress.

Talk to Your Employees

Get to know them and treat them as individuals. Everyone is different and we must get to know each person. Our approach must be on an individual basis and to solve each person's problems we must get to know him individually. The more we know a person the more we understand him.

Overloading

To overload your employees with work will make them depressed. This is cruelty and will slow down their speed of work. Output will be low and efficiency falls. Assign duties that your employees can cope with. Be fair to them. A way to enable them to cope with their duties is division of labour. The Lord said to Moses 'This is what pertains to the Levites: from twenty-five years old and upwards they shall go in to perform work in the service of the tent of meeting; and from the age of fifty years they shall withdraw from the work of the service and serve no more, but minister to their brethren in the tent of meeting to keep the charge, and they shall do no service. Thus shall you do to the Levites in assigning their duties' (Numbers).

Do Not Betray

Do not betray those who have helped you. Leak no secret entrusted to you. Be loyal and faithful to those employees who have been kind to you. We must practice love and kindness in return for the love and kindness that we have received. The retribution for betrayal will end with bad results. Judas betrayed Jesus and had him (Jesus) delivered to the chief priests. When the chief priests and the elders of the people took counsel against Jesus to put him to death, they bound him to Pilate the governor. Judas seeing that Jesus was condemned repented and brought back the thirty pieces of silver to the chief priests and the elders, saying. 'I have sinned in betraying innocent blood'. They said 'What is that to us? See it to yourself'. And throwing down the pieces of silver in the temple he departed; and he went and hanged himself (Matthew).

No Water, No Life

Sun, air and water – the prime factors which decided man's destiny. Take away coal, oil and metals, and a man returns to the type of life led by his predecessors – devoid of modern necessities of life. However, he has a chance to live his natural life. But take away one of the three mentioned – almost immediately man's fate will lead to death. Of the three, water is the most important of all. Thomas Fuller (1642) once said 'We do not know the worth of water till the well runs dry.' Thus we see the important role of rain and seawater in determining life on earth. If human beings were without properly managed drinking water in the care attitude, they may be facing the problem of drinking seawater sooner or later.

Cultivate a Happy Life

A happy life is the outcome of good deeds of a man. It cannot be bought nor can it be sought and it is as simple as 'Always be cheerful and your life will be a happy one'. A happy life has to be earned. If one were to base one's dreams of a happy life on virtual principles and act likewise, such a life could easily be bestowed upon one. Education is another contributory factor in the field of a happy life, as it enables a man to distinguish right from wrong and to have a better understanding between him and his fellow men. Contentment, too, plays an important part in the life of a man. Health is equally important to a happy life. Religion is also a basic factor that helps to create a happy life. It tells a man which path to take and which to avoid, it guides him towards a virtuous and a happy life.

A happy life is essential to every human being. Without it a man feels extremely miserable; his actions trouble him and his thoughts mislead him. He finds that every door is closed to him and eventually welcomes an end to his life as a solution.

Author's Note – Why This Chapter is Needed!

I love talking to teenagers. They are never afraid to tell you what they are going to accomplish in their lives. The more teenagers I talk to the more I realise that, although they dream of becoming successful, there's a problem. They're never taught the essential principles for achieving success.

Society tells teenagers if they go to school they will become successful. School is a very important part of success, but there is more to it than that. A school education is only one part of creating success. The other part of creating success is a REAL WORLD education. Skills such as goal setting, making contacts, communicating with others, choosing a career, managing money, overcoming obstacles and making choices. Teenagers need to learn these principles in order to create a successful future.

As a responsible corporate man and individual, many people have overlooked this part that also we have some role to play in helping the young generations by giving them wise advice and ideal direction to assist them in building their confident and bright future. It is also part of our social responsibility although we are not their parent or immediate family members; they are our future generations and will continue to lead the world. Therefore, I have been taking many years to think about it, put all my thoughts and efforts together to do the necessary research work on this particular area with the objective of how to help others as part of my responsibility to society as a whole.

Tips for Creating a Good Future, Achieving Dreams and Becoming Successful

An open mind is the beginning of self-discovery and growth. We cannot learn anything new until we can admit that we do not already know anything. When you think you know it all, your mind is not open to new ideas and opinions. Make it a point to learn something new through communicating, listening, writing, reading, watching and observing. No one can take an education away from you. Money does not make you successful. A con man has a lot of money, drives a big car and stays in a big house. Does that mean he is successful? Having lots of money does not mean you are successful. There is much more to success than having money. Success is how high you bounce after you hit rock bottom. Hard work always pays off!

There is nothing wrong with wanting to have lots of money. The problem exists when you make money your main focus. You become greedy; your life becomes twisted. Networking contacts is extremely important. The type of people you associate with reflects the type of person you will become. If you associate with positive people who have dreams and goals, then you will develop successful, winning characteristics. Making contacts is very important in our life. Introduce yourself to people, build a rapport, get their address and contact numbers, list them in your address book, then stay in touch forever. The more contacts you have, the more opportunities you will have. It is difficult to soar like an eagle if you hang out with buzzards and chickens all the time.

This chapter is a gift for all who read it. Society tells us if we go to school we will become successful. School is a very important part of success, but there is more to it than that. A school education is only one part of creating success. Skills such as goal setting, making contacts, communicating with others, choosing a career, managing money, overcoming obstacles and making choices. We need to learn these principles in order to create a successful future.

Going through life without goals is like playing 'Blind Life.' Here is another explanation for why goal-setting works. Perhaps you remember the little experiment you probably had to do in school science. Focus the sun's rays through a magnifying glass and start a fire. The sun's rays do not start fires normally, because the heat is diffused over a large area. But focus those rays, and you will start a fire. This is the power of focus.

Getting involved in goal-setting first forces you to focus your thinking, then your resources, then, finally, your actions. There is a chance that you may fail while trying to achieve your dreams. You must understand this. DO NOT GIVE UP. Successful people are not afraid to fail. The way to overcome failure is to, first, realise that it happens, then learn from it. Failure will teach you valuable lessons about succeeding.

The lesson: the people who make a difference in your life are not the ones with the most credentials, the most money, or the most awards. They are the ones that care and love you very much with full social responsibility (Steiner, 1986) without getting any recognition or expecting to receive any reward from you.

I am pleased to receive many letters from my previous readers that this article led them to take a certain course of action leading to a better life and being a responsible person in society. Too many people live life as though it were a dress rehearsal for something in the near or distant future – well it is not. It is the real thing, and it is now! Learn from the past, plan for the future, but live for the present. It is your duty to yourself to make your life exciting; to maintain a clear mind, keep informed, work hard, think smart, and have fun! But not to forget to play your role in 'social responsibility'. I send you my best wishes wherever you are in the world and please keep sending in your comments.

Your have in your hands an important statement, the 'Power of truth' from world famous people.

Please feel free to write to me with any comments and criticisms of this chapter so I may keep improving. Believe me when I tell you that I value every single letter or e-mail I receive. Nothing else to say right now other than I hope you enjoy this chapter.

Last message to you – awareness of poverty!

Love for others, care for others, thought for others who are not as fortunate as we are, then we can see the light and the enlightenment that many in their holy work have seen. Like Mother Theresa, those that 'Dare To Be Doctors' are there for us to follow. These are but few.

In terms of education there is today no real support or rather total support for the unfortunate. We know that just a few people cannot achieve this ideology but as the word spreads there are many who would come forward to chip in, in whatever manner they can to attain what we wish to attain. To really do this we must first radiate love towards others who are less fortunate. We should help humans to improve their standard of living, which is so much more than some companies even sponsoring the zoo to help animals. Are not people more deserving than animals?

The ideology we hold is that without strengthening our position in terms of resources we cannot help others. Each country still needs support from their nations to put the idea into actual functioning. The country needs education to improve the public's standard of living. But how do we do that. We need to have good educational programmes and strong support from those who can afford to help others who are in need. This is because with many people in this world, who are also looking into the same direction as we do we know we can succeed.

Our social responsibilities cannot be just left to others (Crowther, 2002) with only a glimpse of hope but without the real commitment to fulfil the gap we have found missing. We must lead and with this commitment, we have many who will join hands in the lead. We must not just be thinking of ourselves, our improvements, our prospects but have a thought for those who cannot afford to even have a moderate education not to mention a degree.

With this ideology that we have, we trust and we have the faith that the continuation will follow. We invite those who share our philosophy of love for the unfortunate to continue to spread to all those who can afford in whatever way that they can. Little by little we will build a mountain.

We have seen the press publishing articles about individuals who have financial problems and need finance to help them to pay their medical expenses and zoom the cash flow in. What about the multitudes of people who need the help but yet we do not see. Like the holy books have said we have eyes but we do not see.

But, of course, charity must begin at home. When we are strong enough, with your enthusiastic support, then we can really help those who really need help. I feel that the field of education can lead many from poverty to affordability. Love our neighbours especially those who need help from us. We desire to be like a kingdom on earth where we can pour out to the unfortunate like the rain pours down water to us when we are thirsty. We have imagination in our minds of the heavenly Kingdom, which can radiate all goodness. But the little goodness in the earthly Kingdom that we can afford we forget easily. Holiness is here to begin and to share with others, not when we reach the heavenly far. Come join hands with us to the road of education for the unfortunate.[1]

Last but not least, this chapter is full of advice and helpful hints that show people how to get more of what you want out of life and your responsibility to society at large.

The choice is yours as to whether you will apply yourself or take necessary action to improve or change them to your everyday life. Whether you succeed or not in life is up to you. No one can do it for you. Not your parents, brothers and sisters, friends, superiors, teachers or anyone else. You have to decide within yourself.

No one can guarantee or promise what level of success you will achieve in your life. I believe if you put these principles to work through daily practice, then YOU WILL begin to achieve SUCCESS. THE TIME TO START IS NOW.

References

Crowther, D. (2002), 'The Importance of Corporate Social Responsibility to All', address given on receipt of honorary doctorate, Ansted University, November.

Emerson, R.W. (1860), *The Conduct of Life*, many editions.

Fuller, T. (1642), *The Holy State and the Profane State*, many editions.

Gyatso, G.K. (1990), *Joyful Path of Good Fortune*, London: Tharpa Publications.

Kant, I. (1788), *Critique of Practical Reason*, many editions.

Kumar, S. (1967), *Non-Violence or Non-existence*, London: Christian Action Publications.

---

1   One of the goals of Ansted University is to 'foster the unity of our world community through education'.

Peters, T.J. and Waterman, R.H. (1982), *In Search of Excellence: Lessons from America's Best-run Companies*, New York: Harper and Row.
Steiner, R. (1986), *The Philosophy of Spiritual Activity*, Hudson, NY: Anthroposophic Press.

Chapter 12

The Future of Corporate Social Responsibility

David Crowther and Lez Rayman-Bacchus

Introduction

The contributions to this book have applied the full range of meaning to the notion of responsibility. Arguments have concerned *retrospective* responsibility, seeking to allocate blame and reasons for the state of relations between corporation and stakeholders. There has also been concern for *prospective* responsibility, that corporations and governments have obligations and duties to exercise. Some of the debates have also questioned the capacity for corporations to make *moral judgements*. This book has not sought to assess *causal* responsibility, recognising that not all failures or accidents attract blame. Nevertheless much of the debate on corporate social responsibility, within this book and elsewhere, suspect some linkage between corporate actions and a wide range of undesirable social and ecological outcomes.

Together we have ranged far and wide in exploring the terrain of corporate social responsibility and more generally the topic of business ethics. Some contributions have pursued a macro perspective in discussing the relationship between the corporation and society, but locate their discussions within differing frames. Clarke and de la Rama investigate the development of socially responsible investment among the major economies, while Abreu and David compare and contrasts corporate social responsibility practices around the member states of the European Union. Rayman-Bacchus assesses the role of trust and legitimacy against an evolving capitalist landscape. Peters argues that the best basis for generating good corporate citizenship is economic self-interest rather than moral imperatives. Crowther finds that the burden of social responsibility has shifted from the corporation to society. Other contributions have moved closer in to examine processes within particular sectors, a focus on corporations constructing social relations, and closer still outlining how managers should behave within the corporation. Mahon and McGowan suggest there are corporate lessons to be learnt from the contrasting ways that the 'sin' sectors of tobacco and alcohol are evolving, within the USA. Crowther has explored the extent to which corporate reporting is no more than impression management. Haw, drawing on his experience and research has looked at social relations within the corporation, and calls for managers to treat their employees well. Doing so will benefit everyone in the long run. Yet other contributions have focused on technological change and concomitant corporate behaviour. Topal and Crowther, having assessed corporate developments around biotechnology, warn of the dangers to society of failing to regulate corporate responsibilities; Mraović reflects on how the Internet has enabled the transformation of the organisation to the extent that new and unpredictable forms of social relations can be expected to emerge alongside the globally networked organisation.

A number of important and unresolved debates remain embedded within most of these topics. At one level this book may be regarded as a social barometer. The diversity of fears, hopes and propositions being aired about corporate social responsibility broadly reflect the concerns of large sections of society, including ordinary citizens, sectional pressure groups and activists (environmental concerns, individual rights, investor exposure) and policy makers. At another level this book highlights the persistence of a number of underlying debates that reinforce the difficulties facing stakeholders (including governments and corporations), seeking to shape a better world. One of these debates centres on the acceptability of corporate self-interest as a driving force of a capitalist economic system. Another area of difficulty is with the very notion of corporate social responsibility.

Egoism and Altruism

One of those debates concerns the extent to which corporate self-interest is helping or hindering economic and social development in the long run. For our purposes self-interest connotes selfishness, and since the Middle Ages has informed a number of important philosophical, political and economic propositions. Among these is Hobbes' world where unfettered self-interest is expected to lead to social devastation. A high degree of regulation is prescribed in order to avoid such a disastrous outcome, but in the process we sacrifice our rights. Self-interest again raises its head in the utilitarian perspective as championed by Bentham, Locke and J.S. Mill. The latter for example advocated as morally right the pursuit of the greatest happiness for the greatest number. Similarly Adam Smith's free-market economics, is predicated on competing self-interest. These influential ideas put interest of the individual above interest of the collective. Indeed from this perspective, collective interests are best served through self-interest. At the same time this corporate self-interest has come to draw disapproval in modern times, as reflected in many of the arguments within this book. The moral value of individualism has all but vanished.

Has the pendulum swung too far toward encouraging corporate self-interest at the expense of the public interest? Indeed the continuing conversion of public service provision to market testing by many governments suggests a strengthening belief that the two interests are not in conflict. Self-interest and altruism (promoting the welfare of others over self) need not be in conflict. There is ample evidence that encouraging corporate self-interest (and risk taking) does benefit society (albeit unequally from a Marxist perspective). Some of that evidence is contested, as in the case of genetically modified foods. However, as this book shows, there is also abundant evidence to the contrary; that the pursuit of corporate self-interest continues to burden society with hitherto unimaginable costs. Nevertheless, during the last two decades most of the world's nations have set about creating anew, or refining (capitalist) economic and political institutions that encourage corporate self-interest.

While governments and consumers alike look to business to continue delivering economic and social benefits, many observers remain concerned about corporate self-interest; a self-interest that is synonymous with those of the managers. Managerial self-interest is unavoidably driven by a combination of shareholder interests (backed up by markets for corporate control and managerial talent), and occupational rewards and career opportunity. The public interest is easily sacrificed on the altar of these managerial motivators (or constraints). Moreover, public interest is not homogeneous and therefore cannot be simply represented. Public interest has become factionalised into constituencies and stakeholder groupings, each concerned with their particular interests. Consider for example the 'not-in-my-back-yard' protests over the building of recycling plants and mobile telephone masts, yet opinion polls support the former and sales of mobile phones demand more of the latter.

As has often been noted, from a global perspective corporate self-interest seems to be associated with an unequal distribution of economic and social benefits. However it seems unfair to lay the responsibility for such inequality solely at the door of the corporation. National and regional politics, religious conviction and differentiated moral values all play an immeasurable role in shaping a nation's life chances. Nevertheless this book is testimony to the worldwide suspicion that corporate egoism is a significant (if not the most important) influence on economic and social development.

There are many examples of corporations behaving altruistically, from the paternalism of nineteenth and twentieth century industrialists, to modern day donations to charities and the *ad hoc* secondment of managers to community projects. However the perceived value of such giving is tainted by suspicions that many such acts seem self-serving. For example there is room to ask whether Microsoft is giving away computers out of altruism or as part of an aim to reinforce its brand name. Many modern projects of altruism are tied to the purchase of products from the giving corporation, for example Tesco supermarket. Other initiatives are clearly pushing at the boundaries of acceptable corporate behaviour, such as donations to political parties. These examples show that corporate altruism covers a wide range of socially acceptable behaviour, from selfless giving to self-interested giving.

Perhaps one reason for corporate self-interest being such a mixed blessing is that we are overly reliant on evaluating the *consequences* (a notion discussed in our introduction) of corporate action, especially our fixation with the bottom line. Nothing concentrates the managerial mind like performance targets and outcomes. However, as Wilbur (1992) argues, self-interest encompasses not just consequences and results, but also requires freedom of choice and consistency. From this perspective the pursuit of corporate (self-interested) activity should be guided by structured alternatives and consistency, in order to ensure that the self-interest of others is not undermined by selfish action. Sensing that we cannot rely on corporate altruism we the public are demanding our governments to initiate more legislation and tighter regulation. However, even this move has shown important weaknesses. Many of the politicians and policy makers are in the pockets of business. Self-interest is even here, and it is not acceptable to us. These arguments casts doubt on the extent to which we are able to arrange our economic and political institutions in order to harness self-interest to the benefit of society. The functioning of a civilised society includes putting the interests of others before self-interest. As Baron et al. (1992) and Mansbridge (1990) observed, altruism is part of social, political and economic life. However, the exploitative nature of capitalism sits uncomfortably with Kant's (1959) ideal of mutual respect for the interests of others, and even less with Rawls' (1971) desire to see a strong form of egalitarian liberalism. These tensions (between capitalism and liberalism, and between meeting unconditional social obligations and the pursuit of economic value), drives the need for constant vigilance of corporate activity. Since we are unlikely to abandon capitalism, nor escape from the fixation on performance measurement, managerial commitment to upholding the interests of others could straightforwardly be included in the managerial performance appraisal.

Moral Agency or Agency Theory?

The debates within this book share the view that corporations can and should be held responsible for their actions. Indeed, we see this 'responsibility' as self-evident, as we examine the differing ways that corporate social responsibility is being undermined, and consider how we might better align corporate interest more closely with the public interest. While few would argue that corporations should be held responsible for their actions, arguments about *shareholder* versus *stakeholder* interests show there is disagreement about the scope that such responsibility should take. Compounding these disagreements is the argument that corporations should fulfil a range of obligations, described as economic, legal, ethical and discretionary; an assessment given greater force by the claim that the exemplary ones do meet these standards (Carroll, 1991). Nevertheless shareholder and stakeholder supporters will not agree on the relative importance of these obligations. There is a further difficulty in evaluating responsibility, and that lies with the very notion of corporate or collective managerial responsibility. Consider how two models commonly relied on in the business ethics literature generate alternative assumptions and opportunities for assessing corporate responsibility: agency theory and moral agency. The first model helps us approach the evaluation of moral responsibility through the notion that corporations as economic agents of society have a fiduciary duty of care to society. In contrast the second model allows us to assess corporate social responsibility through projecting individual human characteristics onto the corporation. Which provides a stronger purchase on the issues at stake?

Agency theory presumes that corporations are fictional entities. From this view the corporation is simply a convenient meeting place or 'nexus' where agents and their principals contract, (Jensen and Meckling, 1976). Managers and shareholders contract, whether explicitly or implicitly, to maximise shareholder returns in exchange for employment benefits. While the chief concern within this individualist model is how to align the agent's self-interest with those of the principals, as Mitnick (1992) shows there is no unified conception of agency theory. For example the dominant worry is about the costs of maintaining alignment of interests, reflecting an economics tradition. However there are other concerns. Some social scientists, for example, worry about the agent's fiduciary duty (ethical rather than legal) and the implications for trust relations (Shapiro, 1987). According to Mitnick it is by introducing the *law of agency* that we are able to enrich agency theory and say that managers have a fiduciary duty to act in the interests of shareholders or stakeholders. At a higher level of aggregation the corporation can be regarded as having a fiduciary duty to a wide range of constituencies and more generally to the public.

The assumption of obligation and trust that attaches to fiduciary duty introduces a moral dimension to agency theory. From this point we can talk about agents having not just *retrospective* and *prospective* responsibility for their actions, but also assess whether there is a moral outlook in their decision-making. When economists assess the risks or costs of agents deceiving their principals, they are worrying about the moral hazard that principals are exposed to. There is room for further developing the moral dimension within this model. For example to what extent does the corporation's managers share a moral commitment within their organisation? Further, to what extent is this moral commitment shared with policy actors (social institutions) within the external social context? Moral commitment here could mean tacit or reasoned agreement on the limits of, on one hand risk taking, and on the other hand accountability. We might also expect moral commitment to be embedded within, and bridging, a range of social institutions, not limited to the corporation. These questions could shed new light on the contested areas of genetically modified foods, stem cell research, electro-magnetic radiation, and others.

The moral agency view holds that the corporation is a moral entity; it is the individual writ large. This anthropomorphic view draws inspiration from the idea that the rational and independent individual can be held responsible and accountable for their decisions. Within this view the corporation is more than a legal entity. Theorists have set forth conditions for ascribing legitimate moral liability to the corporation. First, since we are able to experience its presence, the corporation is a sociological reality (Coleman, 1990). Second, if a corporation is capable of exercising rational intention, then this qualifies it as a moral entity. As Corlett (1996) and others argue a corporation can be legitimately liable if they act intentionally, voluntarily and knowingly. This projection of human qualities onto the organisation seems to ignore that corporations comprise (many) individuals pursuing their own purposes. In addition corporations commonly host both a formal strategy (for investor consumption) and an informal strategy (reflecting managerial goals). From Davidson's (1980) perspective this layering of strategy does not negate the existence of corporate moral agency; a corporate moral agent can accommodate multiple layers of intentionality. In addition, French (1995) argues that the existence of transparent internal decision structures and corporate policies give rise to collectively arrived at corporate decisions. Taking these arguments together, suggests that while corporations may harbour competing aims they do nevertheless exhibit a distinctive rational behaviour and intention, as decisions to invest in this or that market or technology testifies.

Being a moral agent means being exposed to the possibility of blame and punishment. As Corlett suggests for moral liability to apply there must also be guilt and fault. Further complicating the picture is the need to distinguish between moral and legal liability. Acts of God (floods, earthquakes, lightening) may render the most carefully crafted corporate action redundant. In such circumstances the corporation may not be morally liable, but still be legally liable.

That we need to introduce conditions and refinements suggests that corporate action can never be uniformly equated with individual action. Velasquez (1983) goes further suggesting that corporations cannot be held morally responsibility because they are not individuals. Goodpaster and Matthews (1982) agree that individuals and corporations are not equivalent, but argue that there is value in making the association. For them the 'principle of moral projection' helps us to understand the demands we make on corporations as well as the demands we make of ourselves.

Debates about what model of morally responsible agency best characterises the corporation are important. Corporate leaders and policy makers unconsciously and purposively draw on intellectual frameworks, whether commonsense or otherwise, in developing strategic and legislative frameworks for guiding corporate behaviour. In the process they are unavoidably making moral judgements, based on sets of possibly incomplete assumptions. The two perspectives sketched out above provide discourse frameworks that are at the same time competing and complimentary. Both perspectives understate, if not ignore, the degree to which managers within any given corporation share a particular moral outlook. For example the existence of a shared sense of stewardship or unbridled individualism goes a long way toward understanding the moral attitude of the corporation (Rayman-Bacchus, 2003). Moreover it seems likely that the corporation and other social institutions will share a moral commitment to a particular institutional outlook. For example where there is a common interest in some technological area.

The development of case law (within the USA and UK at least), during the last century does suggest that discourse frameworks for evaluating corporate liability have been evolving; discourse frameworks that increasingly avoid the dangers of equating individual moral liability with corporate liability. Desjardins and McCall (1996: 73) for example show how USA product liability law has evolved without reference to 'our ordinary understanding of our personal liability for harm we cause'. For example corporations may be held liable for injury caused by their products in ways that cannot be equated with injury caused by individuals. There is today an array of public policy sanctions and incentives, and institutional arrangements in place aimed at monitoring, assessing and ascribing corporate liability, and punishing the guilty. These arrangements address an ever-widening range of circumstances, from individual rights to ecological and social conditions. For example, in addition to product liability legislation, there is also protection for employee privacy, consumer data protection, health and safety at work, minimum wage, maximum weekly working hours, job security, protection of the environment, and discrimination (race, gender, disabilities). Some of these arrangements are contested and both corporate leaders and policy makers must remain sensitive to balancing economic imperatives and social costs. For example, the complaint among employers that minimum wage costs will make them uncompetitive, against the need for a living wage among a large proportion of the labour force. These developments suggest a pragmatic engagement between corporations competing and cooperating with other policy actors, each playing a part in constructing the attitudes and expectations of each other and in the process shaping the broad social context in particular directions.

Thus corporate social responsibility seems to be developing within evolving discourse frameworks and social institutions. This is happening without having to commit to methodological individualism, and without discarding attempts to assess corporate responsibility as futile or against the public interest.

Accounting and Accountability

At the beginning of this book Crowther and Rayman-Bacchus argued that the corporate excesses, which are starting to become disclosed and which are affecting large numbers of people, have raised an awareness of the asocial behaviours of corporations. This is one reason why the issue of corporate social responsibility has become a much more prominent feature of the corporate landscape. There are other factors which have helped raise this issue to prominence and Topal and Crowther argue that a concern with the effects of bioengineering and genetic modifications of nature is also an issue which is arising general concern. At a different level of analysis Crowther (2000) has argued that the availability of the World Wide Web has facilitated the dissemination of information and has enabled more pressure to be brought upon corporations by their various stakeholders.

Alongside this recognition that corporations are accountable to their stakeholders has come a development of the principles upon which this demonstration of accountability should be based. Inevitably this is predicated in accounting as a mechanism by which such action can be measured and reported. In generic terms this has come to be called either social or environmental accounting.[1] The objective of environmental accounting is to measure the effects of the actions of the organisation upon the environment and

---

1   Although among academics the terms social accounting and environmental accounting are deemed to denote different aspects of responsible accounting, among practitioners the terms tend to be treated as synonymous and generally called environmental accounting. This approach has been followed here.

to report upon those effects. In other words the objective is to incorporate the effect of the activities of the firm upon externalities and to view the firm as a network which extends beyond just the internal environment to include the whole environment (see Crowther 2000b, 2002). In this view of the organisation the accounting for the firm does not stop at the organisational boundary but extends beyond to include not just the business environment in which it operates but also the whole social environment. Environmental accounting therefore adds a new dimension to the role of accounting for an organisation because of its emphasis upon accounting for external effects of the organisation's activities. In doing so this provides a recognition that the organisation is an integral part of society, rather than a self contained entity which has only an indirect relationship with society at large. This self-containment has been the traditional view taken by an organisation as far as their relationship with society at large is concerned, with interaction being only by means of resource acquisition and sales of finished products or services. Recognition of this closely intertwined relationship of mutual interdependency between the organisation and society at large, when reflected in the accounting of the organisation, can help bring about a closer, and possibly more harmonious, relationship between the organisation and society. Given that the managers and workers of an organisation are also stakeholders in that society in other capacities, such as consumers, citizens and inhabitants, this reinforces the mutual interdependency.

Environmental accounting also provides an explicit recognition that stakeholders other than the legal owners of the organisation have power and influence over that organisation and also have a right to extend their influence into affecting the organisation's activities.[2] This includes the managers and workers of the organisation who are also stakeholders in other capacities. Environmental accounting therefore provides a mechanism for transferring some of the power from the organisation to these stakeholders and this voluntary surrender of such power by the organisation can actually provide benefits to the organisation. Benefits from increased disclosure and the adoption of environmental accounting can provide further benefits to the organisation in its operational performance, beyond this enhanced relationship with society at large. These benefits, it is argued, can include:

- an improved image for the organisation which can translate into additional sales;
- the development of environmentally friendly or sustainable methods of operation which can lead to the development of new markets;
- reduced future operational costs through the anticipation of future regulation and hence a cost advantage over competitors;
- decreased future liabilities brought about through temporal externalisation;
- better relationships with suppliers and customers which can lead to reduced operational costs as well as increased sales;
- easier recruitment of labour and lowered costs of staff turnover.

---

2   See Rubenstein (1992) for fuller details of this argument.

It needs to be recognised however that there are increased costs of instituting a regime of environmental accounting and that these additional costs need to be offset against the possible benefits to be accrued. These increased costs are concerned with the development of appropriate measures of environmental performance and the necessary alterations to the management information and accounting information systems to incorporate these measures into the reporting system. This is particularly problematical for the organisation in terms of justification because the increased costs are readily quantifiable but the benefits are much more difficult to quantify.

This leads to one of the main problems with the accounting for externalities through social and environmental accounting. This problem is concerned with the quantification of the effects of the activities of the organisation upon its external environment. This problem revolves around four main areas:

*   determining the effects upon the external environment of the activities of the organisation;
*   developing appropriate measures for those effects;
*   quantifying those effects in order to provide a comparative yardstick for the evaluation of alternative courses of action, particularly in terms of an accounting based quantification;
*   determining the form and extent of disclosure of those quantification so as to maximise the benefits of that disclosure while minimising the costs of the disclosure and minimising the possibility of knowledge of the firms operational activities being given to competitors.

These are problems which have been addressed by proponents of this form of accounting but it is fair to say that these problems have primarily been recognised to exist rather than being satisfactorily solved. Those that argue in favour of an increased extent of disclosure in this area tend to consider the advantages of the disclosure from the point of view of external stakeholders rather than from the point of view of the organisation itself. Indeed one of the features of the environmental accounting discourse is the polarisation of views between those concerned with the firm, and its owners and managers, and those concerned with the environmental, and thereby certain external stakeholders. The management of stakeholders, and the business on behalf of all stakeholders, is one mechanism for reinforcing the organisational boundary, which becomes less important under a social accounting perspective. Indeed it will be argued that this polarisation of perspectives is an important component of organisational performance reporting. Accordingly it is increasingly apparent that these environmental issues are recognised by organisations as being of importance and the extent of environmental reporting by organisations is increasing and seems likely to increase further in the future.[3]

---

3   But see Deegan and Rankin (1999) for a consideration of the deficiencies of current environmental reporting.

Before the development of any appropriate measures can be considered it is first necessary for the organisation to develop an understanding of the effects of its activities upon the external environment. The starting point for the development of such an understanding therefore is the undertaking of an environmental audit. An environmental audit is merely an investigation and recording of the activities of the organisation in order to develop this understanding (Kinnersley, 1994). Indeed BS7750 is concerned with such audits in the context of the development of environmental management systems. Such an audit will address, inter alia, the following issues:

- the extent of compliance with regulations and possible future regulations;
- the extent and effectiveness of pollution control procedures;
- the extent of energy usage and possibilities increasing for energy efficiency;
- the extent of waste produced in the production processes and the possibilities for reducing such waste or finding uses for the waste necessarily produced;
- the extent of usage of sustainable resources and possibilities for the development of renewable resources;
- the extent of usage of recycled materials and possibilities for increasing recycling;
- life cycle analysis of products and processes;
- the possibilities of increasing capital investment to affect these issues;
- the existence of or potential for environmental management procedures to be implemented.

Once this audit has been completed then it is possible to consider the development of appropriate measures and reporting mechanisms to provide the necessary information for both internal and external consumption. These measures need to be based upon the principles of environmental accounting, as outlined below. It is important to recognise however that such an environmental audit, while the essential starting point for the development of such accounting and reporting, should not be viewed as a discrete isolated event in the developmental process. Environmental auditing needs to be carried out on a recurrent basis, much as is financial or systems auditing, in order to both review progress through a comparative analysis and to establish where further improvement can be made in the light of progress to date and changing operational procedures.

The Principles of Environmental Accounting

In order to understand the rationale for environmental accounting, and the basis on which it is suggested that such accounting operates, it is necessary therefore to consider the principles upon which environmental accounting operates. There are three basic principles (Schaltegger et al., 1996) to environmental accounting:

- sustainability;
- accountability;
- transparency.

and each will be considered in turn.

Sustainability

Sustainability is concerned with the effect which action taken in the present has upon the options available in the future. If resources are utilised in the present then they are no longer available for use in the future, and this is of particular concern if the resources are finite in quantity. Thus raw materials of an extractive nature, such as coal, iron or oil, are finite in quantity and once used are not available for future use. At some point in the future therefore alternatives will be needed to fulfil the functions currently provided by these resources. This may be at some point in the relatively distant future but of more immediate concern is the fact that as resources become depleted then the cost of acquiring the remaining resources tends to increase, and hence the operational costs of organisations tend to increase.[4]

Sustainability therefore implies that society must use no more of a resource than can be regenerated. This can be defined in terms of the carrying capacity of the ecosystem (Hawken, 1993) and described with input – output models of resource consumption. Thus the paper industry for example has a policy of replanting trees to replace those harvested and this has the effect of retaining costs in the present rather than temporally externalising them. Similarly motor vehicle manufacturers such as Volkswagen have a policy of making their cars almost totally recyclable. Viewing an organisation as part of a wider social and economic system implies that these effects must be taken into account, not just for the measurement of costs and value created in the present but also for the future of the business itself.

Measures of sustainability would consider the rate at which resources are consumed by the organisation in relation to the rate at which resources can be regenerated. Unsustainable operations can be accommodated for either by developing sustainable operations or by planning for a future lacking in resources currently required. In practice organisations mostly tend to aim towards less unsustainability by increasing efficiency in the way in which resources are utilised. An example would be an energy efficiency programme.

---

4   Similarly once an animal or plant species becomes extinct then the benefits of that species to the environment can no longer be accrued. In view of the fact that many pharmaceuticals are currently being developed from plant species still being discovered this may be significant for the future.

Accountability

Accountability is concerned with an organisation recognising that its actions affect the external environment, and therefore assuming responsibility for the effects of its actions. This concept therefore implies a quantification of the effects of actions taken, both internal to the organisation and externally. More specifically the concept implies a reporting of those quantifications to all parties affected by those actions. This implies a reporting to external stakeholders of the effects of actions taken by the organisation and how they are affecting those stakeholders. This concept therefore implies a recognition that the organisation is part of a wider societal network and has responsibilities to all of that network rather than just to the owners of the organisation. Alongside this acceptance of responsibility therefore must be a recognition that those external stakeholders have the power to affect the way in which those actions of the organisation are taken and a role in deciding whether or not such actions can be justified, and if so at what cost to the organisation and to other stakeholders.

Accountability therefore necessitates the development of appropriate measures of environmental performance and the reporting of the actions of the firm. This necessitates costs on the part of the organisation in developing, recording and reporting such performance and to be of value the benefits must exceed the costs. Benefits must be determined by the usefulness of the measures selected to the decision-making process and by the way in which they facilitate resource allocation, both within the organisation and between it and other stakeholders. Such reporting needs to be based upon the following characteristics:

*   understandability to all parties concerned;
*   relevance to the users of the information provided;
*   reliability in terms of accuracy of measurement, representation of impact and freedom from bias;
*   comparability, which implies consistency, both over time and between different organisations.

Inevitably however such reporting will involve qualitative facts and judgements as well as quantifications. This qualitativeness will inhibit comparability over time and will tend to mean that such impacts are assessed differently by different users of the information, reflecting their individual values and priorities. A lack of precise understanding of effects, coupled with the necessarily judgmental nature of relative impacts, means that few standard measures exist. This in itself restricts the inter-organisation comparison of such information. Although this limitation is problematic for the development of environmental accounting it is in fact useful to the managers of organisations as this limitation of comparability alleviates the need to demonstrate good performance as anything other than a semiotic.

Transparency

Transparency, as a principle, means that the external impact of the actions of the organisation can be ascertained from that organisation's reporting and pertinent facts are not disguised within that reporting. Thus all the effects of the actions of the organisation, including external impacts, should be apparent to all from using the information provided by the organisation's reporting mechanisms. Transparency is of particular importance to external users of such information as these users lack the background details and knowledge available to internal users of such information. Transparency therefore can be seen to follow from the other two principles and equally can be seen to be a part of the process of recognition of responsibility on the part of the organisation for the external effects of its actions and equally part of the process of transferring power to external stakeholders.

Disclosure in Corporate Reporting

These principles affect not just the accounting for the activities of an organisation but also the reporting of those activities. Thus disclosure is also important and can be expected to increase as corporations engage more in socially responsible activity. In an earlier chapter Crowther has considered this disclosure in the context of reporting and has suggested that in some respects this demonstrates increasing concern for social responsibility and in some respects a desire for window dressing. An examination of the external reporting of organisations does however demonstrate an increasing recognition of the need to include social and environmental information and an increasing number of annual reports of companies include some information in this respect. This trend is gathering momentum as more organisations perceive the importance of providing such information to external stakeholders. It has been suggested however (Till and Symes 1999) that the inclusion of such information does not demonstrate an increasing concern with the environment but rather some benefits to the company itself.[5] One trend which is also apparent however is the tendency of companies to produce separate environmental reports. In this context such reports are generally termed environmental reports although in reality they include both reporting upon environmental impact and upon social impact. Thus the terms social accounting and environmental accounting tend to have been conflated within the practice of corporate reporting and the two terms used interchangeably for the form of performance measurement and reporting which recognises and reports upon the effects of the organisation's actions upon its external environment.

---

5   Till and Symes consider Australian companies where there are tax effects of environmental actions and disclosure benefit companies with increased disclosure. The cultural and legal environments differ from country to country and in the UK such benefits do not accrue. Nevertheless the lack of altruism, or concern for stakeholders, needs to be borne in mind when considering such increased environmental reporting.

While these reports tend to contain much more detailed environmental information than is contained in the annual report the implication of this trend is that such information is required by a separate constituency of stakeholders than the information contained in the annual report. This suggests an impression therefore that environmental information is not necessary for the owners and investors in a business but is needed by other stakeholders. This therefore leads to a further suggestion that organisations view environmental issues as separate from the economic performance of the business rather than as integral to it. This highlights the problematic nature of environmental accounting and some of the problems associated with environmental impact measurement.

The Gaia Hypothesis

While the discourse of accounting was developing the notion of greater accountability to stakeholders during the 1970s, other developments were also taking place in parallel. Thus in 1979 Lovelock produced his Gaia hypothesis in which he posited a different model of the planet Earth; in his model the whole of the ecosphere, and all living matter therein, was codependent upon its various facets and formed a complete system. According to this hypothesis, this complete system, and all components of the system, was interdependent and equally necessary for maintaining the Earth as a planet capable of sustaining life. This Gaia hypothesis was a radical departure from classical liberal theory which maintained that each entity was independent and could therefore concentrate upon seeking satisfaction for its own wants, without regard to other entities. This classical liberal view of the world forms the basis of economic organisation, provides a justification for the existence of firms as organs of economic activity and provides the rationale behind the model of accounting adopted by society. The Gaia hypothesis however implied that interdependence, and a consequent recognition of the effect of one's actions upon others, was a facet of life. This consequently necessitates a different interpretation of accountability in terms of individual and organisational behaviour and reporting.

Given the constitution of economic activity into profit seeking firms, each acting in isolation and concerned solely with profit maximisation, justified according to classical liberalism, it is inevitable that accounting developed as organisation-centric, seeking merely to measure and report upon the activities of the firm insofar as they affected the firm. Any actions of the firm which had consequences external to the firm were held not to be the concern of the firm. Indeed enshrined within classical liberalism, alongside the sanctity of the individual to pursue his own course of action, was the notion that the operation of the free market mechanism would mediate between these individuals to allow for an equilibrium based upon the interaction of these freely acting individuals and that this equilibrium was an inevitable consequence of this interaction.[6] As a

---

6　This assumption of course ignores the imbalances in power between the various parties seeking to enact transaction through the market.

consequence any concern by the firm with the effect of its actions upon externalities was irrelevant and not therefore a proper concern for its accounting.

The Gaia hypothesis stated that organisms were interdependent[7] and that it was necessary to recognise that the actions of one organism affected other organisms and hence inevitably affected itself in ways which were not necessarily directly related. Thus the actions of an organism upon its environment and upon externalities was a matter of consequence for every organism. This is true for humans as much as for any other living matter upon the planet. It is possible to extend this analogy to a consideration of the organisation of economic activity taking place in modern society and to consider the implications both for the organisation of that activity and the accounting for that activity. As far as profit seeking organisation are concerned therefore the logical conclusion from this is that the effect of the organisation's activities upon externalities is a matter of concern to the organisation, and hence a proper subject for accounting in terms of organisational activity.

While it is not realistic to claim that the development of the Gaia hypothesis had a significant impact upon organisational behaviour, it seems perhaps overly coincidental to suggest that a social concern among business managers developed at the same time that this theory was propounded. It is perhaps that both are symptomatic of other factors which caused a re-examination of the structures and organisation of society. Nevertheless organisational theory has, from the 1970s, become more concerned with all the stakeholders of an organisation, whether or not such stakeholders have any legal status with respect to that organisation. At the same time within the discourse and practice of accounting there has been a growth in concern with accounting for externalities and for the effects of the actions of the firm upon those externalities. One externality of particular concern is that of the environment; in this context the environment has been defined to include the complete ecosphere, rather than merely the human part of that ecosphere. These concepts form part of the foundations of a concern with environmental accounting.

A Historic Concern with Social Responsibility

A concern with corporate social responsibility is not of course a new phenomenon. Indeed it was a prominent feature of the 1970s where the performance of businesses in a wider arena than the stock market and its value to shareholders had become of increasing concern. Fetyko (1975) considered social accounting as an approach to reporting a firm's activities and stressed the need for identification of socially relevant behaviour, the determination of those to whom the company was accountable for its social performance and the development of appropriate measures and reporting techniques. Klein (1977) also considered social accounting and recognised that

---

7   In actual fact Lovelock claimed in his hypothesis that the earth and all its constituent parts were interdependent. It is merely an extension of this hypothesis to claim the interrelationship of human activity whether enacted through organisations or not.

different aspects of performance are of interest to different stakeholder groupings, distinguishing for example between investors, community relations and philanthropy as areas of concern for accounting. He also considered various areas for measurement, including consumer surplus, rent, environmental impact and non-monetary values. While these writers considered, by implication, that measuring social performance is important without giving reasons for believing so, Solomons (1974) considered the reasons for measuring objectively the social performance of a business. He suggested that while one reason was to aid rational decision making, another reason was of a defensive nature.

Unlike other writers, Solomons not only argued for the need to account for the activities of an organisation in term of its social performance but also suggested a model for doing this, in terms of a statement of social income. His model for the analysis of social performance is as follows:

	£
Statement of social Income:	
Value generated by the productive process	xxx
+ unappropriable benefits	xxx
– external costs imposed on the community	*xxx*
Net social profit / loss	*xxx*

Figure 12.1   Analysis of social performance

While Solomons proposed this model, which seems to provide a reasonable method of reporting upon the effects of the activities of an organisation on its external environment, he failed to provide any suggestions as to the actual measurement of external costs and benefits. Such measurement is much more problematic and this is one of the main problems of any form of social accounting – the fact that the measurement of effects external to the organisation is extremely difficult. Indeed it can be argued that this difficulty in measurement is one reason why organisations have concentrated upon the measurement through accounting of their internal activities, which are much more susceptible to measurement.

In this respect, Gray, Owen and Maunders (1987) consider social reporting in terms of responsibility and accountability and distinguish between the internal needs of a business, catered for by management accounting, and the external needs, which are addressed for shareholders by financial reporting but largely ignored for other stakeholder interests. Social accounting is an attempt to redress this balance through a recognition that a firm affects, through its actions, its external environment (both positively and negatively) and should therefore account for these affects as part of its overall accounting for its actions.

The evaluation of the performance of an organisation is partly concerned with the measurement of performance and partly with the reporting of that performance, and with the greater importance being given to social accountability the changing reporting needs of an organisation are also being recognised. Thus Birnbeg (1980) stated that accounting is attempting to supply various diverse groups, with different needs for information, and that there is a need for several distinct types of accounting to perform such a function. Similarly Gray (1992) considers the limitations of the traditional economic base for accounting and questions some of its premises.[8] Rubenstein (1992) goes further and argues that there is a need for a new social contract between a business and the stakeholders to which it is accountable, and a business mission which recognises that some things go beyond accounting. Ogden and Bougen (1985) on the other hand consider the disclosure of accounting information to trade unions and state that different conceptualisations of the relationship between management and employees can generate different conclusions regarding the disclosure of accounting information during industrial relations bargaining.[9]

The Future of Corporate Social Responsibility

This concern with social responsibility faded out at the end of the 1970s with the rise of the New Right politics of Thatcher and Reagan and the consequent legitimation of selfish behaviour and greed in the acquisition of wealth. This was positively encouraged at an individual level and spilled over into the corporate world as governments facilitated the free market orientation to the provision of goods and services. Thus markets were progressively opened to competition, corporate taxes were reduced and regulations relaxed in the spirit of the times and the belief in the 'trickle down theory' that this would lead to a benefit to all society.[10] It is only recently that any concern with social responsibility has reappeared. A question therefore remains to be considered as to the extent to which any concern for corporate social responsibility is a cyclical phenomenon which surfaces in times of economic prosperity and disappears when

---

8 Gray in particular argues that there is a need for a new paradigm with the environment being considered as part of the firm rather than as an externality and with sustainability and the use of primary resources being given increased weighting.

9 They argue that increased disclosure can lead to reduced opposition from employees, greater commitment and loyalty and increased legitimacy for intended action. This evidence therefore seems to suggest that greater disclosure of information can actually bring about benefits to the organisation as well as to the stakeholders involved. This is in line with the concepts of social and environmental accounting which are concerned with greater disclosure of the activities of an organisation but with an emphasis upon disclosure of actions and the way in which they impact upon the external environment.

10 Some would argue instead that there was a callous disregard for the majority of society in the promulgation of these policies. Indeed Thatcher is on record as stating that there is no such thing as society.

the economic cycle turns downwards. In other words is the future of this concern with social responsibility one in which this cycle will be repeated and any concern for social responsibility become manifest periodically?

It is always tempting to argue that the current period is different from previous periods and any welcome changes will be sustainable this time around, even without evidence. This time however there is evidence that the concern with corporate social responsibility might be different as it can be seen as related to various other movements which are taking place around the world in the context of increased activism of citizens concerned with what is happening in the global corporate arena. Thus evidence comes from pressure upon the accounting profession through the establishment of groups such as the Association for Integrity in Accounting[11] in the USA, the Association for Accounting and Business Affairs[12] in the UK and the Tax Justice Network,[13] providing evidence of a challenge to the hegemony of corporate activity.

Other evidence comes from such things as the feminist movement and more specifically from the pacifist and anti-militarist strand of this movement (Liddington, 1989). Although initially started as a protest against nuclear weapons the Greenham Common peace ideals were adopted by large numbers of women, many of whom were conventional citizens and consumers, but for some the ideals of breaking with the mores of society assumed prominence. This led initially to the establishment of peace camps at Greenham Common and elsewhere but subsequently to a movement which espoused violence and sought to establish different ways of living. Further evidence comes from the various protest movements which exist at present which are concerned with such things as environmental pollution, animal experimentation, road use and genetically modified crops. Such pressure groups include among their membership many members of society who express their concern not just through this membership but also through their selection of goods and services which they consume. Thus various supermarkets have suffered from a refusal to purchase goods contained genetically modified substances to such an extent that some have withdrawn such products. They have equally been affected by other campaigns such as the refusal to fish when it has been thought that dolphins have been disadvantaged. Similarly Shell suffered from the publicity surrounding their proposed solution for the disposal of the Brent Spar oil platform.

Other activity has been more radical and illegal and has sought to affect society at large. This has been manifest in the violent and destructive tactics of organisations such as the Animal Liberation Front, the obstructive tactics of such people as ecoprotestors in their opposition to road building programmes, and the disruptive tactics of such people as Reclaim the Streets in gaining maximum media coverage from their non-violent program of closing major streets in London for periods of time or in affecting

---

11 Information on the Association for Integrity in Accounting is available at http://www.citizenworks.org.

12 See http://visar.csustan.edu/aaba/aaba.htm.

13 See http://www.taxjustice.net. This organisation is supported by such organisations as War on Want.

the 1998 G8 summit in Birmingham. Other actions of the anti-global movement have been less peaceful, such as what has become known as the battle of Seattle, but equally demonstrate a growing concern with the activities of global corporations. The discourse surrounding such environmental terrorism is one of illegitimacy, depending upon whether one considers that the ends justify the means or not. Their impact upon legitimate organisations tends to be one of increasing transaction costs for the firms targeted, or for society at large, rather than any long-term change in performance measurement and reporting. Chaliand (1987) has argued that a successful terrorist organisation needs a base in society which extends beyond its membership and needs popular support in order to exist and achieve results. Thus it can be seen that such activity enjoys an element of popular support which can become manifest in the general behaviour of individuals as consumers. This popular support can be particularly seen in the activities of the ecoprotestors (Crowther and Cooper, 2001) where their activities can be viewed as the direct action component of a popular movement which concerns large numbers of people.

Possibly a more significant activity as far as organisations are concerned is the increasing use of community based economic activity (Brass and Koziell. 1997). Such activity is manifest in alternative modes of economic exchange and the carrying out of economic activity such as the growing number of local economic trading schemes (LETS), the growing number of economically active organisations such as workers cooperatives and activities such as community banks. Such activity reflects a disillusion on the part of individuals in society with the current mode of organisation of society and is part of a search for alternatives. This kind of activity is relatively small in scale at the present but is growing in size and can be expected to have a significant impact upon organisation to which a response need be sought.

Further evidence of changes in societal mores can be gathered from the existence of the New Age Traveller movement (Earle, Dearling, Whittle, Glasse and Gubby, 1994). The community of travellers has specific strategic objectives. These objectives are not explicitly stated and have not been arrived at by any overt decision making; rather they have developed over time through an unconscious process. Nevertheless these strategic objectives are clearly defined and openly expressed by such travellers (Crowther and Cooper, 2002). These objectives have been expressed by these travellers as seeking to achieve two distinct objectives, which are learning to live differently and developing a community spirit and identity.

By learning to live differently these people mean both that their relationship with nature must be different and that their ability to exist in a peaceable manner must not be driven by the normal societal motives of economic consumption and wealth creation. In this respect therefore they refuse to recognise the proprietary ownership mores of mainstream society as a basis for resource utilisation, and this applies in particular to land which is viewed as a common resource to be used rather than owned. This view of land and its use is of course one of the principal reasons why the traveller movement has so often been in conflict with conventional society and why mainstream publicity about them has been uniformly bad. As with the Leveller movement in the seventeenth century their very existence, and possible survival, can be considered to be a threat to the economic basis of societal existence. The travellers themselves would be pleased to be perceived in this way as this provides a level of support for their ideas of existence. The other main strand of traveller philosophy, which can be seen from their way of life and their general involvement in the ecoprotest movement, is a general concern with the environment and its degradation through developments. This is particularly true when the proposed developments are for the purpose of increasing road transport, or air transport, at the expense of nature.

All of this suggests that the concern with corporate social responsibility is part of a wider social movement in which citizens are seeking to wrest power back from the global corporate world and to demand a share in the benefits of civilisation. Evidence from throughout this book suggests that these corporations are slowly responding to this pressure. So there is ground for optimism but only if the pressure from citizens and concerned stakeholders continues.

References

Baron L., Blum L., Krebs D., Oliner P., Oliner S. and Smolenska M.Z. (1992), *Embracing the other: Philosophical, Psychological, and Historical Perspectives on Altruism*, New York: New York University Press.

Birnbeg, J.G. (1980), 'The Role of Accounting in Financial Disclosure', *Accounting, Organizations and Society*, Vol. 5, No. 1: 71–80.

Brass, E. and Koziell, S.P. (1997), *Gathering Force*, London: The Big Issue Writers.

Carroll, A.B. (1991), 'The Pyramid of Corporate Social Responsibility: Towards the Moral Management of Organizational Stakeholders', *Business Horizons*, Vol. 34: 39–48.

Chaliand, G. (1987), *Terrorism – From Popular Struggle to Media Spectacle*, London: Saqi.

Coleman, J. (1990), *Foundations of Social Theory*, Cambridge, MA: Harvard University Press.

Corlett J.A. (1996), *Analyzing Social Knowledge*, Lanham, MD: Rowman and Littlefield.

Crowther, D. (2000a), 'Corporate Reporting, Stakeholders and the Internet: Mapping the New Corporate Landscape', *Urban Studies*, Vol. 37, No. 10: 1837–48.

Crowther, D. (2000b), *Social and Environmental Accounting*, London: Financial Times Prentice Hall.

Crowther, D. (2002), *A Social Critique of Corporate Reporting*, Aldershot: Ashgate.

Crowther, D. and Cooper, S. (2001), 'Innovation through Postmodern Networks: The Case of Ecoprotestors', in O. Jones and S. Conway (eds), *Networks and Innovation*, London: Imperial College Press: 321–47.

Crowther, D. and Cooper, S. (2002), 'Rekindling Community Spirit and Identity: The Case of Ecoprotestors', *Management Decision*, Vol. 40, No. 4: 343–53.

Davidson, D. (1980), *Essays on Actions and Events*, Oxford: Clarendon Press.

Deegan, C. and Rankin, M. (1999), 'The Environmental Reporting Expectations Gap: Australian Evidence', *British Accounting Review*, Vol. 31, No. 3: 313–46.

Desjardins, J.R. and McCall, J.J. (1996), *Contemporary Issues in Business Ethics*, 3rd edn, Belmont, CA: Wadsworth Publishing Co.

Earle, F., Dearling, A., Whittle, H., Glasse, R. and Gubby (1994), *A Time to Travel?*, Lyme Regis: Enabler Publications.

Fetyko, D.F. (1975), 'The Company Social Audit', *Management Accounting*, Vol. 56, No. 10: 645–7.

French, P.A. (1995), *Corporate Ethics*, Forth Worth: Harcourt Brace.

Goodpaster, K.E. and Matthews, J.B. Jr (1982), 'Can a Corporation Have a Conscience?', *Harvard Business Review*, January–February.

Gray, R. (1992), 'Accounting and Environmentalism: An Exploration of the Challenge of Gently Accounting for Accountability, Transparency and Sustainability', *Accounting, Organizations and Society*, Vol. 17, No. 5: 399–425.

Gray, R., Owen, D. and Maunders, K. (1987), *Corporate Social Reporting: Accounting and Accountability*, London: Prentice-Hall.

Hawken, P. (1993), *The Ecology of Commerce*, London: Weidenfeld and Nicholson.

Jensen, M.C. and Meckling, W.H. (1976), 'Theory of the Firm: Managerial Behaviour, Agency Costs and Ownership Structure', *Journal of Financial Economics*, Vol. 3: 305–60.

Kant, I. (1959), *Foundations of the Metaphysics of Morals*, trans. L.W. Beck, New York: The Liberal Arts Press.

Kinnersley, D. (1994), *Coming Clean: The Politics of Water and the Environment*, London: Penguin.

Klein, T.A. (1977), *Social Costs and Benefits of Business*, Englewood Cliffs, NJ: Prentice-Hall.

Liddington, J. (1989), *The Road to Greenham Common*, New York: Syracuse University Press.

Lovelock, J. (1979), *Gaia*, Oxford: Oxford University Press.

Mansbridge, J. (1990), *Beyond Self-Interest*, Chicago: University of Chicago Press.

Ogden, S. and Bougen, P. (1985), 'A Radical Perspective on the Disclosure of Accounting Information to Trade Unions', *Accounting, Organizations and Society*, Vol. 10, No. 2: 211–24.

Rayman-Bacchus, L. (2003), 'Contextualising Corporate Governance', *Managerial Auditing Journal*, Vol. 18, No. 3: 180–92.

Rawls, J. (1971), *A Theory of Justice*, Cambridge, MA: Harvard University Press.

Rubenstein, D.B. (1992), 'Bridging the Gap between Green Accounting and Black Ink', *Accounting, Organizations and Society*, Vol. 17, No. 5: 501–8.

Schaltegger, S., Muller, K. and Hindrichsen, H. (1996), *Corporate Environmental Accounting*, Chichester: John Wiley and Sons.

Shapiro, S.P. (1987), 'The Social Control of Impersonal Trust', *American Journal of Sociology*, Vol. 93: 623–58.

Solomons, D. (1974), 'Corporate Social Performance: A New Dimension in Accounting Reports?', in H. Edey and B.S. Yamey (eds), *Debits, Credits, Finance and Profits*, London: Sweet and Maxwell: 131–41.

Till, C.A. and Symes, C.F. (1999), 'Environmental Disclosure by Australian Mining Companies: Environmental Conscience or Commercial Reality?', *Accounting Forum*, Vol. 28, No. 3: 137–54.

Velasquez, M.G. (1983), 'Why Corporations are not Morally Responsible for Anything they Do', *Business and Professional Ethics Journal*, Vol. 2 (Spring): 8.

Wilbur, J.B. (1992), *The Moral Foundations of Business Practice*, Lanham: University Press of America.

Index